Simplified Project Management for the Quality Professional

Simplified Project Management for the Quality Professional

Managing Small and Medium-size Projects

Russell T. Westcott

ASQ Quality Press
Milwaukee, Wisconsin

American Society for Quality, Quality Press, Milwaukee 53203

© 2005 by American Society for Quality

All rights reserved. Published 2004

Printed in the United States of America

12 11 10 09 08 07 06 05 04 03   5 4 3 2 1

Library of Congress Cataloging-in-Publication Data

Westcott, Russ, 1927-
   Simplified project management for the quality professional :
     managing small and medium-sized projects / Russell T. Westcott.
       p. cm.
   Includes bibliographical references and index.
   ISBN 0-87389-636-X (alk. paper)
   1. Project management.   I. Title.

   HD69.P75W467 2004
   658.4'04—dc22   2004014822

ISBN 0-87389-636-X

Publisher: William A. Tony
Acquisitions Editor: Annemieke Hytinen
Project Editor: Paul O'Mara
Production Administrator: Randall Benson
Special Marketing Representative: David Luth

ASQ Mission: The American Society for Quality advances individual, organizational, and community excellence worldwide through learning, quality improvement, and knowledge exchange.

Attention Bookstores, Wholesalers, Schools, and Corporations: ASQ Quality Press books, videotapes, audiotapes, and software are available at quantity discounts with bulk purchases for business, educational, or instructional use. For information, please contact ASQ Quality Press at 800-248-1946, or write to ASQ Quality Press, P.O. Box 3005, Milwaukee, WI 53201-3005.

To place orders or to request a free copy of the ASQ Quality Press Publications Catalog, including ASQ membership information, call 800-248-1946. Visit our Web site at www.asq.org or http://qualitypress.asq.org.

∞ Printed on acid-free paper

Quality Press
600 N. Plankinton Avenue
Milwaukee, Wisconsin 53203
Call toll free 800-248-1946
Fax 414-272-1734
www.asq.org
http://qualitypress.asq.org
http://standardsgroup.asq.org
E-mail: authors@asq.org

ASQ
AMERICAN SOCIETY
FOR QUALITY™

Contents

Figures and Tables

Preface

There are two primary reasons for reading and following the applicable guidelines presented in this book. First, as a quality professional, you understand the concept of variation. You realize, perhaps have already experienced, the chaotic business climate we work in: the instability and vulnerability of employment; organizations merging and divesting; and the continual shift from manual work to predominantly knowledge work.

A second reason, and related to the first, is the need for quality professionals to make a serious effort to add project management skills and experience to their repertoire of competencies. More and more the quality professional, whether a manager or a technician, is called upon to either lead a project team or participate on a project team. Most certainly if you are employed in a consulting role, either inside an organization or external to your clients, you will be expected to have demonstrated competency in project management.

So there you have it. Organizations are rapidly changing to embrace a project-style of managing and you, in order to remain an employable professional, need competency in planning and managing projects. Gone are the days when you might be tossed into a project situation, with no training or experience, and get by with mediocre performance. An assigned project can make or break you. Your professional career is on the line. Higher management now expects you to have the knowledge, experience, skills, aptitude, and attitude (KESAA) to apply your technical and managerial quality skills in a project environment. I discuss this in greater detail in Part 1.

The assumption made in this book is that it is unlikely that you, as a quality professional, will be assigned or initiate a megadollar project of long duration and great complexity. Such projects tend to be led by established project managers—often from outside the organization. From this perspective, I develop basic guidelines for the smaller project and build upon these guidelines for a medium-sized project. Dollars and duration are the two major determinants, with complexity a third factor in the medium-size project. How you choose to define "smaller project" and "medium-size project" is for you to decide. Your decision is contingent upon your overall organization's size, the resources available, and the criticality of the desired outcome. Of course if the project outcome is mandated, you will find a way to achieve the outcome or suffer the consequences. If you absolutely need me to give you a rule of thumb, then consider the short term as up to three months duration, the long term from three to 18 months.

Part II takes you through the basics of planning, implementing, managing, and closing a project. Inasmuch as you may have the opportunity to initiate a project (as opposed to being assigned to one), Chapter 3 discusses how to envision the project outcome and how to obtain the all-important top management buy-in. Chapter 4 introduces you to basic planning tools. Chapter 5 addresses the issues you need to consider in forming and leading a project team. Chapter 6 adds additional tools to handle the medium-size project. Chapter 7 discusses the implementation of the project, as well as tracking and measuring progress. Chapter 7 also provides guidelines for evaluating, documenting, and closing down the project.

Part III, Chapter 8, provides a variety of examples and excerpts from actual small- and medium-size projects.

Leveraging project management is discussed in Part IV from two viewpoints. Chapter 9 discusses developing your personal competency for your own development and growth. Chapter 10 suggests how to build and promote project management as a key core competency and competitive edge for your organization.

Many chapters are sprinkled with "short takes" illustrating various project management situations and applications. Diagrams and forms you can modify for your use are provided throughout the book. Each chapter ends with a quiz you can use to test your knowledge up to that point in time. Also, additional information is provided on available resource material, and there is a glossary of terms.

To conclude, many organizations' approach to planning and implementing quality initiatives has been less than effective. Until recently, the quality profession has been slow to address the need for quality professionals with the needed project management competency. But, the working climate and the needs are changing at near lightning speed. As the quality professional moves upward in the organizational hierarchy, she or he must have the KESAA (knowledge, experience, skills, aptitude, and attitude = competency) to succeed in a project-oriented environment. The mission of this book is to guide you toward attaining that competency. Therefore, you may want to adopt/adapt the following personal objectives.

Upon completing the reading of this book and applying the appropriate project management techniques and tools to a small project within your work unit, you will be able to demonstrate to your management:

1. A capability to plan and manage a project

2. The value (time and money) of using proven project planning and management techniques and tools

3. The potential value of documenting the initiation steps, project plans, implementation plans, tracking methods, and project close-out—for future training and planning purposes

4. The potential value of establishing protocols, procedures, and standard practices to attain consistency in applying the project management techniques and tools within the organization—and to provide a baseline for improving the project management process itself

5. An awareness of how demonstrated project management competency could become a major factor in the organization's marketable core competencies

Further, the reader may wish to set additional personal objectives to:

1. Build the project management competency (KESAA) to position oneself for internal promotional and/or job enrichment opportunities.

2. Make oneself more marketable should the need or opportunity arise for considering employment elsewhere.

This is a guidebook; how you use it to plan and pursue your project management journey is up to you.

Notes to Readers

Planning a project is a process, an iterative process. Project planning, for all but the simplest projects, is best done by a project team and, if feasible, includes the recipient of the project's results. This means that the initial project planning done to obtain approval to start the formal project planning is usually rudimentary by comparison with the revised planning produced once the team is formed and functioning. The team adds clarity to the project's definition and projected outcomes, and depth to the plans to achieve those outcomes. When the project plans are submitted to the approving authority prior to a full-scale project launch, the plans represent the most informed and definitive thinking of the collective expertise of the team.

The approved project plans combine the plans for managing the project itself as well as the plans for the work needed to produce the desired results from the project (the execution of the plans). In actuality, two projects are being worked on simultaneously—the defined project and the management of the defined project.

Given enough time and money, just about anyone can run almost any project. Your project planning and management competency is the key to planning and managing a project that is constrained by time, funds, and other resources. You may face a situation where time is short, funds are tight, resources are scarce, resistance and interpersonal conflicts are prevalent, and the organization's culture and management are not especially supportive. "Tag, you're it!" You're the person who is expected to lead a project to successful completion, often while performing your "regular" duties. You've had no, limited, or a less than wonderful experience with planning and managing a project. You need proven techniques and tools in order to achieve success. That is the intent of presenting a "simplified" process.

A question frequently arises about whether to use commercially available project management software. My answer is a No/Yes answer. If you were the person responsible for heading an occasional small or medium-size project (the targeted reader), my answer would tend to be "No." The reason is that the costs (time and money) of using the software could override the value of the project itself. For example:

- Effectively using project management software requires some basic knowledge of project planning and managing (no better way to learn the basics than to use the basic tools—the traditional way).

- Already acquired basic skills in using word processing and a spreadsheet program will most often suffice.

- Project management software purchase price may not be justified.

- Your time and cost in learning to use the project management software may outweigh the value obtained.

- Your skill fade-out between using the software this time and a potential distant need to use it again means relearning (time and money).

- Potential obsolescence of both the software and the computer on which the software is installed before the software is needed again.

On the other hand, you may want to look at software if the project is fairly large—for example, if the project involves:

- Many tasks and task interdependencies

- Many resources involved (e.g., people with diverse expertise, facilities, equipment)

- Many never-been-done-before type tasks

- Long project life cycle

- Very critical deadline and critical milestones

- Potential for many plan changes as project progresses

- Sizable expenditures

- Critical strategic importance (economic, competitive, regulatory pressures)

- Funding cap

- Customer mandated use of project management software

If many of the above factors are involved, then my answer is "Yes" to some form of computer-based project management software. However, the above factors take the project out of the realm of the small to medium-size project for which you, the intended reader, are only occasionally required to manage. Many of the resources at the end of this book address the use of project management software.

Heed Kipling's direction and use a few simple techniques and tools. That may be all you need!

> I keep six honest serving men
> (They taught me all I knew);
> Their names are What and Why and When
> And How and Where and Who.
>
> Rudyard Kipling
> *The Just-So Stories [1902].* "The Elephant's Child."

Acknowledgments

My work life has consisted of a variety of projects, large, small and in between. Many projects were initiated at a point in time when I knew little or nothing about "project management." Some projects were successful, many could have been more successful if only I knew what I know now—and some failed.

I acknowledge, belatedly, the sound advice and knowledge learned from my parents (now deceased). They encouraged me to try new and challenging endeavors, to think things through, and to apply good old simple common sense.

I acknowledge and applaud the enduring love and support of Jeanne Westcott, my wife and closest friend for over 55 years. She endured the many upsets as we moved back and forth around the country for me to accept more responsible positions in the corporate world and again as I broke away from corporate stability to form my own businesses. Jeanne provides the "reality checks" I need to stay the course as I continually reinvent myself to meet new challenges.

Since the early 1990s my business relationship and personal friendship with my partner, George W. Offerjost, in the work-life planning and career-coaching arena have been rewarding and beneficial. Our "big project," the establishment of The Offerjost-Westcott Group, has been a great satisfaction to our clients and to each of us personally. All of our clients who have completed our work-life planning and coaching process have reached their career goals.

In more recent times I have been fortunate in linking-up with colleague Duke Okes in several writing and training projects. I exchange "stories" about my business experiences for his insights, suggestions, and mentoring in areas that are weaknesses for me. Duke's dedication and focus on our joint projects, such as cowriting/editing *The Certified Quality Manager Handbook,* meant giving up months of his business and personal time to produce a product on schedule—a book that became a Quality Press bestseller and is continually acclaimed as most helpful in exam preparation. In addition, the handbook was recently translated into Chinese.

Further, I acknowledge the tremendous learning experience I have had in working with experienced editors (too many to name) on the *Quality Progress,* Quality Press, *Quality Digest, Quality Forum,* and *Informed Outlook* editorial staffs.

Thank you one and all.

PART I

Introduction to Project Management

KEY LEARNING POINTS

CHAPTER 1   **Why Organizations Need Project Managers and Quality Professionals Need Project Management Skills**

■ Organizations are becoming project-oriented and project-structured.

■ You need project management competency to further your professional development and upward mobility.

■ Project managers are in demand.

CHAPTER 2   Overview of Project Management

■ Project planning and project management may employ a wide variety of techniques and tools—know the best tools to use and when.

■ The Plan-Do-Check-Act cycle is applicable.

■ Project management involves knowing the scope of the work to be done and for whom, what work is to be done, who will do the work, when and where it will be done, and how the work is to be accomplished.

■ There are five stages to project management:

–Visualizing, selling and initiating the project.

–Planning the project.

–Designing the processes and outputs—the deliverables.

–Implementing and tracking project progress.

–Evaluating and closing-out the project.

■ Outputs are what the project produces; outcomes are the effects the implementation of the project has on the stakeholders.

1

Why Organizations Need Project Management and Quality Professionals Need Project Management Skills

Organizations Need Project Management

Many organizations that serve a particular industry tend to be structured with a project orientation. Organizations supplying state-of-the-art, high-tech systems and hardware, especially to government entities, are primary examples. The businesses that produce computer software are usually built around projects. Organizations embarking on process-quality improvement initiatives typically are partially structured on a project basis, such as Six Sigma efforts, process improvement teams, and lean management applications.

While not every organization may be wholly oriented to a project-based structure, odds are that one or more "projects" are under way in most organizations, even though they may not formally be called projects. Examples include creating job descriptions for all jobs, reorganizing sales territories, upgrading computer programs, relocating the receiving docks to better accommodate just-in-time deliveries, establishing a manufacturing cell to facilitate one-piece flow, and launching a new product.

In essence the project approach to structuring an organization creates a business within the business—a "child" of the "parent." A project structure touches upon most aspects and functions of the parent organization. Elements of the five basic business functions exist within each project: marketing, engineering, production, finance, and human resources.

Marketing includes exploring the potential for a new or changed process, product, or service with potential customers, internal and/or external. It involves selling the project concept and obtaining management's support. It also includes getting "buy-in" from customers of the project's outcomes.

Engineering design and development furnishes the translation of customers' wants and requirements into the language of production.

Production turns Engineering's designs into finished products or services and delivers the output to customers.

Finance participates in estimating benefits and costs and developing a budget.

Human Resources provides qualified personnel to carry out the project activities and safeguard the health, safety, and well-being of project team members.

The project-oriented organization tends to foster an entrepreneurial culture. Project members typically coalesce into a highly motivated team dedicated to achieving the project's objectives and to overcoming obstacles encountered along the way. Participating in a project frequently provides individuals with a broadened perspective of business life and an appreciation for the diversity of a business leader's responsibilities. Project work often offers opportunity to actually or vicariously experience what it's like to run a business.

A project-based organization structure allows the parent organization flexibility in using resources. Project members can be cross-trained (from different task assignments or by rotating through different projects), providing a pool of multiskilled and experienced personnel. A project orientation also provides easier ways to expand or shrink the resource levels based on needs. This is especially feasible when contract personnel augment a core of experienced personnel.

In some industries there are customer requirements, actually mandates, under which the provider dedicates resources wholly to the customer's project. This requirement does limit the provider's flexibility, but, if the provider is well compensated, the pay may outweigh the disadvantages.

There are downsides to the project-oriented structure. Personnel may be underused during slack periods in the schedule. In an effort to keep highly qualified personnel on board, the affected personnel may be assigned to work for which they are overqualified, leading to dissatisfaction and even poor performance. Further, an overall project structure is not always best for all types of organizations. Examples include a continuous process plant such as an oil refinery or a "job-shop" type of operation providing data input services or machining parts.

The flexibility a project structure offers the overall organization can negatively affect individuals' employment and development. While a project is under way, the team member may be productively and intelligently employed. When the project ends, or the end is near, the team member faces the possibility of not getting assigned to another project. Another worry is the situation a member faces on a long-term project assignment. That uncertainty is the possible loss of opportunity to continue to build new professional competence or to miss a promotional opportunity because of the project's needs. Not every employee is willing or able to accept the job security risks of the project assignment. This is especially prevalent among employees performing lower-level, repetitive tasks, employees who may lack competence or confidence that they can survive displacement.

Regardless of the pros and cons, a project orientation among organizations of nearly every stripe is occurring. Witness the appearance of so many seminars, courses, and certifications in the project management field. If your organization has not embraced the basic approach and tools of project management, ask why not. You may uncover a new need that can help your organization and yourself.

Quality Professionals Need
Project Management Skills

Assume that some form of project management fits your organization's needs. This could range from a total restructuring to an overall project orientation or merely to apply project management techniques and tools to the myriad initiatives launched within the organization. In this book we won't deal with totally restructuring your organization to a project orientation nor will we deal with the really large, long-term and complex project. We will provide guidance for your involvement in the smaller, less complex activities that may not even be called projects, but really should be.

For example, in organizations, following the ISO 9001 standard, there is often confusion as to what is a *preventive action*. Without engaging in the debate that often ensues, the preventive action taken should, generally, be handled as a project. If the proposed preventive action can be planned and completed within a short time frame, such as a week up to three months, and is not complex, such as involving several other organizational functions or a significant capital expenditure, then a simple *Action Plan* may be adequate. This "mini-project plan" will be discussed in Chapter 4. As a quality professional you will likely be involved in preventive actions and therefore need the expertise to produce effective results.

Reasons for acquiring project management competency[1] include the following:

Marketplace demand—The project orientation is permeating almost all industries and organizations. There is a demand for competent project managers. Furthermore the most popular quality initiatives require project management competency, that is, Six Sigma and lean approaches.

Project success enhances your professional status—Completion of a successful project puts you on the road to additional and more responsible project assignments. These assignments fast-track you toward enhanced professional status within your organization and ultimately within your profession.

Portability of your competence—As you build your repertoire of project management knowledge, experience, and skills you will likely be considered for additional project assignments. These assignments may be similar to the project just completed or they may involve you in a larger, more complex and challenging project. Furthermore, opportunity may arise to work in or head your organization's "project office," with responsibilities for overseeing multiple projects as well as training others in project management. And, should a chance for an improved position become available outside your present organization, you have the qualifications to take your expertise to another employer.

Planning for contingencies—We are all aware of the vulnerability of employment in today's work environment. Organizations merge, split apart, downsize, and expand in new directions . . . and some collapse.

As a quality professional who has acquired a broad repertoire of knowledge, experience, and skills and has the aptitude and attitude to succeed, you have a higher probability of surviving should you find your employment threatened. Project management competency can be your "life preserver."

Job enrichment—Project involvement develops your business knowledge and skills. You learn how to "sell" a project concept. You learn how to budget, how to obtain resources, assess risks, and estimate time, costs, and resource requirements.

Working in a project team, you sharpen your listening skills and learn win-win ways to manage conflict. You develop your interpersonal leadership and followership skills, and you learn how to get people to cooperate with one another.

Additionally, you develop managerial competence in planning, organizing, staffing, directing, and controlling. You learn how to plan project work, logically organize the work, locate and procure qualified team members, direct the project activities, and control the expenditures of time, resources, and costs.

Further, you enhance your technical competencies, for example, problem solving, process analysis, and negotiation.

Job enlargement—It is likely that your project assignment will increase your responsibilities, perhaps empowering you to make decisions you typically couldn't expect to make in your "old" or "regular" job. You may find you are working in an assignment with a broader work scope. This enlarged perspective offers more visibility of your capabilities and opens prospects for ever-higher levels of project assignments and promotions.

Career change—Because of your higher visibility and demonstrated competence you may have opportunities to explore and ultimately transition to a career change. The career change may be within the same overall organization, for example, a headquarters position, or in a different organization—perhaps even a different industry or field.

Increased compensation—The bottom line is that all of the reasons mentioned above can lead to more pay. More pay can mean an improvement in lifestyle, greater financial security for yourself and significant others, and an enhanced professional stature.

Increased personal satisfaction—Consider your outcomes from developing and applying project management concepts, techniques, and tools. With one or more successful projects completed, you have increased your competency, gained recognition from peers and the boss for work done well, achieved respectability among your professional colleagues, and from family and friends.

I hope I've made a case for why quality professionals need project management skills. Following is my story of one of my most significant projects.

In the mid-1970s I was employed as a Human Resources director of a 2000-person division of a major corporation. From my vantage point I became increasingly aware of the external pressures upon the company, the inadequacy of the company's responses to customer complaints, and the frustration of employees in not having the support to improve processes. Of the six divisions, my division ranked last on every measure by which divisions were evaluated. Clearly something had to be done. Unfortunately, there was a long history of failed attempts, each followed by punitive actions. Most actions were aimed at the employees who did the work rather than targeting management-controlled policies, procedures, and systems over which the average employee had no control.

Sensing an opportunity to make a difference, I proposed a performance improvement project to my vice president. The gist of the proposal was to allow me to handpick 12 supervisory people, buy some training materials, be released from my HRD role, and launch a performance improvement program. (Estimated expenditures were $8500.) The training and support enabled the participants to identify a project for their own work area, seek approval, and then plan and implement the improvement with their work unit's employees. The estimated annual net payoff from the 12 teams was $20,000. My VP approved the proposal except for releasing me from my HRD responsibilities. (Placing my job on the line, I even said the VP could fire me if the project failed. He readily accepted the stipulation!)

The first group implemented 12 separate projects, applying the improvement training skills learned. The annualized net payback was $72,000, a return-on-investment of 8.4:1. Approval was obtained to continue until every management person received the training (200 people) over a three-year period. The status at the end of three years showed over a $1 million payback (1976 dollars), and that did not include final results of the last group trained that had not yet implemented their projects.

In this approach, each work unit supervisor became a project manager. I managed the "project office," provided the training, monitored overall progress, and sustained management's commitment and support. The outcome was twofold. First, the division moved into first place within the company (the second-place division was far behind), the organization's culture changed from punitive to one that reinforced good performance, and employee morale made a complete, 180-degree turnaround. Second, I enjoyed the learning experience and the challenge and decided to leave to become a self-employed consultant (see Chapter 8, project j).

I mention this experience because it supports the reasons given earlier for building project management expertise. Initially, the project was small, but it expanded until it encompassed all 2,000 persons in the division. The approach also demonstrated that even in a fairly hostile work environment it was possible to make a difference—as well as reinvent oneself.

Of course your opportunity to gain project management competency may take a different road than mine. Instead of exposing yourself to a high risk as I did, you might seek a chance to participate as a project team member, perhaps emphasizing your specific knowledge, experience, and skills. For example, if you hear of a proposed new product launch you could volunteer to participate as a "subject matter expert" (SME) in the use of certain quality tools, such as design of experiments, failure mode and effects analysis. In exchange for your SME role you could negotiate a means to obtain project management expertise, such as attendance at a training workshop or course, or books, videos, or other self-directed learning media.

In conjunction with serving on a project team, you could study for and qualify for the Professional Project Manager (PPM) designation.[2]

Summary

We have looked at some of the reasons organizations need project managers. Perhaps you realize that project management, and project managers, attempt to bring structure and order to an otherwise chaotic situation. Except for maybe the simplest of projects, projects are replete with potholes and perils (read: chances to screw up). If all projects were well defined from the outset, supported with ample funding and other resources, presented no technological, legal, or ethical challenges, and the results were eagerly awaited by the project's customers, who would need the special skills of a project manager? Reality differs. Rarely does a project play out exactly as planned. Does this mean that planning is useless? The answer is: not at all. If there was no plan the project might never be finished, or incur unrealistic costs, or cause irreparable harm, or . . . The point is that a plan is needed if you are to know where you expect to go, how you expect to get there, how you will know when you've arrived, and whether the project produced positive results.

Organizations usually have a number of efforts either under way or in the contemplation stage, efforts that really should be formally considered projects. These efforts tend to be run by persons lacking knowledge, experience, and skills in project management. Absent this expertise, these efforts can be poorly planned—if planned at all—and sloppily implemented. Waste results: wasted time, wasted resources, and less than optimum results, perhaps even failure. The aim of subjecting such efforts to the discipline of project management is not to impose unneeded administrative requirements but to ensure a better, more effective result.

The terms *project* and *project manager* are frequently misused, just as the term *system* has been so widely misused. A project is a one-time, defined effort with a beginning and an end, usually worked on by a temporary team. Repetitious jobs and tasks are not projects. Project management includes the planning, scheduling, and controlling of the tasks leading to meeting the project's objectives. A project manager is the person with the responsibility for ensuring project management takes place. While a project manager may have duties other than managing a project or projects, such other duties, for example, supervising a work unit performing daily repetitive functions, are not "project manager" duties. As a quality professional, assigned to a one-time effort, such as implementing an instrument calibration process, you may perform all the project management tasks by yourself. This is a one-time project, with a beginning and an end, and is not a repetitive function. You are the "project manager" and you employ the project management tools pertinent to the project, however scaled to the small size of the project.

As to why you should acquire project management competency, the answer is simple: if you want to stay in the game you've got to learn the plays. The quality professional lacking project management competency will be bypassed, if not now, then in the near future.

Chapter 2 provides an overview of the project management process.

Notes

1. Competency = Knowledge, Experience, Skills, Aptitude, and Attitude (The KESAA factors). © 2003, R. T. Westcott & Associates.
2. Pass the examination given by the Project Management Institute (*See* Resources, p. 221).

QUICK QUIZ
NUMBER 1

1. What are at least two reasons why organizations need project management?

2. As a quality professional, what are at least three reasons why you need to develop a competency in project management?

2

Overview of Project Management

Background

Project management is a collection of proven techniques for proposing, planning, implementing, managing, and evaluating projects, combined with the art of managing people. Project management, in various forms, has been used for thousands of years. The building of the Egyptian pyramids is often mentioned.

Interest in and practice of project management has peaked and slumped over the years, depending upon economic conditions and the prevailing business climate. Now, after a long period of relative dormancy, project management has moved to the forefront. The reasons are many, but at the top of the list are advances in technology that make the managing of projects easier, customers who are more discerning and demanding, a workforce with better skills, and economic pressure to "run lean."

An aspiring project manager may now locate a wide range of public courses: college-based, association-based, and consultant-sponsored courses are now offered. The Project Management Institute offers certification as a Project Management Professional (PMP)[1] to those who pass a rigorous examination and demonstrate their proficiency with planning and managing a successful project. Project management has regained, even exceeded, its former popularity—and is definitely "in" these days.

Be aware that while there is an extensive portfolio of project management techniques and tools, there is a big difference in applying these methods to a large, complex, multiyear construction project, a 12-month ISO 9001 quality management system implementation, or a three-month process improvement and machinery upgrade project. The basics apply in all situations, but the methodology has to be scaled to fit the benefit-to-cost ratio. A not too uncommon error is failure to use techniques and tools appropriate to the anticipated outcomes of the project and the resources available. Poor judgment can cause either overkill or underuse of techniques that could have been effective. Table 2.1 lists common techniques and tools.

Table 2.1 Project management techniques and tools for improvement initiatives.

Project purpose & intended outcome	Timelines
• Charter (contract) • Mission statement • Scope • Goal and objectives • Stakeholder requirements: deliverables	• Gantt/Milestone chart • Activity Network Diagram (AND) • Critical Path Method (CPM chart)
Analysis of risks and feasibility	**Person(s) responsible**
• Benefit-cost analysis • Payback period • Net present value (NPV) • Internal rate of return (IRR) • Potential return on investment (ROI) • Estimated return on net assets (RONA)	• Linear Responsibility Matrix (LRM) **Project budget** **Quantifiable measurements** • Time expenditure • Resource usage • Project costs versus budget
The team	**Postproject evaluation/lessons learned**
• Team formation • Team building training • Conflict management training • Team facilitation	• Outcomes and ROI achieved • Time schedule met • Budget met • Postmortem of project planning and execution • Documentation to knowledge base
Breakdown of work to be done	
• Work Breakdown Structure (WBS) • Resource Requirements Matrix	

From *Stepping Up to ISO 9004:2000*, by Russell T. Westcott, published by Paton Press, 2003. Reprinted with permission.

The Project Planning Process

The life cycle of a project may be defined in five stages:

1. Visualizing, selling, and initiating the project

2. Planning the project

3. Designing the processes and outputs (deliverables)

4. Implementing and tracking the project

5. Evaluating and closing out the project

Stage 1: Visualizing, Selling, Initiating the Project

Projects come about because of various conditions and may be initiated from a number of different sources. For example, if in your position you are asked (assume "required") to either head a project initiative or join a project team, you arrive on the scene after the visualizing, selling, and initiating has mostly been done. You come aboard after the approval, for at least the planning stage, has been obtained. If you are reading this book because you are in this situation you may skip over Chapter 3 (but do read that chapter later).

However, let's say that in your role as a quality professional, either managerial or technical, you uncover a need for improvement; for example, business is being lost because of lengthy order-to-delivery cycle time. Whether or not your present job description includes initiating a project, you are closest to understanding the need and possible solution, so you pump up your courage and seek approval to launch an improvement project. You share your idea with your boss, receiving any one or more of these reactions:

- "That's not your job, you haven't got time to get into it."

- "You don't have the know-how to tackle anything like that."

- "We do what we're told to do, and fooling around with that idea can only get both of us into trouble. Forget it."

- "I'll give you credit for having the nerve to even think you could do something about that situation. But you'd need a lot more than nerve, and my O.K., to do it. Nice idea, but leave it up to those on high to come up with it. I'd be severely criticized for letting you work on this. Spend your efforts improving your own performance."

- "Don't bother me with your wild ideas, just do your job."

The scenarios may be endless, but they all add up to one thing—your idea has not gained the support of your boss—and probably won't now that you've approached him or her as you did. Did you do something wrong? Well, maybe not ethically or morally wrong, but your approach was ineffective. An adage states: It is nearly impossible to gain subsequent approval from the person who initially said "no way" when first approached.

The only effective way you are going to get buy-in for your idea is when you can link your idea with what is important to the person you are approaching and you can demonstrate that you are openly soliciting his or her input. Human nature being what it is, it is a rare person who will immediately accept your idea without your having to somehow involve the person in shaping the concept. "Not invented here" is a strong barrier to consider, whether admitted to or not, in overcoming resistance. Chapter 3 discusses ways to present your visualization, techniques for selling the project concept, and initiating the project. Before you take a chance of "killing off" your great idea, do your homework first.

Stage 2: Planning the Project

Assuming the project concept and feasibility have been determined, the "Plan-Do-Check-Act" cycle (Figure 2.1) is directly applicable to project planning and management.

Begin your plans by defining the scope of the project. Establish the date when the project will be started and when it should be finished. Document the key planned outputs and the expected outcomes (results and benefits) for completing the project successfully as well as any consequences for failing to meet the targeted dates and budget.

For a medium-size project (MP) it may be helpful to draft a project charter providing the projected outcomes to be achieved by the project, who will head the project, to whom the project head will report, what statutory or regulatory rules are applicable, what organizational policies, protocols, and practices are to be observed, and what constraints may apply. For an MP, prepare a listing of the stakeholders who may be affected or impacted by the project and its outputs and outcomes.

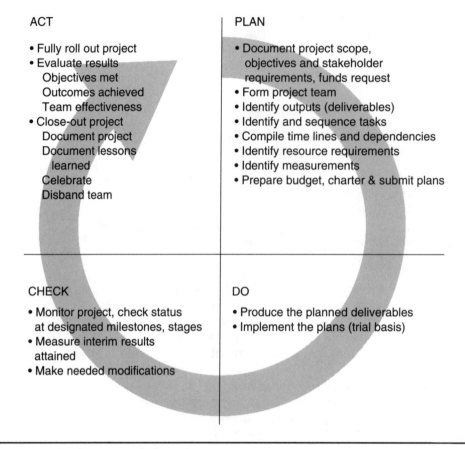

ACT

• Fully roll out project
• Evaluate results
   Objectives met
   Outcomes achieved
   Team effectiveness
• Close-out project
   Document project
   Document lessons
      learned
   Celebrate
   Disband team

PLAN

• Document project scope,
   objectives and stakeholder
   requirements, funds request
• Form project team
• Identify outputs (deliverables)
• Identify and sequence tasks
• Compile time lines and dependencies
• Identify resource requirements
• Identify measurements
• Prepare budget, charter & submit plans

CHECK

• Monitor project, check status
   at designated milestones, stages
• Measure interim results
   attained
• Make needed modifications

DO

• Produce the planned deliverables
• Implement the plans (trial basis)

Figure 2.1   Using the PDCA cycle for projects.

Except for a very small project (SP), you will need to select and form the project team.

Consider how many and what type of people you need on the team. Determine if members should be selected only from the work unit affected by the project outputs, or would a cross-functional team be more appropriate? Should you have multiple disciplines represented on the team? What selection criteria will you use and what if any selection tools would be useful (for example, the Myers-Briggs Type Indicator® [MBTI] or other tools)?

If the project team members will also maintain their regularly assigned responsibilities for the duration of the project, consider what arrangements are needed to ensure adequate release time for team participation. If team members are to be dedicated solely to the project team, what arrangements are necessary to ensure they can return to their regular work when the team is disbanded? How will their developmental, promotional, and compensation progression be protected during their absence?

Determine whether you will want a trained team facilitator to assist the team as the team progresses through the typical team stages (e.g., forming, storming, norming, and performing).[2] Estimate what training the team members will require for being effective as team members. If training will be needed, how, when, and by whom will such training be provided?

Refine the list of outputs the project team will produce. These may include:

- Documents for planning and managing the project

- Protocols for reporting project status

- Computer programs

- Databases

- Project plans for preimplementation approval

- Project implementation plans and schedule

- Documentation of postimplementation outcomes

Identify and sequence the tasks required to achieve the project objectives; typically this takes the form of a Work Breakdown Structure (WBS). The WBS format for SP can simply be a hierarchical listing (outline format) of the tasks and subtasks needed. The format for a MP or more complex project may be a pyramidal structure of categorized functions and tasks. Chapter 4 discusses this tool in greater detail.

Develop the time durations and time dependencies for the primary tasks or task categories. The format is usually a Gantt chart listing the tasks vertically on the left, with the weeks or months shown as horizontally headed columns and horizontal bars representing the time period in which each identified task or task category is to be started and finished. For an SP, with fewer tasks, the Gantt chart does suffice to depict the time dependencies among the tasks. Chapter 4 discusses the preparation of a Gantt chart.

More complex and longer projects require a more sophisticated chart of task dependencies to enable scheduling and monitoring of the project. Three tools are available:

- AND—the arrow network diagram shows dependencies among tasks. However, by itself it does not consider task duration time and cost.

- CPM—the critical path method charting tool is used mainly when experience allows reasonably accurate estimating of time durations for each task. The determination of critical path (the time to accomplish all the designated tasks on the longest path) is based on one time estimate for each task.

- PERT—the program or project evaluation and reporting technique is used for projects for which previous experience may be lacking. The tool allows for three time estimates (optimistic, most likely, pessimistic) and requires a computer program to process. Estimated costs may also be included in the computations.

Chapter 6 discusses the AND and CPM charting methods. PERT charting is usually for large, long-duration, complex projects and will not be discussed in this book.

For some SPs and for MPs, it is appropriate to identify and develop resource requirements lists or matrices. For an SP a simple listing of the personnel required (with types of competency and time frame required) may be sufficient. For an MP you may find that several types of resource requirements matrices may be advisable, such as for personnel, facilities, equipment, materials, and outside contractors. Resource requirements matrices are discussed in more detail in Chapter 4.

After the time lines and project requirements have been determined, it's time to prepare the project budget. The budget should include at least two stages, the project design and launch, and the ongoing after-launch benefits and costs. In very small projects they may be combined. Chapters 4 and 6 include more about the budget preparation.

Tracking the progress of the project and evaluating the results of the project itself and the ultimate results of the implemented project will require you to identify the measurements that will be used as well as the methodology for monitoring and measuring. You will need to determine who needs what data, in what format, and when, in order to monitor project progress and determine if project objectives and outcomes have been met.

In most cases, the project team has made modifications to the initial draft documents. It's time now to prepare the final recommended Project Plan for higher-level approval (this may require several iterations until approval or final rejection is received). If the project is terminated or fails to receive approval, the team completes its documentation by debriefing itself and documenting "lessons learned," then disbands.

Organizations that employ proven project management techniques and tools impart structure and discipline to quality initiatives. Effective project management enables an organization to plan for improved outcomes. Okes and Westcott outlined a 15-step project planning sequence, which appears in modified form in Table 2.2.[3]

Stage 3: Designing the Processes and Outputs (Deliverables)

When the project is approved, the project team proceeds with the content design and with the procurements needed to implement the project. Definition of measurements, the monitoring method, status reporting protocols, and establishing evaluation criteria are part of the design process. Design of the ultimate processes and outputs is completed. Implementation schedules are prepared using a task assignment list or an implementation WBS, an implementation Gantt chart, with interim milestones affixed, or both a Gantt chart and a critical path chart tracking program.

Stage 4: Implementing and Tracking the Project

The project design team may also implement the project, possibly augmented by additional personnel. A trial or test implementation may be used to check out the project design and outputs to determine if they meet the project objectives.

Using the planned reporting methods, the implementation team monitors the project implementation and reports on status to appropriate interested parties at designated project milestones. Measurements of interim results may also be communicated to interested parties. The implementation team makes necessary course corrections and trade-offs that may be necessary and are approved.

Table 2.2 Typical project planning sequence.

Seq.	Tool/Technique	Comment
01	Define the idea or concept and draft a clear statement	The kernel of an idea or the basic concept visualized is translated to a clear statement of the problem, deficiency, or opportunity to be realized. Careful definition at this point later helps clarify the scope of the project.
02	Conduct a risk assessment and justify the project	Risk analyses and assessment (payback period, NPV, IRR, ROI, ROA, and benefits/cost). Go/No-go decision is made.
03	Draft: project scope and project objectives	These documents clarify the overall direction of the project and what it is to accomplish, the breadth and depth of the project, and the objectives by which progress and completion is to be measured.
04	Document stakeholder requirements	Stakeholders would consist of two groupings: (1) those with a direct commitment to the project team, such as a process manager who provides a skilled person to serve on a process improvement team working to reduce machine downtime; and,(2) those without involvement but who can influence or be influenced by project results, such as the purchasing department, which selects the vendor for a new machine; customers; and owners.
05	Form the project team	Team members should be selected based on the need to represent a stakeholder group and/or specific skill sets required. Stakeholder groups not represented on the project team should have opportunities to provide input. Some members may be required only as needed. Whenever possible the interests, values, and personality profiles of individuals nominated should be considered. The relative success of a project frequently hinges on effective team selection and management.
06	Update project scope and project objectives	Team members refine the original drafts. A benchmarking study may be appropriate to help define target outcomes.
07	Document the contractual requirements and deliverables	All requirements (outputs and outcomes) of the project are identified, defined, and documented.
08	Prepare a work breakdown structure (WBS)	Project work is further defined by breaking the work down into a hierarchy of work categories (families of like work clusters), down to the work package level. Boxes on a WBS may be annotated with "person/work unit responsible," "resources required," "cost estimates," and various cross-references, and so forth.
09	Prepare a Gantt chart	Major project work packages or task clusters are listed vertically on a time line chart with each such item's estimated start to finish time depicted as a bar across the chosen time intervals (weeks, months, quarters). As the project progresses, the same chart may be used to chart the actual time expended below the estimated time. Major milestones are shown as points along the time bars.

Continued

Continued

Seq.	Tool/Technique	Comment
10	Prepare a time-dependent task diagram (AND, CPM, PERT charts) and determine the critical path	Depending on the size, complexity and duration of the project, it may be necessary to plot the time dependencies of each work package (WP) to each other WP. An Activity Network Diagram depicts the interrelationships of each WP, or WP cluster, in the project. A Critical Path Method chart adds the dimension of a single time estimate to complete WPs and allows for computing the critical path (longest time line) through the project. A Program Review and Evaluation Technique chart adds two additional time estimates for each WP (optimistic, most likely, pessimistic), allowing further "what if" planning. Typically AND is used for shorter-term, simpler projects, CPM is used where data are available for reasonably accurate time estimates, and PERT is most often used for projects for which there may be little or no prior experience.
11	Prepare resource requirements matrices	One or more RRMs delineate the types of resources needed (e.g., personnel, facilities, equipment, materials, consultants), quantity, when needed, and cost.
12	Prepare a linear responsibility matrix	A LRM, for larger projects, defines the interfaces: who has what responsibility for what tasks, and to what degree (e.g., primary, secondary, resource only, need to know).
13	Prepare the project budget	A detailed, itemized budget, often in a cash-flow format, is prepared based on the time and cost estimates prepared by the team.
14	Establish the measurements to be used	The quantifiable measurements by which project progress and determination that project objectives have been achieved are defined. The progress monitoring process, methods for analyzing data gathered, reporting protocols, and checkpoints for initiating corrective action are determined and documented.
15	Prepare final project plan, draft project charter, and submit for approval	Final approval of the project and authorization for product launch/execution is given.

Stage 5: Evaluating and Closing Out the Project

The implementation team officially closes the project when the scheduled tasks have been completed. Usually evaluations are done to determine:

- Objectives met versus objectives planned

- Actual tasks and events scheduled versus planned

- Resources used versus planned resource usage

- Costs versus budget

- Organizational outcomes achieved versus planned outcomes; any unplanned outcomes

- Effectiveness of project planning team (optional)

- Effectiveness of implementation team (optional)

- Team's compilation of project documents, evaluations, and lessons learned

The project is then officially closed out. Team participants are recognized for their contributions, and the team is disbanded. For some types of projects, many organizations find a postimplementation assessment of the outcomes achieved from implementing the project is valuable, after several months.

Outputs and Outcomes

Frequently the terms "outputs" and "outcomes" are used as if their meanings were interchangeable. The meanings are not the same.

Outputs are what the project produces. Project outputs may be an improved process, installation of a new machine, a benchmarking study, and so forth. Outputs of the project team process itself may be project plans and supporting documents, status reports, and so forth.

Outcomes are the effects that the implementation of the project has on the overall organization and should support the strategic direction of the organization. Outcomes may consist of measurable improvements in customer satisfaction, profits or cost containment, improved market position and market penetration, and so forth. For ease of understanding, outcomes are usually expressed as dollar values. Figure 2.2 shows the relationships of organizational factors and actions on project outcomes.

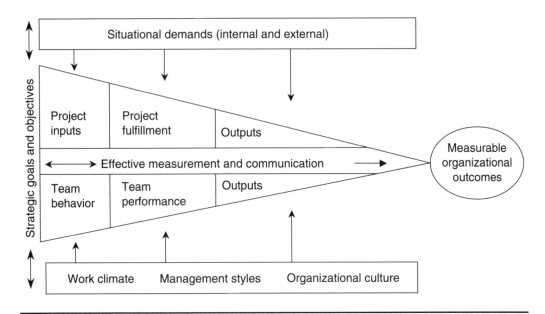

Figure 2.2   Achieving measurable outcomes from projects.

Conclusions

Project management, with its plans, tools, and controls, provides the organization with a clear path to success. Quality initiatives such as Six Sigma, an ISO 9001/9004-oriented quality management system, or the application of lean thinking cry out for sound project management.

Organizations are progressing toward greater flexibility, speedier responses to customer demands, increased employee involvement, more customer and supplier alliances, and continual improvement efforts. A project orientation is emerging as a primary organizational need. This means quality professionals must add project management competence to their repertoire to survive and grow now and into the future.

Part 2, Chapters 3 through 7, defines the process and tools for planning and managing a project.

Notes

1. The Project Management Institute's Standards Committee has published a document available on the Web (http://www.pmi.org) that can help your organization decide what tools will be most applicable to its situation and identify areas in which organizational competence should be developed. Information about the Certificate Program is also available.
2. Defined by B. W. Tuckman, "Developmental Sequence in Small Groups," *Psychological Bulletin 63,* no. 6 (November–December 1965): 384–399.
3. Okes, Duke, and Russell T. Westcott, eds. *The Certified Quality Manager Handbook,* 2nd ed. Milwaukee: ASQ Quality Press, 2001 (Chapter 14).

QUICK QUIZ
NUMBER 2

1. Name the five stages of a project life cycle.
2. If you were contemplating suggesting a process improvement project based on your findings from a process audit, what approach would you take in gaining approval to move ahead?
3. For what purpose is a critical path useful?
4. Define "deliverables."
5. Differentiate between "outputs" and "outcomes."

   —Are they both "deliverables"?

   —Is there a time dimension associated with each term?

   —Are they both measurable?
6. What are the primary differences between a very large project and a very small project?

   —Do the same principles, techniques, and tools apply in planning and managing both types?

   —Is it better or worse to use project management tools that are not essential to the project, just to be sure you have control?

PART II

Defining the Process and Tools for Planning and Managing a Project

KEY LEARNING POINTS

CHAPTER 3   Visualizing, Selling, and Initiating Projects

- Transforming your vision into reality
- Selling your project
- Determining feasibility—techniques and tools
- Setting project objectives
- Requesting funds to cover the project planning stage

CHAPTER 4   Planning Projects—Basic Model

- Task Schedule approach
- Action Plan approach
- Nine-step basic project planning model

CHAPTER 5   Forming and Leading a Project Team

- Team structures
- Team roles and responsibilities
- Selecting team members
- Team stages
- Leading the team

CHAPTER 6   Planning projects—Additional Considerations

- Estimating and task duration
- Network diagramming and critical path
- Outsourcing
- Scheduling and plan changes
- Cash-flow budgeting
- Project charter and communications
- Implementation planning
- Project management office
- Six Sigma

CHAPTER 7   Implementing, Tracking, Evaluating and Closing Projects

- Managing the project activities
- Tracking, measuring, and reporting
- Lessons learned and closing the project
- Evaluating the outcomes

3

Visualizing, Selling, and Initiating Projects

Background

Projects may emanate from four broad categories:

1. Vision (yours or another person's)

2. Strategic plan

3. Mandate from some authority or an emergency response to a critical situation

4. Need to improve processes, products or practices

As a quality professional you may have little influence over whether or not to initiate a mandated project, such as changing a process to respond to an environmental legal action or seeking ISO certification of a management system to retain or obtain a major customer. However, you may have influence over how the project is planned and managed.

Depending upon your position in your organization you may participate in projects emanating from top-level strategic planning. If top management is aware of your project management competency you could be designated as the project manager for a project to implement a segment of the organization's strategic plan.

In your role as a quality professional you will likely uncover a potential change that could significantly affect your organization's outcomes. Such an idea may be your own or a synthesis of ideas derived from peers and other professional colleagues, inside or outside the organization. Initiating a project resulting from your idea can be difficult because it must be "sold" to management in order to be funded.

If your organization has initiated a process or quality improvement, such as Six Sigma or lean thinking, you may find yourself either on a team to further the goals of the initiative, or the project team leader.

This chapter will address more extensively those projects that result from a vision and that you, personally, would like to initiate and manage. Other types of projects will still require some of the same expertise, but to a lesser degree.

Visualizing the New Reality

Let's look at an example:

> Art, the quality manager of a logistics management company at one of his company's five locations, developed a facility auditing process that internally aided his organization in better meeting customer requirements and reducing costs. Art visualized offering this process to his company's clientele, as an add-on service and for a fee. Part of this vision was a countermeasure to meet the mandate from management to cut internal costs. A cut would mean a reduction in personnel. If implemented, Art's vision would not only expand the company's service offerings but also provide funding to support his existing number of professionals, perhaps even to hire additional professionals as the new service became attractive to clients.

There is a difference between a dream or fantasy, an idea and a vision. A person with a dream sees something different but usually without considering practicality. The person with the idea has a "brilliant flash" about something that would be nice or good but, at the time, hasn't a clue about how to transform the idea into reality. One who has a vision usually sees something changed in the future, with certain difficulties overcome, and often a path to the new reality. Moreover, the vision includes the benefits and at least some of the disadvantages and what the net effect can be.

Regardless of whether you agree with the above concepts or not your visualization must take on some substance before it can be "sold" to potential supporters. You may generate dreams and ideas by the barrel, but until you add substance to your idea of the changed reality you have little other than your initial dreams and undeveloped ideas. You have an unclear vision. Another example:

> Basking in the success of my first book, I dreamed of doing another book. It wasn't even clear what the subject would be. At that point there was just a dream. Gradually a topic emerged: project management slanted to quality professionals (idea). Work began by thinking through what the book would address, why it was needed, who would benefit from reading it, what competitive books existed, how the book would lay out, how many pages it might have, a projected publishing date, and what sample chapters to submit (the vision) to a potential publisher. The book began to take on shape, and a book proposal was submitted to the publisher (the start of the selling stage). Following reviews by the publisher's panel of experts and numerous e-mail exchanges between the publisher and me, a revised proposal was accepted. Developing a project plan for delivering the draft manuscript by the target date and carrying out the editing and revision plan was my responsibility. The publisher's responsibility included determining the feasibility of the project, evaluating my capability to produce the manuscript, consideration of other projects under way at the publishing house, projecting the potential book sales and the costs of publishing, and distributing the book (product launch stage).
>
> You are reading the output from this collaborative effort. The outcomes are yet to be realized, that is, book sales, favorable reviews, author royalties, and acknowledgment of widespread value derived from the guidance offered.

As a quality professional, where might you expect to find the opportunity to envision an improvement project? While the answer may be, "Just about anywhere," let's look at some of the obvious places where opportunities may lurk:

- Customer complaints are mounting, both in the total number and their severity:
  - Product or service quality.
  - Timeliness of delivery.
  - Responsiveness of supplier people to customers' needs and wants.

- Scrap rates are mounting.

- Production cycle time appears excessive.

- Customers' requirements are not clearly defined, causing waste.

- Production is not capable of producing what Sales has sold.

- Poor quality material is received from suppliers.

- Poor quality work is done by subcontractors.

- Internal processes are producing errors; mistake-proofing may be useful.

- Processes are inefficient and not cost-effective.

- Too many of the following instances are occurring:
  - Decisions are being made to not open a corrective action request (CAR) when a CAR should be opened.
  - Repetitive CARs for the same situation are occurring, indicating the root cause has not been found and corrected.
  - Instances are occurring where CAR investigators who should have explored the potential for a similar situation elsewhere in the process didn't, resulting in CARs for problems in other processes similar to the ones already resolved.

- Preventive action requests (PAR) are not being used when opportunity knocks:
  - Process owners are failing to dig deep enough into their process to uncover the potential for error.
  - PAR investigators who should have considered a breakthrough-type improvement chose only an incremental improvement, resulting in an outcome less than optimal.
  - Work-in-process awaiting inspection is held up at bottlenecks in the process.

- Suppliers are having difficulty meeting your requirements for quantity, quality, and/or delivery time.

- A critical shortage of trained workers is anticipated.

- A new competitor with a brand-new facility and process has entered the marketplace.

- Workplace accidents are on the rise.

- Worker absences are increasing.

- Machine downtime is increasing.

- Newly expanded yard storage of raw material is close to the riverfront and poses a risk from potential flooding.

- In-house information technology is ineffective in keeping pace with industry norms and customers' needs.

- Strategic plans call for applying for the Baldrige Award within the next three years.

From an initial idea a vision emerges: what the change will be, the impact of the change, and a potential path to achieving the vision. As the quality manager, how do you translate the vision into action—then sell and initiate a project?

Selling the Project

The concept of "selling" is anathema to many professionals (even some sales people). It is an all too common belief that if you tell someone about your fantastic idea they will immediately see the advantages of funding your idea. It rarely happens that way. The "not invented here" syndrome is strong with many people, causing them to reject a suggestion of change from someone else for no other reason than it wasn't their idea. Of course, they will seldom confess to that and instead provide some other reason for rejection, such as "We tried that two years ago and it didn't work." Suffice it to say, one of the more difficult tasks in turning an idea into a vision and a funded project is gaining the necessary support.

Support must be sought from several places before you can successfully launch a project. Some places from which you should seek support for your vision are:

- The person from whom you take direction (e.g., supervisor, boss)

- The person or persons within any organization that will be affected by the change you envision

- Peers or subject matter experts from whom you will have to seek knowledge or expertise to bring your vision to fruition

- The person or persons from whom resources will have to be obtained to implement your project

- The primary person or persons who will most benefit from the output of the change resulting from your project

- The persons who will most recognize the organizational outcomes derived from the outputs of your project

- The person, if not included above, who must authorize the project and/or funding request

- The significant other in your personal life who will be most affected by your success or failure

Consider this example:

Harry, a newly hired graduate quality engineer, is in his first week on the job. He observes a major bottleneck in his employer's order fulfillment process. As an avid student of the theory of constraints and the techniques involved, he speculates that a change could shorten cycle time from two weeks to three days. He scribbles a few notes on paper and tells his boss about his great new idea. In telling about his idea, he is stopped short as the boss tells him, "You're too new on the job to be messing with that stuff. That's not your job." Harry is shot out of the water before getting to the third sentence!

What mistakes did this disillusioned but initially enthusiastic engineer make? He:

- Presented it as *his* brilliant idea.

- Did not have a plan to seek his boss's viewpoint on the bottleneck before mentioning the idea.

- Had no facts to substantiate the idea.

- Had no rationale for spending time on something that was not his or her official job or concern.

- Had little concept of what it might take to implement the change or what potential impact it could have, either negative or positive.

- Had poor timing (too little time on the job).

- Had not taken the time and effort to understand what the boss might view as important, what the boss's needs might be, and on what criteria the boss was measured by his superior (e.g., finding the "hot button").

- Did not have enough time on the job to build a good performance record in the job for which he was hired.

- Was too new to have gained "friends" in the organization and therefore had no known supporters for the idea.

- Had no knowledge, skill, or experience in planning and managing a project and therefore would have been an unlikely person to be allowed to run the project, if he had gotten that far.

Assuming the zealous engineer's perception was correct, but a plan did not get off the ground, who lost out? He did and the company did. They both lost because he did not know how to create and sell the vision. If it were possible to compile a list of the rejected opportunities passed up by organizations because the ideas and visions were never sold properly, the list would startle all of us.

Another example:

Paula, a quality engineer at Omega Bearings, learned that to gain approval for a new expenditure of any magnitude required making a presentation to the president and his direct-reports (the board). Paula was not high in the organization's hierarchy.

However, Paula took a very proactive approach to her job and constantly looked for ways in which Omega could improve both its quality and productivity. For example, in performing a quality management system process audit, under the ISO 9001 standard, Paula observed a deficiency in the process that often resulted in mistakes being made in communicating customer order requirements.

Over several weeks, while performing her regular duties, Paula found time to talk with some of the people involved in the process in question, gathered some opinions and facts, and got support for a change, providing she took the initiative to propose the change. She analyzed her data, spoke with the finance people about how to estimate the value of the change, and picked up some pointers on how to present the financial impact of the change.

Paula discussed the observations with her boss, received his suggestions, and gained his support, including permission to contact members of the board. She then visited all the "president's men" and solicited their suggestions on what to do. Out of five board members, Paula gained committed support for her vision from three. Paula then asked for help from the Art Department, the department that assisted members of the board in formalizing their proposals and creating presentation materials.

With a mock-up of her presentation, Paula went separately to her boss and the three top-level supporters to give each a run-through of what they would see at the next funding meeting.

She emphasized how she had incorporated their suggestions. After receiving constructive criticism and making finishing touches, Paula gave her boss a trial run of the presentation and asked her boss to arrange an appointment for her to present the proposal to the board. The project was approved, and Paula was designated project manager.

What happened? All board members had been exposed to the vision in advance and had been asked for suggestions and support. Three had supported the vision immediately. During the meeting it was clearly evident that three of the board members immediately bought in and were supporting the vision from the outset. Following Paula's presentation, the remaining two board members nodded their approval. The president approved the initiation of the project. A done deal.

Paula, virtually unknown to top management, sold her vision by carefully "covering the bases" up front. Intuitively or otherwise, she knew you couldn't spring something new on people, especially if you're an unknown, without doing your homework first. She also knew she needed hard facts to prove her case and that those numbers must correlate with the criteria by which the people she was selling to were evaluated.

Paula had an advantage; she worked in an organization that did not openly discourage new ideas—or women taking the initiative. Some readers might not enjoy this advantage. If so, selling the vision—getting the buy-in—will be a tad more difficult.

O.K., you have the vision. You've achieved buy-in to move ahead. You do not, however, yet have all the resources to plan and launch a project. Prudent management is going to expect you to provide a rationale for the project. This may require a formal funding request, or at the minimum, a memo requesting the initial resources you will need. Management, in its responsibility to its stakeholders, will want an assessment of the potential risks involved.

Risk Assessment
(Determining If the Project Is Feasible)[1]

All projects will require some resources, such as employees, facilities, equipment, tools, supplies, subcontractors, and the funds for the resources. Additionally one other resource (nonreplenishable) is required—time. Committing such resources places a burden on the ongoing operation of the organization. Some organizations have been able to justify additional people and facilities for the duration of a project. This is a rare occurrence. Mostly, an organization has to find ways to absorb a project activity while still "making the donuts."

Let's look in on Alice:

> Alice is the quality assurance manager at Sweet Takes, a distributor of snack foods to outlets throughout the mid-Atlantic states. She has gotten her management to agree to a cycle-time reduction project. The vision Alice has for this project is to shorten order processing and product delivery to the 496 outlets served by Sweet Takes by installing new technology to directly link the outlets to Sweet Takes. This technology will allow Sweet Takes to know, real-time, exactly what products from Sweet Takes each outlet is selling and when the items are being sold. From this "pull-type" of data, Sweet Takes will be able to schedule shipments to outlets as well as "pull" stock from Sweet Takes' suppliers. Alice foresees the time when Sweet Takes will no longer stock product but, with information received directly from the outlets, will be able to order "drop shipments" from their suppliers directly to the outlets.
>
> Management can enjoy the vision of better satisfying its customers, better efficiency in order handling, and better cash flow. But management also recognizes the burden the project will place on the existing operation until the technology is in place and working. "What's this going to cost us, in time, money and business disruption?" and "How will the benefits pay for the costs involved?" are the questions Alice must answer before receiving the green light to launch the project.

A first consideration is the resources required for the project, as if it were a standalone project. Will the benefits of the project substantially outweigh the costs, and how soon? Assuming the project estimates meet this initial review, the next consideration is the impact of project planning and implementation on the ongoing operations, including other projects that may be under way. If Alice can clear both these hurdles by an acceptable margin she should be able to obtain approval to proceed with the planning. Of course, there will be another hurdle, as Alice will have to get the actual project plans approved before moving into implementation.

Remember, at this point Alice has no people authorized to work on the project, just some supporters who have expressed interest. Alice has several alternatives:

- Try to attempt the risk analysis and project authorization (charter) on her own.

- Find a mentor who can tutor her in what to do and how to do it.

- Convince a supporter to help, "free of charge."

- Partner with a person or persons in the organization who have the needed expertise and willingness to help, in trade for participation in the project when approved.

- Offer the project concept to one of the supporters for the supporter to champion, with Alice's help.

- Give up.

Alice considers her options and decides to continue as the champion of the project. She will obtain the help of an accounting person who understands the funding process and has access to cost records, and she will convene a group brainstorming session with participants from all the key processes and functions potentially affected when the change is made. From this session she plans to excite one or more individuals who will offer their time and energy, without charge, in helping to prepare the risk assessment and project planning funds request.

From the brainstorming session, attended by supporters and skeptics, a long list of resources needed and issues were generated. In a second session, the attendees amended the list and then constructed an affinity diagram.[2] Based on the affinity diagram, the group prioritized (through multivoting)[3] the key resources to be addressed and the critical issues to be resolved. Most attendees agreed to accept responsibility for one or more of the identified items and to obtain the needed data by a stated deadline.

With her "friend" in accounting, Alice worked with the submitted data to prepare a risk assessment and compiled the information in the proper format for requesting the planning funds. Alice distributed the compiled report to the session attendees and set a date to meet to review the draft document.

Alice reviewed the draft document with her brainstorming compatriots. Several changes were suggested, and some were approved. Following the meeting, Alice reworked the funding request and sent a copy to her contributors. Receiving no substantive suggestions for further modification, Alice submitted the funding request.

Note: The approach Alice followed not only helped her through a difficult data gathering and analysis process but also served to build additional buy-in for the project. Some members of her ad hoc group requested to join her project team once approval was received.

Dr. Deborah S. Kezsbom and Katherine A. Edward provide a sample table with "Criteria for Classifying Risks as High, Medium, or Low."[4] Several other tools may be used in assessing the organizational risks involved, such as:

- Benefits versus cost analysis
  - Project ranking
  - Payback period
  - Net present value (NPV)
  - Internal rate of return (IRR)
  - Potential return on investment (ROI)
  - Estimated return on assets (ROA)

- Portfolio analysis

- Project selection decision analysis

Benefits versus Cost Analysis

A *benefits-to-costs analysis* is typically prepared first, using anticipated monetary benefits and projected costs. Although it is difficult to introduce real precision and certainty to this analysis because of so many unknowns,[5] it does provide an indication of the potential net value of the results from a proposed project. For a very small, uncomplicated project of short duration and involving few people to plan and implement, a benefits-to-costs analysis may be sufficient to "sell" the project.

The formula for computing a benefits-cost ratio is:

$$\frac{\text{Sum of all the } \textbf{net} \text{ benefits anticipated (e.g., \$576,000)}}{\text{Sum of all the } \textbf{net} \text{ costs anticipated (e.g., \$85,400)}} = \$6.74$$

This means a projected benefit of $6.74 for every dollar of costs, also expressed as "6.74:1."

"Net benefits" represents the dollar value of all the advantages to the organization resulting from the project, less the dollar value of all the disadvantages to the organization. "Net costs" represents the dollar value of all costs involved in planning and implementing the project (costs incurred by both the project team as well as costs incurred by the recipients of the project outputs in making the changes emanating from the project, less any ancillary savings to the project sponsor (e.g., value of improvements to the project planning process, establishment of a project data base for use in training project personnel and in estimating future projects).

The relationship of the time frame represented by the benefits and the time frame for the costs must be compatible. In the medium-size to larger-size projects, the incurring of project costs may cease or substantially diminish after the project is implemented, whereas the full benefits may not materialize until some years have passed. For example, if the project took two years to fully implement, but the payments on acquired facilities and machines extend for ten years, the benefits-to-cost computation may rightly encompass a ten-year period.

For a small project the benefits should be realized in a relatively short period. Often the benefits-to-cost ratio is computed for yearly periods dating from the completion of implementation, that is, "first year," "second year," and so on until all costs have been absorbed. For the small and medium-size projects to which this book is addressed, the realization of benefits should typically occur fairly quickly. The majority of smaller projects, especially those implemented in less than one year, are computed on an annualized basis. As noted later, a return-on-investment figure may be the same result as a benefits-cost analysis, depending on the cost and benefit factors used.

To estimate the projected benefits consider five possible outcomes, or a combination thereof:

1. A cost savings, including process efficiencies

2. An increase in productivity

3. A cost avoidance

4. An increase in sales or services delivered

5. An increase in customer retention

Determine which type or types of benefit the proposed project will emphasize. Project what the changed process or system will likely cost to operate on an ongoing basis. Compute the net increase or decrease (variance) in ongoing operating costs of the process or system once the change has been implemented. If the variance from the costs of the changed system or process is greater than that previous to the change, use this variance as part of the cost figure for computing the ratio. If variance from the costs after the change is lower than present costs to operate the system, use this variance as part of the benefit figures used in computing the ratio.

Determine the projected costs of planning and implementing the change to the process or system. Add these costs to any projected net increase in operating costs to sum all anticipated costs.

Based on the type or types of outcome anticipated from implementing the projects estimate, conservatively, what benefits may accrue from the change. Estimating cost savings will probably be the easiest to estimate—the change will either eliminate or reduce a type of cost, such as scrap, machine downtime, tool wear, or incorrect deliveries. Using figures from a cost of quality study[6] may add credence to the benefits-cost analysis.

Estimating an increase in productivity and its value to the organization is somewhat more speculative. Care must be taken to ensure the increase in productivity is real. For example, if an operator's time is reduced by a half-hour per day, the benefit is calculated based on the value of the work the operator accomplishes in the saved time, not the pay of the operator for the half-hour. Unless the plan is to send operators home a half-hour early, without pay, there are no savings from just the time saved. The value lies with the additional product produced with the time saved. (Keep in mind that increasing productivity is only as valuable as there is demand for the product produced. Just creating more inventory is not productive.)

Determining the benefits from cost avoidance is partially based on past history of costs. There may have been significant costs involved with resolving legal issues, lost-time accidents, failures under performance-based contracts, and so on. If either organizational history or industry history indicates costs and the frequencies for a given type of incident, there is a basis for projecting "what if this happened" costs. It is best to be very conservative in these estimates; the objective of the benefits-costs analysis is to be able to show a sufficient benefit to make the project worthwhile, so don't go overboard. Remember, when dealing with rising costs of this nature, this may also affect insurance premiums. A cost avoidance may in fact reduce or prevent further escalation of insurance costs, another benefit.

Benefits to be derived from an increase in sales, or in service deliveries for not-for-profit organizations, are difficult to forecast, but possible. Sales have increased costs associated with the sales increase. Sales are predicated on many factors, not the least of which is customer demand. Increasing sales may also require expansion of present plant, personnel, and equipment, if there is insufficient capacity to handle the increase. Not that this is necessarily a bad thing, but it does involve factoring in additional costs—and consideration of the risk that sales cannot be sustained to support the expanded facilities and workforce.

Computing the benefits-to-cost ratio for increased customer retention is based on knowing what the value of a given customer-base segment is (i.e., how much do customers in this segment spend, on average over, say, five years?), thereby providing a figure representing the value for the loss of a customer. For example:

> The average annual expenditure at the only in-town supermarket for a three-person household (all adults), such as mine, is $5,500. The figure jumps for a larger family and families with several small children. Ours is a small town, which means that continually losing customers who spend this amount per year and having little opportunity to obtain enough new customers could mean the ultimate demise of the store. Competing supermarkets exist in adjacent towns.

The loss-value times the average number of lost customers times an estimated percentage of improvement equals the benefit side of the equation. Frederick Reichheld and Claus Fornell published a useful formula for computing the value of a customer.[7] Reichheld discussed the value of customer retention in great detail in a later book.[8]

Of the several possible outcomes from the proposed project, process improvements and other types of direct cost savings are the easiest numbers to compile. If the numbers used are conservative and a substantial benefit is shown, the value of moving ahead is obvious.

Be aware that there are shortcomings in using the benefit-cost analysis approach, such as:

- The formula does not consider the time value of money, which is important when a proposed project is expected to extend over several years.

- The formula itself does not consider the impact on the ongoing operation during project implementation.

- The approach does not account for the priority the proposed project should be given relative to other proposed or current projects.

- While the proposed project may show monetary benefits, it still takes money up front to implement the project. This may require funds an organization does not presently have or be in a position to borrow.

Another perspective in computing a benefit-to-costs analysis comes from segregating costs and benefits as *direct* and *indirect*.[9] Direct costs may include equipment, labor (wages and salaries), training, and machines. Indirect costs may include displaced workforce, idle time, and opportunities lost. Direct benefits may include increased sales, increased production, reduced delivery costs, eliminated deficiencies, and reduced warranty costs. Indirect benefits may include better-trained employees, improved work environment, and greater customer satisfaction. A positive benefits-to-cost ratio based on direct costs and direct benefits is an easier "sell" than a ratio primarily based on indirect data.

If the "ballpark" ratio generated by the benefits-cost analysis fails to produce a ratio of three or above, recheck the figures; if the answer remains the same, the project is likely not worth launching. On the positive side, the vast majority of cost-reducing, efficiency-raising, process-type improvements tend to generate a ratio often in the hundreds. However, when some authority mandates the project or when a crisis exists, it's likely the project must be done regardless of whether there is a favorable ratio or not.

Project Ranking

There are several tools for ranking project feasibility and acceptability, such as:

- Payback period
- Net present value
- Internal rate of return
- Potential return on investment
- Estimated return on assets
- Portfolio analysis
- Project selection decision analysis

Each of these tools may be used as stand-alone decision tools, but in actuality combined use of two or more is typical.

Payback Period

Payback period is the number of years it will take the results of the project to recover the investment from net cash flows. It is a measure of the speed with which cash invested in the project will be returned. Projects with more rapid returns are considered less risky than those extending over a longer period. The determination is simple:

Cumulative net cash flow is negative until the third year. Payback period is in the third year.	
Year 1 Costs ($20,000), benefits ($0)	= Cumulative net cash flow (–$20,000)
Year 2	Costs ($12,000), benefits ($8,000) = cumulative net cash flow (–$24,000)
Year 3	Costs ($2,000), benefits ($65,000) = cumulative net cash flow ($39,000)*
Computing a breakeven point is similar. The breakeven point occurs when the total dollar value of all the benefits is equal to the total dollar value of all associated annualized costs.	

For all small and most medium-size projects the payback period should occur soon after the project is implemented.

Net Present Value

Net present value (NPV) takes into account the time value of money. This computation would usually not be necessary for shorter-term projects with payback periods within the first or second year. However, the three steps are:

1. Determine the present value of each cash flow, using a discount rate ascertained from the cost of capital to the organization and the projected risk of the flow. A higher risk means a higher discount rate is required.

2. Compute the project's NPV by adding the discounted net cash flows.

3. Determine whether the project is right for the organization, which it is when NPV is positive.

This computation can be done using spreadsheet software with the appropriate mathematical function.

Internal Rate of Return

Internal rate of return (IRR) is a computation of a discount rate that causes NPV to equal zero. When an IRR is greater than a minimum rate set by the organization for other capital investments, the project is likely to be approved. This sophisticated computation is used primarily when longer-term capital budgeting decisions must be made. Spreadsheet software may be used to make the calculation.

Potential Return on Investment

Potential return on investment (ROI) is a ratio computed from the cumulative benefits divided by the cumulative investment amount. Depending on the numbers chosen for inclusion, it may or may not differ from the ratio derived from the benefits-cost analysis.

Estimated Return-On-Assets

Estimated return on assets (ROA) is a ratio used primarily when a project may involve a substantial acquisition of physical assets. Capital invested in the assets is recovered from use of the assets over the usual life of the assets. A variation is RONA, return-on-net assets. An example of the ROA computation for a capital acquisition project follows:

> Acquisition of a $500,000 laser-cutting machine, with a useful life of 10 years. The estimated salvage value at the end of its useful life is $5,000. An interest rate of 6% is used. The estimated benefit derived from use of the equipment over its useful life is $7,600,000.

$500,000 ÷ 10 years = $50,000 + [$50,000 × .06] = $53,000 (asset cost per year)

$53,000 × 10 years = $530,000 (gross estimate of asset's cost for useful life)

$530,000 − $5,000 = $525,000 (asset cost less estimated salvage/sale value)

$7,600,000/$525,000 = $14.48 (estimated ROA),

$14.48 return for every $1 of asset invested.

Additional factors complicating the above ROA determination are:

- Adjusting for the time value of money (not included above).

- Fluctuating rates at which benefits are realized during the life of the asset; an example is economic perturbations.

- Payment for the asset over several years, which impacts the cash flow. The investment is delayed and interest cost may vary for different time periods.

Direct costs and primary benefits may be used to develop a ballpark estimate for determining the overall feasibility of initiating the project.

Thomas Pyzdek, in a *Quality Digest* article, discusses how software can help in selecting winning projects.[10] Ronald Snee and William Rodebaugh Jr. offer their belief that project selection is the most difficult element of Six Sigma implementation. Their article differentiates "hard" and "soft" savings.[11]

Any or all of the above computations may be used to aid in determining the feasibility of a project and in ranking the proposed project against other anticipated expenditures. Note that some of the same tools may be used, along with others, in assessing and managing risks during the life of the project.

Portfolio Analysis

Portfolio analysis is a process for relating the comparative values of proposed projects to potential impacts on the resources of the organization. Too frequently projects with favorable ratios are approved without sufficient concern for how the projected resource requirements will impact the organization. The intent of *portfolio analysis* is to weigh the relative impact of a portfolio of projects on the organization. A matrix may be used to record the weights decided upon by a review group. Any combination of critical factors may be used in the analysis. The matrix in Figure 3.1 shows the relative weights of a portfolio of five proposed projects and the potential effect upon the organization.

Project Selection Decision Analysis

Project selection decision analysis is the process of screening projects so that the projects having the most merit are proposed for approval. As mentioned previously, projects may have the potential of producing a high ROI and a speedy payback but may still not be economically sound for an organization. A clear understanding of the relationship between the organization's strategic objectives, its financial status, and other potential impacts is critical. The techniques and tools discussed above provide the numbers but, in the end, it is a judgment call as to whether the project is worth the risk at the present time. For example, say the organization has faced hostile takeover attempts in the last two years and may be facing these again soon. The organization might put large new projects on hold until the threat is minimized or eliminated. A decision matrix may be constructed, such as in Figure 3.2.

The cells in a comparative matrix may be filled with either a number that is a ratio (e.g., benefit-to-cost, return-on-investment, return-on-assets), the NPV, the IRR, or the payback period. In Figure 3.2 a group of nine persons voted (five votes per person) for the priority ranking of five projects under consideration. In spite of the fact that project 2 had a huge potential ROI it was ranked low because of the lengthy payback period and the strategic concern for the economic slowdown already beginning. The purpose of project 3, in spite of a more favorable ROI than project 5, caused the group to rank project 3 lowest.

Returning to Alice, let's assume her proposed project has survived the feasibility analysis. Alice is ready to develop the objectives for the project.

Table 3.1 Portfolio analysis—weighting factors impacting the organization (5 = highest impact).

Project	ROI	Personnel	Facilities	Equipment	Material	Funds	Total of Weights	Rank
1	2	2	4	3	2	4	17	4
2	1	5	5	5	5	5	26	5
3	4	4	2	0	0	3	13	3
4	3	1	3	0	1	2	10	2
5	5	3	0	0	0	1	9	1

Table 3.2 Project selection matrix (9 persons voting, 5 votes apiece) (1 = highest rank).

	Project 1	Project 2	Project 3	Project 4	Project 5
NPV	107.6K	2518K	80.7K	71.6K	53.5K
Payback—yrs.	2.75	5.3	3.67	1.0	3.0
ROI	23.48	91.33	10.15	22.93	3.19
Votes	12	4	2	21	6
Rank	2	4	5	1	3

Developing Project Objectives

A handy model for guiding the development of objectives is the S.M.A.R.T. W.A.Y. © (discussed Chapter 4).[12]

Submitting the Project Proposal/Request for Funding

Alice is ready to prepare and submit the project proposal or funding request, depending upon the policy, procedures, and protocol of her organization. This is where her friend from accounting will be very helpful in guiding her through the preparation and submission stage. If the project involves a large sum of money and perhaps more than a year to implement, Alice will probably have to physically make a presentation to top management. This means Alice may also need help in preparing visual aids (slides, charts, etc.) in addition to presenting a well-written executive summary of the proposed project. Those supporters of the project who are also members of the top management group and who will be present at the presentation should be tapped for their advice as to what the approving body likes to see and hear.

Figure 3.3 presents a sample request form for project funds. Every organization will have its own procedures and protocols for funding the project-planning phase. The options used by different organizations may range from an informal "go ahead" to requiring a very detailed presentation.

When the project funding is approved, Alice has her authorization to begin to officially put together a project team and commence the project planning.

REQUEST FOR FUNDING FOR THE PREPARATION OF A PROJECT PLAN

Project name: _____   Project no.: _____

Request initiated by: _____   Date submitted: ____/____/____

Department: _____

Expected start date: ____/____/____   Expected plan finish date: ____/____/____

Process(es) affected: _____

Project objective:

Project overview:

Justification/reason for project:

Project planning funding requested:

   Planning team: ____ employees $_____;   ____ sub-contractors $_____

   Facilities: $_____;   Equipment: $_____;   Services: $_____

   Materials: $_____;   Other: (specify) _____ $_____

                                       Total: $_____

   Comments: _____

Projected investment required to implement project plans:

   Personnel: $_____;   Facilities: $_____;   Equipment: $_____

   Other: (specify) _____ $_____

   Years to implement project plans: _____   Total: $_____

   ROI ratio: _____;   Payback period: _____;   NPV @ ___% = $_____

Alternatives considered and why each was not chosen:

Consequences if project not implemented:

Funding for preparation of project plan up to $_____ approved by:

                                     Date: ____/____/____

_____
[   ] Supporting documents are attached.

Figure 3.1   Request for planning funds.

Observation

The scope of projects typically encountered by the quality professional include:

- Process improvement projects, some where similar solutions have been documented previously and those, such as often found in a Six Sigma initiative, where there is no known previous solution.

- Other process reengineering or systems development projects such as implementing an ISO 9001/9004-based quality management system, restructuring production scheduling.

- Small to medium-size capital equipment projects.

What's Next?

Chapter 4 will detail the steps, techniques, and tools needed to develop the plans for small to medium-size projects. As mentioned earlier, this book will not explore the larger, complex project arena, such as major construction projects, reengineering an entire facility and its production processes, or implementing a total enterprise requirements planning process. These larger projects employ the same concepts and more sophisticated versions of the same tools but are usually assigned to an experienced project manager, often from outside the organization.

Notes

1. Portions of this section on *Risk Assessment* have been adapted from Chapter 14 "Projects," in *The Certified Quality Manager Handbook,* 2nd ed., edited by Duke Okes and Russell T. Westcott, ASQ Quality Press, 2001, and are used with permission.
2. The Affinity Diagram is one of the "seven quality management tools."
3. Multivoting is a quick and easy way for a group to identify the items of the highest priority in a list.
4. *The New Dynamic Project Management,* Deborah S. Kezsbom, Ph.D., and Katherine A. Edward. 2001. New York: John Wiley & Sons, pp. 247–248.
5. Estimating costs and benefits can be aided if your organization has detailed records of past projects from which knowledge can be gleaned.
6. *Principles of Quality Costs,* 3rd ed., Jack Campanella, ed. 1999. Milwaukee: ASQ Quality Press.
7. Reichheld, Frederick, and Claus Fornell, "What's a Loyal Customer Worth?" *Fortune,* December 11, 1995.
8. Reichheld, Frederick F., *The Loyalty Effect.* Boston, MA: Harvard Business School Press, 1996.
9. *The Certified Quality Manager Handbook, second edition*, Duke Okes and Russell T. Westcott, eds. 2001. Milwaukee: ASQ Quality Press.
10. Pyzdek, Thomas, "Selecting Winning Projects," *Quality Digest,* August 2000, p. 26.
11. Snee, Ronald D., and William F. Rodebaugh, Jr., The Project Selection Process," *Quality Progress,* September 2002, pp. 78–80.
12. S.M.A.R.T. W.A.Y. © is used with permission of Russell T. Westcott.

QUICK QUIZ
NUMBER 3

1. In your position as a quality professional, where and when might you identify opportunities for improvement?

    —What actions would you take to sell management on initiating an improvement project?

    —How would you attempt to overcome any resistance to your project idea?

2. What steps would you take to identify and lessen potential risks to a new project?

3. Is computing a benefits-cost value important in determining a project's feasibility? Why?

4. What can you do to analyze a proposed project's benefits to costs if you have no documented figures available?

5. For any project, except perhaps a very small one, why is it logical to do some ballpark estimating, then seek approval for funding to prepare the detailed project plans, rather than spend more time and effort up front (without funding) only to find out the project will be rejected?

4

Planning Projects—Basic Model

From Concept to Reality

Let's assume that you've received the approval to proceed with planning your project and the funding to do so. You've sold the concept and now it's time to prepare the detailed plans needed to launch the project and produce the desired results.

If yours is to be a very small project of short duration, you probably will work the project by yourself. If the project may take a longer time, is more complex, and crosses functions, you'll probably need a team effort. Regardless of the project size, you'll need to answer four basic questions:

1. What work needs to be done?

2. Who will do the work?

3. When will the work be done?

4. How much time and cost will it take to accomplish the work?

To answer these questions you'll need a:

- Clear statement of the project's scope, objectives, deliverables, and authorizations

- Clear breakdown of the tasks required and who is responsible for each task

- Schedule of when the tasks are to be started and finished

- List of resources needed and when needed

- Budget

- Means for tracking, measuring, and reporting progress and results

The Task Schedule Approach

Let's begin with a bare-bones tool for planning a very simple project, the *Task Schedule*. This tool is usually sufficient when the responsibility for the project rests with a small number of people and the handoffs are clear and simple to manage. The tool is easy to set up using either the table format in your word processing software (see Figure 4.1) or a spreadsheet program.

Project name: _____

Task Schedule

ID	Task Name	Days	Start	Finish	Dep	Comments	Actual

Figure 4.1 Task schedule.

This simplistic approach and tool could be easily expanded to a Gantt chart (discussed later in this chapter) and/or an Activity Network Diagram (discussed in Chapter 6). The point in presenting the Task Schedule is to demonstrate that you should use only what you need in order to accomplish your project objectives.

My research has found that many project managers launch into more detailed project planning and project managing techniques and tools than are often necessary. There is a cost, both in time and dollars, involved in planning and managing a project. This cost must be weighed against the needs of the specific type of project, the number and expertise of the persons to be involved in the project, the anticipated costs of the project outputs, the sensitivity issues generated by the project, and the outcomes expected from the project.

Chapter 8 defines a project using the Task Schedule. Figure 8.1 shows a partially completed Task Schedule.

Let's move on to a slightly more comprehensive approach to project planning.

The Action Plan Approach

Projects that will involve several people on a team, perhaps from different functions within the organization, from outside contractors, suppliers, and internal customers, usually call for more detailed planning. *Action Plans,* really mini–project plans, may suffice as the tool of choice to enable you to plan many quality/performance improvement projects. The types of projects you typically encounter involve short-term design, implementation, and execution stages and may affect only one organizational function. A suggested format for action planning is shown in Figure 4.2.

ACTION PLAN

Project name: _____

Description: _____

_____

_____

Linked to what (strategic objective, contract, policy, procedure, process, corrective or preventive action, customer mandate, or regulatory requirement)?:

_____

_____

Plan No:	
Date Needed:	
Date Initiated:	
Approval by:	
Team Leader:	
Team Member:	
Team Member:	
Team Member:	
Team Member:	

Project objectives:

_____

_____

Scope (Where and for whom will the solution/implementation be applied? What limitations & constraints?):

_____

_____

Deliverables (include Outputs re: Content, Outputs re: Project Management, and Outcomes):

_____

_____

By what criteria/measures will completion and success of project be measured?

_____

_____

Assumptions made that might affect project (resources, circumstances outside this project):

_____

_____

Describe the overall approach to be taken, data needed, processes to apply:

_____

_____

When should the project be started to meet the date needed/wanted? _____

Estimate the resources required (time, personnel, facilities, equipment, tools, materials, money):

_____

_____

Is there sufficient organizational capacity and are resources sufficient to meet the objectives?

_____

Estimate the benefits versus costs value:

_____

_____

Outline the major steps and dates on page 2.

Figure 4.2a   Action plan (front).

ACTION PLAN—STEPS

Outline the *major steps* to be taken, a projected *start and finish date* for each step, and the *person to be responsible* for each step. Attach any backup data.

					Plan No:
Step No.	**Activity/Event Description**	**Depends on step**	**Start date**	**Finish date**	**Person responsible**

Page 2

Figure 4.2b   Action plan (back).

Some of the advantages of the Action Plan approach are that it:

• Ensures that even the simpler project has been carefully planned with the aim of lowering the potential for less than optimal results or outright failure.

• Forces answers to critical questions such as:

–What triggered the initiation of the project?

  • Tactical planning resulting from the organization's strategic plan

  • A corrective action resulting from a process audit, analysis of complaints, and/or nonconformities

  • A preventive action to improve a process

  • A customer or regulatory mandate

  • New or changed policy, procedure, or process

–Is there a clear understanding of what the project is to accomplish?

–What constraints or limitations will influence the project?

–By what measures will the progress and success of the project be determined?

–Will the resources required be available as needed?

–Are the competencies needed to produce a quality and cost-effective project outcome available to the project team?

–Are the work environment conditions favorable for the success of the project?

–Are the benefits projected worth it to the impacted organization(s)?

- Establishes the basis for project tracking and measurement to facilitate followup and decisions when the schedule, resources, and costs may require adjustments to meet planned objectives.

- Contributes to building project planning and estimating competence through documented "before and after reviews" coupled with benefits-to-costs analysis.

Potential disadvantages of the Action Plan approach are:

- If the typical "get-to-the-solution-quickly" mentality is dominant, action planning may be treated lightly or inadequately.

- Action planning may be ignored when the project is small enough to involve only one person. This may be especially true if that person feels very competent and knows exactly what to do and how to do it. Bypassing a formalized planning stage leaves little or no documented evidence of the approach used, no basis for subsequent evaluation of the effectiveness of the methodologies used, and no knowledge base for training future project leaders encountering similar projects. (See the previous discussion of the Task Schedule as a tool to use when the details of the Action Plan are deemed unnecessary.)

- Because action planning is simplistic, there is a danger it may be tried for larger, more complex projects. When there are many tasks with critical time and sequence dependencies, the Action Plan approach is inadequate for determining the critical path and managing schedule and resource changes.

- The Action Plan document, in itself, is insufficient for detailing extensive resource requirements, stakeholder requirements, budget line items, and so forth.

Adding to the Project Manager's Toolbox

Now, let's look at more detailed planning, such as a process improvement project:

You are the QC manager for Linear Printing Inc. (LPI), a contract printer of flexible packaging material used by a large producer of gourmet coffees. LPI has two continuous process printing lines. Line 1 employs an 18-year-old multicolor printing machine and runs three shifts, five days a week, with a total crew of 15 (including a lead operator for each shift). Line 2 performs a similar operation, with a newer machine and with a total crew of 12 people; it runs 25 percent faster than line 1.

Both lines have been experiencing costly breakdowns, resulting in loss of productivity, delayed product deliveries, and, more recently, defective product reaching the customer. Oddly, line 1 accumulates fewer overall problems, and definitely fewer color separation and registration problems.

You have turned your idea into a vision and received approval to establish a process improvement team (PIT) as the first stage of what could ultimately be a long-term, multistage project. Stage I is authorized for a three-month trial, with three persons and yourself. The initial budget constraint is $8000 and the anticipated outcome is a minimum of $40,000 in improvements.

When you personally prepared your proposal for approval, you based it on preliminary data gathered, some assumptions based on your knowledge and experience, and your best guess as to potential benefits. You felt your 5:1 ratio of benefits to costs was conservative and attainable. Now that you have the green light, you have three months, authorization for three people to help you, and up to $8,000 to make your vision a reality.

Stage I is a small project but if successful could become the basis for a much larger project. You ask yourself: "What is a good approach to take? What techniques and tools would be most useful for a project of this scale? What risks are there?"

A cautionary note: Be careful to distinguish between the approach, techniques and tools your team will use for planning and managing the project and those that pertain only to results or products of the project. For instance, a schedule for the project tasks is derived from the project management *process*. This differs from a scheduling procedure that is designed as one of the system outputs generated from the improved process, a project *output* or *content*.

Continuing the example above:

In your proposal you made some broad statements about what the project would achieve and your ballpark estimates of benefits and costs. So, you have a fairly good grasp of what needs to be done and a feel for the types of people you'll need on the team. You may even know exactly who you want to have on the team. (Incidentally, in your proposal, did you include obtaining the authority to select the team members you need?)

If you were launching a medium-size project that might require a sizable number of team members drawn from several work units and with a range of disciplines and experience, you would have a different situation. If that is the case you should consider preparing a detailed description of the types of "talent" you need and the criteria you will use to make your request. Further, you would be wise to also prepare a Resource Requirements Matrix (RRM), a spreadsheet laying out the types of "talent" and number of hours for each type spread over the duration of the project. The RRM is discussed later in this chapter.

You have chosen the best and usually the busiest people for your team. Having approval authority to select these individuals doesn't mean you will easily get what you want. You want to "borrow," for some period of time, the operating management's best people. Trust me, you'll encounter resistance. And you thought selling your proposal was hard! Now you want to pull off-line some of the organization's key people. Aside from calling for a direct order from top management (a very last resort), you need to help the operating management understand "What's in It for Me" (WIIFM, pronounced whiff-um). Keep in mind that the manager from whom you want to borrow a person is measured on some other basis than the success of your project. Your best hope is to succeed in establishing a "partnership" whereby the output of the project directly benefits the line manager's operation and the project outcome is the result of your joint venture. (Sharing the credit for success is always a smart move.)

You have sold your vision and obtained approval to launch your project with the needed project team members and funding. You and your team need to get to work on more detailed plans. Table 4.1 includes nine basic steps and tools for planning stage 1 of your approved project.

Project Scope

Establishing the project scope is documenting a summary statement of what your project will include and pertinent exclusions. The project scope must be clear enough to be understood by all team members, as well as by those affected by the results (outputs and outcomes) of the project. "Scope creep" can occur when more work (e.g., additional data gathering and analysis, more outputs, etc.) gets tacked on to the project as it progresses. By having a clear statement of the project scope, project additions can be more easily identified and can either be rejected or subject to negotiation for any additional resources needed.

If not done for your initial project proposal, an Analysis of Stakeholder Requirements is an essential addendum to the statement of project scope. An example of a stakeholder requirements analysis is shown in Figure 4.3.

Table 4.1 Basic model of planning steps.

Step	Technique/Tool	Action
1	Project scope • Stakeholder analysis • Exclusions	Document summary statement of project scope Outline stakeholders' requirements List pertinent exclusions
2	Project objectives • S.M.A.R.T. W.A.Y.©	Establish key project objectives using model
3	Project deliverables	List outputs from project results List project management outputs
4	Work breakdown structure	Break work down into a hierarchy of work levels
5	Gantt/milestone chart	Establish time lines for each major project step
6	Resource requirements matrices	Lay out requirements for key resources (personnel, facilities, equipment, supplies, etc.) by type and time period in which they are required
7	Project budget	Prepare a budget of anticipated expenditures, by line item and time period
8	Measurements	Delineate metrics to be used to track & evaluate project progress and results
9	Project plan submission	Assemble planning documents, prepare an executive summary & submit for project launch approval

Stakeholder	Requirements	Impacts
Project team	• Project plans • Project management	Approval Successful implementation
Customer	• Timely initial response • Courteous response • Timely call-back response, if needed • Satisfaction with action taken or reasonable explanation as to why no action will be taken	Satisfaction with complaint response and resolution process
Customer service rep (CSR)	• Effective procedures, tools, and techniques for handling customer complaints • Positive reinforcement for work done wel. • Organizational objective to achieve a balance between serving volumes of customers quickly and serving customers satisfactorily • Well-trained and available support/supervision	Productivity loss due to overload of inadequately handled customer complaints. Customers' mood and satisfaction with responses. CSRs' demeanor and satisfaction in serving customers. CSRs' morale and motivation.
Complaint Investigators (experienced CSRs removed from customer contact duties)	• Reduction in number of complaints to investigate • Reassignment of CSRs to customer contact duties	Elimination of complaints escalated to CEO's office. (Average = 2000/month with investigation cost of 20 CSRs/month)
Customer service management	• Senior management commitment to customer satisfaction as top priority • Revised measurements that reflect more appropriate balance between achieving customer satisfaction and productivity	More satisfied customers Lower operating costs Less employee turnover, fewer grievances and disciplinary actions Time better spent on preventive actions
Operations management	• Senior management commitment to preventive action to reduce occasions causing customer complaints	Reduction in customer complaints
CEO	• No poorly handled customer complaints to deal with	Time better spent on future planning, attracting and retaining investors
Stockholders	ROI	Investor confidence in company

Figure 4.3   Customer response project—stakeholders.

Project Objectives

Establishing clear project objectives is critical in the choice of metrics to be used to track and evaluate project progress and results (measurements are discussed later in this chapter). A suggested model for setting objectives is the S.M.A.R.T. W.A.Y.©, where the letters remind you to:[1]

S　Focus on *specific* needs and opportunities.

M　Make each objective *measurable*.

A　Make each objective challenging and *achievable* in order to stimulate *achievement* and a feeling of *accomplishment* when achieved.

R　Ensure that each objective is *realistic*. Stretching the objective is good; however, being reachable is critical.

T　Indicate a *time* frame or phases for achievement for each objective.

W　Be confident that each objective is *worth* doing.

A　*Assign* responsibility for each objective.

Y　Ensure that all objectives *yield* desired results.

Consider the following steps in constructing objectives:

1. Specify a single outcome and any pertinent conditions, such as "Given a project budget of $xx,xxx, complete documentation of all procedures needed before the ISO 9001 audit, by February 1, 2004."

2. Select a quantifiable method for measurement ($, %, #, Y/N).

3. Set up an ambitious but realistic target.

4. Establish a time to complete the project, and/or milestone dates.

5. Include a cost parameter (if practical).

6. Be clear, brief, and easy to understand (Keep It Simple Sam/Sally).

7. Write objectives as action statements. For example:

   –"Given the installation of a model z ultrasound testing device, decrease widget defects detected at final inspection from xx per hundred to yy per thousand, by November 1, 2005."

   –"Reduce scrap rate from 20% level (6/04), to 5% by January 1, 2005."

   –"Complete Project W, within the $x,xxx budget, by October 31, 2005."

8. Collaborate with affected parties in writing objectives and choosing measurements.

   Typically, project objectives relate to the anticipated outcomes derived from the completion of the project. It's important to distinguish between project outputs or deliverables and project outcomes. Project outcomes are the impacts or effects resulting from the work done on the project. Examples of categories of outcomes are:

–Effect on the customers served by the organization

–Effect on the profitability of the organization

–Improvement in production cycle time

–Reduction in waste

–Growth in the organization's market share

–Impact on the organization's culture

–Effect on organization's image: to the public, to customers, to employees

–Reduction in risk to the organization

Project Deliverables (Outputs)

Project outputs may be reports of various types, an addition or deletion of a machine, a procedure—a tangible thing. Project outputs are separated between planning and controlling documents used in managing the project itself versus the products of the project activities. Deliverables are those outputs the project team has agreed to provide to the affected stakeholders, including those deliverables involved with project management. Figure 4.4 is a hypothetical sample of a deliverables list.

Name of Deliverable	Description/Purpose of Deliverable
Project Management Outputs	
Time and cost tracking system	Procedure, software to collect project data
Progress reports	Weekly "exception" reports of variables
Evaluation report	End of project evaluation of results
Project documentation	Critical documents for knowledge base
Team effectiveness evaluation	Members performance evaluated
Team celebration	Members recognized for contribution
Project Work Outputs	
Engineering specifications for machine	For use in selecting and purchasing machine
Vendor selection criteria	For use in selecting vendor
Purchase order	For purchase-lease of machine
Floor plan	Layout for new machine workspace
Installation plan	For replacement of old machine with new
Operator training plans	For offsite and onsite operator training
Trial-run plans	To test new machine, acclimate operators
Revised work instructions	For changed process
Revised plant scheduling system	For changes in production scheduling
Turnover plans	Turning over responsibility to production
Postinstallation process audit	To determine if planned outcomes were achieved

Figure 4.4 Deliverables (hypothetical).

Project Outcomes

Outcomes are the effects that the implementation of the project has on the overall organization. They should support the strategic direction of the organization. Examples of outcomes include measurable improvements in customer satisfaction, increased profits, improved cost containment, improved market position, and market penetration. Outcomes are usually expressed as dollar values. Figure 2.2 (Chapter 2) shows the relationships of organizational factors and actions on project outcomes. Most often outcomes are realized at some future period after the project is officially closed. Also, outcomes are typically the primary, long-term benefits from completing the project.

Work Breakdown Structure

A *Work Breakdown Structure* (WBS) is a detailed outline of the categories of work and the necessary activities involved in completing the project. A WBS is created in either an outline format (see Figure 4.5) or a diagram, a graphical hierarchy of interlocking tiers and boxes (see Figure 4.6).

ID #	Activities	Resp. Person	Start Date	Finish Date	Time Est.	Cost Est.	Depends Upon
02	New garage project	Russ	040104	092204	102	42,125	0
02.01	Purchase drawings	Russ	040104	040104	1	25	02
02.02	Select builder	Russ	040104	041204	2	0	02.01
02.03	Obtain permits	Russ	041404	043004	1	150	02.02
02.04	Order building materials	Bud	050504	052704	2	3,000	02.03
02.05	Construct garage	Bud	050504	091304	88	36,150	02.04
02.05.01	Lay foundation	Bud	051704	052704	5	3,500	02.05
02.05.01.01	Prepare lot	Ron	051704	052004	3	1,500	02.05.01
02.05.01.02	Set forms & pour concrete	Bud	052404	052704	2	2,000	02.05.01.01
02.05.02	Erect structure	Bud	060704	081104	45	19,350	02.05.01.02
02.05.02.01	Framing	Pete	060704	063004	15	6,750	02.05.02
02.05.02.02	Roof	Bill	062104	071904	12	5,400	02.05.02.01
02.05.02.03	Windows & doors	George	072104	073004	3	450	02.05.02.02
02.05.02.04	Siding	Al	072204	081104	15	6,750	02.05.02.03
02.05.03	Finishing structure	Bud	072604	091304	38	13,300	02.05.02.03
02.05.03.01	Electrical work	Oscar	072604	081804	15	5,250	02.05.03
02.05.03.02	Plumbing work	Tony	072804	082004	10	3,500	02.05.03
02.05.03.03	Interior finish, painting	Stan	082304	083104	7	2,450	02.02.03.02
02.05.03.04	Exterior finish, painting	Stan	083104	091304	6	2,100	02.05.03.03
02.06	Property reconstruction	Bud	081604	092204	8	2,800	02.05.03.02
02.06.00.01	Driveway	Rashid	081604	083104	4	1,400	02.06
02.06.00.02	Landscaping	Rashid	083104	092204	4	1,400	02.06.01

Figure 4.5 Work breakdown structure (WBS)—building garage (outline format).

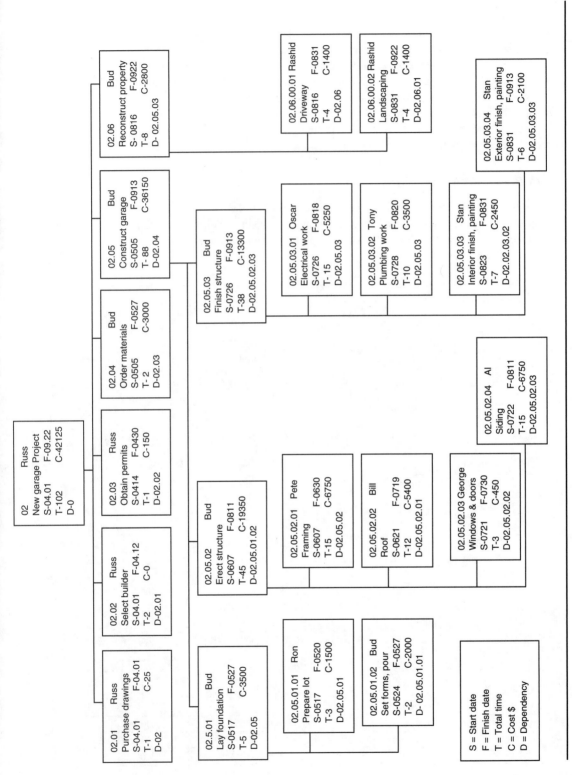

02
New garage Project
S-04.01   F-09.22
T-102   C-42125
D-0

02.01
Purchase drawings   Russ
S-04.01   F-04.01
T-1   C-25
D-02

02.02
Select builder   Russ
S-04.01   F-04.12
T-2   C-0
D-02.01

02.03
Obtain permits   Russ
S-0414   F-0430
T-1   C-150
D-02.02

02.04
Order materials   Bud
S-0505   F-0527
T-2   C-3000
D-02.03

02.05
Construct garage   Bud
S-0505   F-0913
T-88   C-36150
D-02.04

02.06
Reconstruct property   Bud
S-0816   F-0922
T-8   C-2800
D-02.05.03

02.5.01
Lay foundation   Bud
S-0517   F-0527
T-5   C-3500
D-02.05

02.05.02
Erect structure   Bud
S-0607   F-0811
T-45   C-19350
D-02.05.01.02

02.05.03
Finish structure   Bud
S-0726   F-0913
T-38   C-13300
D-02.05.02.03

02.05.01.01   Ron
Prepare lot
S-0517   F-0520
T-3   C-1500
D-02.05.01

02.05.01.02   Bud
Set forms, pour
S-0524   F-0527
T-2   C-2000
D- 02.05.01.01

02.05.02.01   Pete
Framing
S-0607   F-0630
T-15   C-6750
D-02.05.02

02.05.02.02   Bill
Roof
S-0621   F-0719
T-12   C-5400
D-02.05.02.01

02.05.02.03 George
Windows & doors
S-0721   F-0730
T-3   C-450
D-02.05.02.02

02.05.02.04   Al
Siding
S-0722   F-0811
T-15   C-6750
D-02.05.02.03

02.05.03.01   Oscar
Electrical work
S-0726   F-0818
T- 15   C-5250
D-02.05.03

02.05.03.02 Tony
Plumbing work
S-0728   F-0820
T-10   C-3500
D-02.05.03

02.05.03.03   Stan
Interior finish, painting
S-0823   F-0831
T-7   C-2450
D-02.02.03.02

02.05.03.04   Stan
Exterior finish, painting
S-0831   F-0913
T-6   C-2100
D-02.05.03.03

02.06.00.01 Rashid
Driveway
S-0816   F-0831
T-4   C-1400
D-02.06

02.06.00.02 Rashid
Landscaping
S-0831   F-0922
T-4   C-1400
D-02.06.01

S = Start date
F = Finish date
T = Total time
C = Cost $
D = Dependency

Figure 4.6   Work breakdown structure (WBS)—building garage (diagram format).

At first glance, the diagrammatic format may resemble an organization chart. On closer examination you will see that the boxes contain data about the activities that are to occur. Further, you will note that the diagram depicts an upward combining of activities until all levels converge at the top—the project level.

Although the names for these levels vary, the typical levels, from top to bottom, of a WBS are:

1. Project level

2. Subproject level

3. Work unit/Component level (optional)

4. Work Package level

5. Task level (optional)

Not every level is needed for every project. For example, the plans shown in Figures 4.5 and 4.6 extend only to the Work Package level. If further definition and control were desired, the task level could have been included: for "Framing" Work Package 02.05.02.01 could have been expanded to:

- 02.05.02.01.01   Flooring

- 02.05.02.01.02   Outside wall frames

- 02.05.02.01.03   Inside wall frames

- 02.05.02.01.04   Door and window frames

Objectives of a WBS are:

- To identify discreet work activities and tasks for which resources will be needed

- To present a visual "picture" of the entire project to aid comprehension

- To provide a basis to track time and costs

- To observe potentially redundant work efforts which may be combined for better use of resources and performance effectiveness

- To identify potential conflicts in performer assignments

- To aid in detecting potential shortfalls in needed human competencies, plant/ facilities capacity, and process capabilities

While the outline format shows the same basic data as the chart and is somewhat easier to compile, the outline lacks the visual advantage of seeing the project as a whole picture. In using the diagrammatic approach to a WBS, the following additions to the task boxes can further enhance the usefulness of the "big picture":

- Person or function responsible.

- Start and finish dates. Note: The duration is the total time period required and may be greater than the time applied in doing the activity/task (for example, recording incoming data for one hour per day, over eight weeks = total duration of eight weeks).

- Time estimate (added after timelines and resources have been established).

- Cost estimate (added after timelines and resources have been established).

- "Depends upon _____" (the activity or task that must occur before this activity/task is started).

An activity/task number is usually added to aid in aggregating estimated time and costs, both planned and actual. For example: "12.06.13.07" signifies Project 12, Subproject 6, Work Unit 13, Work Package 7.

(Note: Figures 4.5 and 4.6 reflect the addition of time and cost estimates after resource requirements have been determined.)

If projects tend to have repetitive work packages, either within the project itself or over time within other projects, a dictionary of such common work packages can be compiled and a unique identifier assigned to each. This identifier can be used as a reference to allow for summarizing time and dollars across the WBS (horizontally) and/or for all projects incorporating these repetitive work packages. This data can be useful for future estimating.

In larger projects, each Work Package may be supported by a Work Authorization containing:

- Work Package Description and number

- Assigned to and date

- Authorized by and date

- Any budget restraint

- Tasks, with descriptions, contained within the Work Package

- Estimated completion dates for each task

- Estimated dollar costs for each task (optional)

- Estimated personnel time for each task (optional)

- Inputs to each task

- Deliverables (outputs from each task)

While the additional data suggested in the previous list can be very useful, time and cost are involved in generating the data, making changes during planning, and in accumulating, evaluating, and reporting actual versus planned performance. Your planned effort must be scaled to the size, complexity, and benefit value of your project.

Details from the WBS are generally used as input to develop:

- Staffing chart/resource requirements matrix identifying the number and types of personnel required at different critical stages of the project

- Sequenced network of activities and events, identifying the critical path and any potential slack time in the schedule

- Linear Responsibility Chart

- Cost Estimate/Budget

- Project organizational structure

- Basis for a risk analysis

- Basis for tracking, measuring, reporting, and evaluating the project

Here are hints for developing the WBS:

- Think through the level of detail needed to manage the project effectively.

- Do you wish to collect time and costs relative to given deliverables?

- Be careful not to overburden the collection of data and reporting by assigning unnecessary work packages or tasks.

- What type of reporting system will be used to monitor the project progress, build your WBS to fit that system, or change the reporting system as needed?

- Whenever feasible, use computer-based systems so changes can be made quickly and easily.

- Use a team approach to developing the WBS. Having more eyes and expertise will tend to bring up issues that need addressing as well as sharpen estimating.

The WBS should usually include the project management process itself. "Project Management" may be excluded from the very small, simple projects. Managing the project is "project work"; it does involve resources and it does incur costs.[2] When project management work is included in the WBS, it should be included in the Gantt chart, any pertinent resource requirements matrices, and the budget.

The WBS has several benefits:

- It provides a clearly understood structure for understanding and managing the myriad details.

- It uncovers need for details often overlooked in less structured approaches.

- When time and money constraints are critical, the WBS provides the project manager with the input needed to plan for resource allocations to meet time and dollar budgets.

- It often uncovers opportunities to improve the project management, the outcomes of the project, or both.

- Combined with other project documentation, it provides a record that can prove very useful in planning future projects and in training project managers.

Gantt/Milestone Chart

The Gantt chart, named after its original designer, Henry L. Gantt, a military advisor in World War I, is used both as a planning document and as a place to document actual performance. Planned timelines are drawn for each major activity (work package or component level) and are positioned on a time grid so as to depict the planned start and finish times and activity duration. Columns may be added to show, in date format, the planned start and finish dates for each timeline. Also, planned equivalent time (in days usually) and estimated costs may be added for each line item. The person responsible can also be added on each line. The chart is also referred to as a "milestone chart" when it indicates critical review and decision points, with a symbol, along the major timelines.

For simpler projects, the activity interdependencies are readily apparent. Figure 4.7 shows a Gantt chart for the garage project laid out in Figures 4.5 and 4.6.

(Note: Figure 4.7 reflects the addition of time and cost estimates after resource requirements have been determined.)

The Gantt chart can also be used as a recording and reporting device for documenting actual performance during the course of the project. To do this, each planned timeline is double-spaced, that is, an additional line below it is used to record actual dates, times, costs, and a bar is added to show the actual task duration.

A Gantt chart can be created either by using a spreadsheet program or the "table" function in your word processing program. Figure 4.7 was originally created in Microsoft Word. A detailed WBS provides data for compilation and posting to a Gantt chart.

Resource Requirements Matrix

When a project will involve several people with diverse levels of expertise at different periods of time, creating a personnel Resource Requirements Matrix (RRM) is a wise investment. Likewise, if there are multiple sites, suppliers, customer involvement, or equipment needed, an RRM for each is suggested.

The RRM is a simple format. For example, the breakdown of the types of personnel required is quantified (number of people plus hours, days, or weeks of equivalent time) and allocated to the time period in which such personnel are required. Figure 4.8 is a hypothetical personnel RRM.

A detailed WBS provides a basis for estimating requirements and posting to RRMs.

Project Budget

Estimating Time and Costs

One of the most challenging chores in the project planning cycle is the estimating of time and costs. If possible, it is wise to refer to similar tasks that have been performed before to gain a sense of the approximate time a given task will take. Time and cost

Gantt Chart–Garage Building Project–Project #02
(hypothetical)

Week ending →

ID#	Activity /task	S	F	Days	$	April	May	June	July	August	Septmeber
02	New garage project	0401	0922	102	42125						
02.01	Purchase drawings	0401	0401	1	25						
02.02	Select builder	0401	0412	2	0						
02.03	Obtain permits	0414	0430	1	150						
02.04	Order materials	0505	0527	2	3000						
02.05	Construct garage	0505	0913	88	36150						
02.05.01	Lay foundation	0517	0527	5	3500						
02.05.01.01	Prepare lot	0517	0520	3	1500						
02.05.01.02	Set forms and pour	0524	0527	2	2000						
02.05.02	Erect structure	0607	0811	45	19350						
02.05.02.01	Framing	0607	0630	15	6750						
02.05.02.02	Roof	0621	0719	12	5400						
02.05.02.03	Windows & doors	0721	0730	3	450						
02.05.02.04	Siding	0722	0811	15	6750						
02.05.03	Finish structure	0726	0913	38	13300						
02.05.03.01	Electrical work	0726	0818	15	5250						
02.05.03.02	Plumbing work	0728	0820	10	3500						
02.05.03.03	Interior finish, painting	0823	0831	7	2450						
02.05.03.04	Exterior finish, paint	0831	0913	6	2100						
02.06	Property reconstruction	0816	0922	8	2800						
02.06.00.01	Driveway	0816	0831	4	1400						
02.06.00.02	Landscaping	0831	0922	4	1400						

Legend: ▬▬ Total project ▬▬ Sub-project - - - - Component ·········· Work package > Single day (Task level is not shown)

Figure 4.7 Gantt chart—garage building project.

Personnel Resource Requirements—Project #5
(hypothetical)

#	Talent required	Level	Equiv Days	April				May				June				July				August			Septmeber		
	Week ending ⟶			2 9	1 6	2 3	3 0	7 4	1 4	2 1	2 8	1 1	1 8	2 5	9 6	1 6	2 3 0	3 6 0	1 3 0	2 0 7	2 3 7	1 0 7	1 7 4	2 4
1	Project manager from quality function	5	62																						
1	Engineering—laser-cutting machine specs and evaluation	4	14																						
1	Machine installer	3	5																						
1	Installer helper	1	5																						
1	Production supervisior	4	47																						
1	Cutting machine operator and trainer	2	32																						
1	Work instruction documenter	4	10																						

Figure 4.8   Personnel resource requirements—project #5.

estimates are built up from the lowest project level chosen, such as the Work Package level. Suggested places to look for guidance are:

- A previous project of similar scope and containing similar work packages is a likely place to look. If a knowledge database of documented completed projects is maintained you may be able to find just what you need.

- Some industry trade associations standardize and catalog routine task times and make the catalog available to association members.

- Consult a group of experienced workers from your own organization who are doing, or have done, the type of task for which you need a time estimate.

- Ask one or two workers to simulate doing the work package for which you need a time estimate. Time the work, including preparatory steps, movement of material, storage of product, lookup steps, and data entry steps.

- Ask someone on or outside the project team who is good at visualizing doing a task to visualize the task for which you need an estimate.

- Contact outside organizations doing similar work and ask for their assistance.

- When all else fails, poll the project team members for their best guess and select the answer you are most comfortable with, perhaps an average of the estimates.

An estimated work package timeline is usually expressed in "equivalent days." If a performer is to start a task on Monday and finish on Thursday, it is assumed for the timeline that the equivalent time period, or duration, is four days. However, for estimating personnel costs for the same work package, it may be that the anticipated time to be spent will total six hours spread over the four days. Therefore, for estimating time lines, the total anticipated time period, or duration, is used. However, when estimating personnel costs the actual time expected to be spent doing the work is more precise and realistic. In the example just given, the work package time duration is four days, the personnel cost associated with the work is the estimated time to do the work (six hours) times the compensation typically paid for the type of person assigned to the work package. Some projects for some customers may require more finite estimating, such as half days, quarter days, or even hours.

Estimating personnel costs means finding out the specific pay rate for the individual(s) who are planned to do the work (difficult to impossible in many organizations). A typical alternative is to obtain pay ranges for the job levels needed, from your human resources/personnel department, and choose the pay rate within each range that most reflects the experience and longevity of the type of individual you expect to be assigned. Other alternatives are:

- For quality professionals, ASQ publications, *Quality Progress* and the *Quality Digest* publish annual salary surveys, as do other industry publications.

- Asking project team members to guess at the pay rate for the types of individuals needed for each activity or task.

- Obtaining industry figures for average pay rates.

Regardless of the method used to obtain a base pay rate for specific types of performers, you need to be sure the rate includes the "benefits" figure typical for your organization. The benefits package can range from a very low to a high percentage (35–40 percent added to the base is not uncommon). The benefits percentage can be much higher for persons of higher rank within the organization. Additionally, your organization may use "burdened" pay rates to allocate "overhead" costs. Be careful to use the right percentage. It has a substantial impact on overall costs.

Compiling the Budget

In preparing a project budget, consideration must be given to organizational policies, procedures, guidelines, and sometimes contractual mandates. A decision must be made regarding the level of control essential to organizational fiscal responsibility, the experience level of the project manager and the project team, and the sensitivity of the project's outcomes on the organization. The more granular the budget the more effort is required in estimating and the more effort must be committed to tracking, measuring, and reporting. In an earlier example, the plans shown stopped at the work package level because if the budget were to track time and dollar expenditures in much more detail, the cost of maintaining the system might reduce the return on the project investment.

Preparing the budget consists of compiling the estimated costs shown at the lowest WBS level established as the control level, for example, the work package level. In this case, the first pass was taken by the individuals responsible for the work of each work package. These estimates were reflected as time (T) and cost (C) figures on the WBS. (See Figures 4.5 and 4.6, and the Gantt chart, Figure 4.7.)

If there is a predetermined time to complete (there usually is) and a predetermined cost cap (there often is), the aggregated time and cost estimates must not exceed the established cap. In rare cases it may be possible to renegotiate a higher cap. It would be better to return to the estimating and "sharpen your pencil." Revisit the estimates of critical activities:

- Look for any opportunity to combine activities and reduce personnel costs.

- Rethink the process flow to determine if some activities may be removed.

- Break some activities into segments, some of which could be achieved with lower-cost personnel.

- Determine if any labor-saving equipment or alternative approach can reduce costs, such as:

–Outsourcing activity

–Using temporary workers

–Replacing manual activity with a computer program (be careful to consider the added cost of learning and building efficiency in using a new program)

Any revised estimates should be changed on all pertinent documents. When the estimates have been reviewed and brought into line with any imposed constraint, the compilation of equivalent days and estimated costs constitutes the budget, or the sum of all lowest-level estimates (see Figure 4.9).

Some projects, usually contracted by the customer, may require planning by stages. A "go/no go" decision is to be made at the conclusion of each stage. For this situation the budget would be laid out by the specified stages. The result is similar to a cash-flow budget presentation. See Figure 4.10 for an example.

Always keep in mind the time and cost of creating and maintaining the documentation in relation to the size, complexity, and value of the project. Minimal acceptable detail (the MAD approach!) is better than overkill.

Measurements

Measurements are established for two main purposes:

1. Measurements used while the project is under way; metrics are used to:

   –Detect any deviance from plans that could affect the successful completion of the project and allow for making "course corrections" to bring the project back into alignment with the plans.

   –Monitor usage of resources in order to ensure that adequate resources are available as needed.

   –Monitor effectiveness of project team.

2. Measurements used to evaluate outputs and outcomes from the project; metrics are used to determine whether:

   –Project has exceeded, met, or not met stated objectives, including scheduled deliverables.

   –Stakeholders' requirements have been exceeded, met, or not met.

   –Budget is on target or there is a cost overrun or underrun.

   –Project's return on investment (ROI) is positive or unfavorable.

   –Resource use has been under target, as planned, or over target.

   –Lessons learned have been identified and reviewed, actions to improve have been initiated, and the lessons have been documented.

Project Charter

Before the proposed Project Plans are submitted, a Project Charter should be drafted. The charter is the approval document that authorizes launching of the project activities. The charter is not only the official sign-off that the plans have been approved but is also the formal authorization for the acquisition of resources and the appointment

ID #	Work Package	Equivalent Days	Cost
02.01	Purchase drawings	1	$25
02.02	Select builder	2	0
02.03	Obtain permits	1	150
02.04	Order materials	2	3,000
02.05.01.01	Prepare lot	3	1,500
02.05.01.02	Set forms, pour	2	2,000
02.05.02.01	Framing	15	6,750
02.05.02.02	Roof	12	5,400
02.05.02.03	Windows & doors	3	450
02.05.02.04	Siding	15	6,750
02.05.03.01	Electrical work	15	5,250
02.05.03.02	Plumbing work	10	3,500
02.05.03.03	Interior finish	7	2,450
02.05.03.04	Exterior finish	6	2,100
02.06	Reconstruct property	8	2,800
Totals		102	$42,125

Figure 4.9   Project budget—garage project.

of the project manager and team. The charter, when approved, is distributed to appropriate stakeholders as official notification of what the project is about and the organizational outcomes the project is expected to generate. Figure 4.11 is a sample Project Charter form. Preparing the Project Charter at this point assumes that the "planning stage" has been authorized and funded earlier. If the project is small enough, there may be no need for a "funds to plan" approval stage.

Project Plan Submission

The project manager, with the team's collaboration, prepares an executive summary of the project plans, emphasizing the outcomes. Depending on the organization's policies and practices, the plans are submitted, in some form, as a written request for approval. There may or may not be a need for a formal oral presentation to the approving authority, although this is an excellent way to deal with questions and any resistance face-to-face.

Following the plan submission there may be need for further tweaking of the plans to satisfy the needs and wishes of the approving authority, assuming the plans have not been completely rejected. In reality, the larger and more sensitive the project is, the more likely it is that several iterations with major alterations will be required before a green light is obtained.

Assume a project has four stages and five team members.
Prepare budget for each stage.

Member	Planned Hours per Stage				$ per hour
	1	2	3	4	
Beth Esda	10	15	15	25	$20
Anna Lyst	8	8	6	12	$15
Ed Ifye	0	15	25	20	$18
Jule Ly	0	20	20	25	$9
Ali Ghator	10	5	10	15	$10
Total	28	63	76	97	

Labor Hours Budgeted per Stage

Stage	Hours	%	Cum %
1	28	10	10
2	63	24	34
3	76	29	63
4	97	37	100
Total	264	10	

Labor Dollars Budgeted per Stage

Member	Hourly $	Stage 1	Stage 2	Stage 3	Stage 4
Beth Esda	$20	$200	$300	$300	$500
Anna Lyst	$15	$120	$120	$90	$180
Ed Ifye	$18	$0	$270	$450	$360
Jule Ly	$9	$0	$180	$180	$225
Ali Ghator	$10	$100	$50	$100	$150
Total		$420	$920	$1,120	$1,415

Non-labor Expenses = $2,800

Stage	%	Dollars
1	0	$280
2	24	$672
3	29	$812
4	37	$1,036
Total	100	$2,800

Project Budget

Stage	Labor	Non-labor	Total
1	$420	$280	$700
2	$920	$672	$1,592
3	$1,120	$812	$1,932
4	$1,415	$1,036	$2,451
Total	$3,455	$2,520	$5,975

Figure 4.10 Budget example.

PROJECT CHARTER						Sheet 1 of 2

PROJECT CHARTER   Sheet 1 of 2

Project name: _____   Project No.: _____

Planned start date: _____   Planned finish date: _____

Project purpose:

_____

Project scope (including key stakeholders and deliverables):

_____

Projected outcomes (how much, by when?):

_____

Budget (by primary type of expenditure, by cash flow over life of project):

	Totals					
In-house personnel						
Contract personnel						
Facilities						
Equipment & tools						
Materials						
Permits						
Other _____						
Other _____						
Totals						

Decision constraints placed on project manager and on project team:

_____

Special issues, parameters, or conditions specifically affecting this project:

Continued

Figure 4.11   Project charter (form).

Continued

PROJECT CHARTER		Sheet 2 of 2

Project name: _____ Project No.: _____

Planned start date: _____ Planned finish date: _____ Sheet 2 of 2

Project Team

Names	% Time on project
Project Manager:	
Team member:	
Team member:	
Team member:	
Team member:	
Team member:	
Team member:	
Team member:	
Team member:	
Team member:	
Team member:	
Team member:	

Project Plan Approvals

Approval Authority	Signatures & Organization Title	Date signed
Project Manager		
Project sponsor		
Key stakeholder (customer)		
Key stakeholder (customer)		
Key stakeholder (customer)		
Key stakeholder (customer)		
Final authority (within org.)		

Summary

This chapter has taken you through three levels of planning complexity:

- Task Schedule approach
- Action Plan approach
- Basic nine-step model for planning

Chapter 6 will add several more techniques and tools for handling medium-size projects of longer duration and larger costs.

You have seen that, except for the most rudimentary short-term project, project planning and management is far more than just getting a few colleagues together and setting a schedule. However, you now have a basic understanding of the fundamentals of project management, and you have a basis for building your knowledge and skills for more challenging project assignments.

When you work with others on a project, either as a project leader/manager or as a member of a project team, it is beneficial to understand how teams are formed and how they are managed. Chapter 5 digresses from the techniques and tools of project planning to provide guidelines for team formation and management—the people who will plan and execute the plans.

Notes

1. © 1999 R.T. Westcott & Associates, reprinted with permission.
2. Eric Verzuh, in his book *The Fast Forward MBA in Project Management*, John Wiley & Sons, 1999, suggests that project management should be included in the plans under "Managing the project."

QUICK QUIZ
NUMBER 4

1. What are the major differences between a Task Schedule and a list of things to do?

2. How would you differentiate between when it would be appropriate to use an Action Plan and when it would not?

3. Based on your reading from this book, and supplemented by reading from other sources, what is the purpose of Project Scope, and what should be included?

4. In any project except a very small one, what one document is most essential as the foundation for developing project plans and managing the project?

5. Should the steps needed to plan and manage the project be considered in the:

   —Project feasibility analysis?

   —Project Scope?

   —Work Breakdown Structure?

   —Schedule?

   —Network diagram?

   —Project budget?

   —Project Charter?

   —Project Status Reports?

   —Project Evaluation?

   —Project Closeout Report?

   —Lessons Learned documentation?

6. What are at least two major reasons for preparing Resource Requirement Matrixes?

7. Why is a Gantt chart sometimes referred to as a Milestone chart?

8. Compare a cash-flow budget to a Resource Requirements Matrix. In what ways:

   —Are they similar?

   —Do they differ?

9. Assuming that the Project Charter officially authorizes the launching of a project and the formation of the project team, which of the following statements will most likely be true?

   —The initial project planning documents will undergo extensive reworking as the team begins to work out the details for completing the project.

   —The approval obtained for the *Project Charter* means strict adherence to the approved plans is mandatory.

10. What are some of the circumstances that could cause "scope creep," and what should be done to prevent it?

5

Forming and Leading
a Project Team[1]

In Chapter 4, it was assumed that you were planning a small project. If you required talent to work with you, those additional heads and hands probably would have been people you knew quite well and with whom you had worked before.

In this chapter it will be assumed that you are to lead a medium-size, more complex project of longer duration and that you're not going it alone or working with a few old buddies. You're going to have to:

- Specify the competencies you require.

- Determine how and from where team members will be selected.

- Decide how the team will be organized.

- Identify what team roles team members will play.

- Estimate the amount of time team members will need to spend on the project.

- Plan how to address the inevitable conflict that will occur between the project needs and the ongoing responsibilities of each member in their "real job."

- Establish where and when team members will work on the project.

- Attend to team members' concerns about the potential for losing out on promotions, preferred assignments, and pay raises resulting from being partly or fully out of the mainstream.

- Ascertain what knowledge and skills training team members will need and possibly arrange for education or training in:
  –Teamwork
  –Project planning and management
  –Developing new or enhancing existing technical and social skills
- Communicate to members the means and frequency by which their project performance will be measured and evaluated.

- Facilitate the establishment of team behavior rules and guidelines.

- Sharpen your personal competency in:

  –Forming and leading a team

  –Handling team dynamics

  –Project management techniques, practices and tools

  –Negotiating and dealing with diverse stakeholders, including higher management—especially people over whom you have little or no authority

  –Working under a spotlight where you and your team's every move may be scrutinized

Team Structures

The structure of your project team may take one or a mix of several different forms, such as:

- Natural teams

- Process improvement teams

- Cross-functional teams

- Dedicated project teams

- Self-directed teams

- Virtual teams

A work unit or group is of itself not a team. However, an entire or substantial part of a work unit may function as a team, that is, a team to create something or to accomplish a complex task. Thus, when a single work unit functions as a team to achieve a specific objective, but with members coming from only the single work unit, it is called a "natural team."

Process improvement teams focus on improving specific business processes. The team may be composed of persons from various functions and with a variety of expertise. If the team is focused on a major breakthrough, it is a cross-functional team and a perhaps a dedicated project team and, perhaps even a virtual team. If the team members are concerned with "incremental" process improvements within their own work unit, they are a natural team.

Natural teams, cross-functional teams, process improvement teams, dedicated project teams, and virtual teams can all be self-directed. Self-directed (self-managed) teams are empowered to make a wide range of decisions relating to the project's administration, allocation of work, work standards, safety and quality issues, conflict resolution, and so forth. Self-directed teams often select their own project leader.

Virtual teams may be composed of two or more persons who are affiliated with a common organization and work on a common project but are not necessarily employees. Virtual project team members, typically geographically dispersed, conduct their work either partly or wholly via electronic communication. Virtual project teams may or may not be cross-functional in terms of competencies and they may or may not be self-directed. For example, the author has participated on three virtual project teams in the writing of two books and one training program for ASQ.

Project Team Roles and Responsibilities

Table 5.1 outlines the roles, responsibilities, and attributes of project team members.

Several roles within the project team may be combined, depending upon the size of the team and its purpose. For example, an experienced project team may not require the services of a facilitator, at least not throughout the project's life. Members also performing in other roles may assume the roles of timekeeper and scribe. The timekeeper and scribe roles may be rotated to remove the onus of bias. Even the project leader's role may be rotated. On-call subject matter experts (SMEs) may or may not be designated as project team members. In some situations, the roles of champion, sponsor, and project team leader could be the responsibility of one person.

> I once listened to a talk by the president of a 90-person company. He felt so strongly committed that he assumed the role of champion, sponsor, and project leader of the project team that successfully implemented the organization's quality management system. They received ISO 9001 certification in the first time through their audit.

Linear Responsibility Chart

For projects involving many people and where each person or position interfaces with the project for different reasons, laying out the team members' responsibilities clarifies the responsibilities for the entire team. The linear responsibility chart (LRC) is a matrix showing task activities and events, review and oversight roles, and other supporting roles. Stakeholders of the project and approval authorities may also be included. Typically the roles and responsibilities are listed vertically and the persons or positions responsible are spread across the top of the matrix. Usually symbols are used in the intersecting boxes to indicate the level of responsibility, such as primary responsibility (P), secondary or support responsibility (S), subject matter expert on-call (E), approving authority (A), and need-to-know only (K). Of course other types of symbols may be used depending on the intended use of the LRC. Figure 5.1 is a sample LRC.

Team Size

The ideal size of the project team may be five members, but many factors influence the size, for example:

- Project objectives

- Planned project outcomes

- Size and complexity of the tasks of the project team

- Size of the organization in which the project team will be formed

Table 5.1 Roles, responsibilities, and performance attributes of quality project team members.

Role Name	Responsibility	Definition	Attributes of Good Role Performance
Champion	Advocate	The person initiating a concept or idea for change/improvement	• Dedicated to see it implemented • Absolute belief it is the right thing to do • Perseverance and stamina
Sponsor	Backer, Risk Taker	The person who supports a team's project plans, activities, and outcomes	• Believes in the concept/idea • Sound business acumen • Willing to take risk and responsibility for outcomes • Authority to approve needed resources • Upper management will listen to her or him
Project Team Leader	Change agent; Chair; Head	One who: • Staffs the team, or provides input for staffing requirements • Strives to bring about change/ improvement through the team's outcomes • Followers entrust her/him to lead them • Has the authority for and directs the efforts of the project team • Participates as a team member • Coaches team members in developing or enhancing necessary competencies • Communicates with management about the project team's progress and needs • Handles the logistics of project team meetings • Takes responsibility for project team records	• Committed to the team's mission and objectives • Experienced in planning, organizing, staffing, controlling, and directing • Capable of creating and maintaining channels that enable members to do their work • Capable of gaining the respect of team members; a role model • Is firm, fair, and factual in dealing with a project team of diverse individuals • Facilitates discussion without dominating • Actively listens • Empowers project team members to the extent possible within the organization's culture • Supports all team members equally • Respects each team member's individuality
Facilitator	Helper; Trainer; Advisor; Coach	A person who: • Observes the project team's processes and team members' interactions and suggests process changes to facilitate positive movement toward the project team's goals and objectives • Intervenes if discussion develops into multiple conversations	• Trained in facilitating skills • Respected by project team • members • Tactful • Knows when and when not to intervene • Deals with the team's process, not content • Respects the team leader and does not override his or her responsibility • Respects confidential information shared by individuals or the team as a whole

Continued

Continued

Role Name	Responsibility	Definition	Attributes of Good Role Performance
		• Intervenes to skillfully prevent an individual. dominating the discussion, or to engage an overlooked individual in the discussion • Assists project team leader in bringing discussions to a close • May provide training in team building, conflict management, etc	• Will not accept facilitator role if expected to report to management information that is proprietary to the team • Will abide by the ASQ Code of Ethics
Timekeeper	Gatekeeper; Monitor	A person designated by the team to watch the use of allocated time and remind the team when their time objective may be in jeopardy.	• Capable of assisting the project team leader in keeping the project team meeting within the time limitations predetermined • Sufficiently assertive to intervene in discussions when the time allocation is in jeopardy • Capable of participating as a member while still serving as a timekeeper
Scribe	Recorder; Note taker	A person designated by the team to record critical data from project team meetings. Formal "minutes" of the meetings may be published to interested parties.	• Capable of capturing on paper, or electronically, the main points and decisions made in a project team meeting, and providing a complete, accurate, and legible document (or formal minutes) for the team's records • Sufficiently assertive to intervene in discussions to clarify a point or decision in order to record it accurately • Capable of participating as a member while still serving as a scribe
Team Members	Participants; Subject matter experts (on call)	The persons selected to work together to bring about a change/improvement, achieving this in a created environment of mutual respect, sharing of expertise, cooperation and support.	• Willing to commit to the purpose of the team • Able to express ideas, opinions, suggestions in a nonthreatening manner • Capable of listening attentively to other project team members • Receptive to new ideas and suggestions • Even-tempered, able to handle stress and cope with problems openly • Competent in one or more fields ofexpertise needed by the project team • Favorable performance record • Willing to function as a project team member and forfeit "star" status

	Project Responsibilities						
Work Package	Project Leader RTW	Engineer ERT	Systems Analyst MKY	Programmer STM	Technician PAC (vendor)	End User WCJ (customer)	Project Sponsor BFG
Project planning & management	L, M	M	M	M	E	E	A, K
Perform needs assessment	M	L	M			A	
Prepare system specifications	M	L	M	M	E	E, A	
Code & test program	K	E	E	L	E		
Conduct trial run(s)	K	E	M	L	E	E	K
Review & modify program	L	M	M	M	E	E, A	K
Final test & user signoff	L	M	M	M	E	A	K
Project closeout & documentation	L	M	M	M			A, K

Symbols:
    L = Lead role
    M = participating team Member
    E = Expert on call
    K = need to Know (be kept informed)
    A = Approver

Figure 5.1   Sample linear responsibility chart (truncated).

- Type and structure of the project team

- Duration of the project team's work and frequency of meetings

- Degree of urgency for the outcomes of the project team's efforts

- Resource constraints, such as funding, availability of appropriate personnel, facilities, equipment

- Team management constraints, such as minimum and maximum number of team members needed to achieve the project team's objectives and outcomes

- Organizational culture; organizational policies and practices

- Predominant managing style of the organization to which the project team reports

- Regulatory requirements

- Customer mandates

Selecting Project Team Members

The basis for a strong, successful team is in the careful selection of its members. (See Table 5.1, Roles, Responsibilities, and Performance Attributes.)

Team members are often selected because of their knowledge and past achievements. Membership choices for smaller and shorter-duration teams are frequently based on informal referrals. Some instruments and formal methods may be employed in staffing larger and longer-duration teams, especially where candidates may be unknown to the sponsor or team leader.

Although it may help, neither charisma nor superiority (e.g., position, education, longevity, or political clout) is the primary criterion for choosing a potentially effective team leader. For example:

A floundering project team, formed to design and implement a substantive information technology project, failed to reach any of its first-year goals, other than spending the $100,000 (1970 time period) allocated for the project. The small team of three, augmented by personnel from a software design firm, was led by a person who had an in-depth knowledge of present systems, the organization, and the principal people in the organization. He had been with the company his entire working career and was within two years of retirement when first assigned. A systems analyst and an accomplished computer programmer were the other in-house project team members.

When the CEO became concerned that nothing visible was occurring he ordered that a new project manager be assigned with the directive to find out what was going on, with an objective to then recommend project continuance or abandonment. The new project manager assessed the situation and confirmed that the three project incumbents had sufficient expertise, with help from the software firm, to complete the project with a one-year extension and with additional funding.

The recommendation was approved and the now four-person team proceeded under new direction. Formal project management practices were instituted, and a tight timeline with interim milestones and clear objectives for the work were established. Measurements and monitoring were instituted, along with weekly progress reviews. Much of the earlier work had to be discarded. Agreements had to be obtained for the analyst and the programmer to ensure their reentry to their former work units when the project was completed. The contract with the software house had to be renegotiated, with applicable performance penalty clauses. Working conditions for the team were improved. Means for recognizing their contribution were created.

Relieved of his project manager responsibility, the former leader poured newfound energy and his extensive knowledge into the detailed design of the system, eager to retire with a success. Assured of getting their jobs back after the project was completed, the analyst and the programmer were committed to making the project successful.

The successful completion of the project, 10 months later, was due in large part to the new team leader's project management competency. He succeeded without having the specific detailed knowledge and skill sets of his team members.

Ideally, a profile of what attributes are being sought for each member of a team establishes the criteria for guiding selection. Let's begin by asking two questions. First, how do you define competency? Second, how do you ensure that you acquire people with the level of competency you need to support your project's requirements? Competency consists of five factors (see Figure 5.2):

Knowledge—Formal education, degrees, education certifications, professional certifications, self-study achievements

Experience—Years spent applying knowledge and skills, in types of organizations, in kinds of industries, in jobs/positions held

Skills—Skill certifications, training received, demonstrated proficiency in use of pertinent tools and equipment

Aptitude—Natural talent, capability, capacity, innate qualities, deftness, knack, adaptable to change, natural ability to do things requiring hand-eye coordination, fine-motor skills

Attitude—Manner of showing one's feelings or thoughts; one's disposition, opinion, mood, opinion, ideas about, belief, demeanor, condition of mind, state of feeling, reaction, bias, inclination, emotion, temperament, disposition, mental state, frame of mind, ease in accepting and adopting new or changed plans and practices

Seeking and selecting people who possess the needed KESAA factors begins with an analysis of the work to be done. For each identified body of work the analyst probes for the KESAA factors that are required as well as the relevant level of each such factor. For example:

Sure-Shot, a manufacturer of missile launchers for the U.S. Army, is seeking a quality professional to lead the introduction of a Six Sigma–based quality initiative. The person hired will report directly to the vice president of operations. This position, new to the company, requires the analyst to do some research in learning how other companies have defined the requirements of the position. The resulting analysis addresses the KESAA factors as follows:

- *Knowledge:* Formal education—mechanical or electronic engineering degree, MBA (desired)
- *Experience:* 3–5 years as a quality manager in a defense industry company; 7–10 years in applying statistical-based quality design and control tools; 1–3 years in leading one or more process improvement teams, 1–3 years performing in a middle or upper management position
- *Skills:* Master Black Belt, ASQ-Certified Quality Engineer and/or Certified Six Sigma Black Belt, proven project leadership skills, Project Management Professional certification (desired)

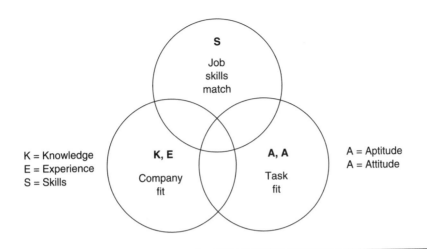

Figure 5.2 The KESAA factors.

- *Aptitude:* Demonstrated ability to adapt rapidly to changing work conditions, company strategy, new techniques and tools, and customer requirements
- *Attitude:* Clearly enjoys a challenge, takes extreme pride in leading a team to achieving objectives; has no objection to working in the defense industry

Using KESAA to Build a Process Improvement Project Team

In addition to basic selection criteria for new positions, identifying the KESAA factors for selecting candidates for roles on a project team is especially useful. Usually project team members comprise a cross-functional and cross-discipline collection of diverse individuals. Knowing what tasks are to be done by team members and what KESAA factors are critical to those tasks can substantially influence "getting the right mix." For example:

Figure 5.3 shows KESAA factors most desirable for fulfilling the Work Package "Train project managers in using new Microsoft Project software." This Work Package is a subset of a project entitled "Select and Implement Project Management Software." The more analysis is done to identify the KESAA factors for each Work Package/task on the work breakdown structure the greater likelihood of selecting the best persons to accomplish those tasks.

Selecting and hiring the right people for the right job, at the right time, and for the right reasons is almost totally neglected in the quest for quality. Requisitioning "one degreed quality engineer" for your project does little to guide the selection process in seeking and fitting candidates to the key tasks the incumbent will need to perform.

PROJECT STAFFING—KESAA REQUISITES ANALYSIS

[Define KESAA factors for each key project participant planned on the resource requirements matrix—personnel]

Task/Work package name: Train project managers in using new Microsoft Project software
Task/WP Number: 3.10.01.01
Job/Position Category/Title: Application software specialist

Knowledge	• Knows proven techniques for designing and delivering software training to people with diverse knowledge, experience and skills • Extensive knowledge of project planning and management techniques, tools and practices • Received Microsoft certificate for completing the advanced MS Project five-day training program, within last four years • Earned college degree (software major)
Experience	• Has instructed project teams in use of MS Project at a previous employer, two or more times • Used MS Project on two or more previous large-scale projects • Has demonstrated proficiency in providing software technical support for MS Project users working on large-scale projects • Has demonstrated proficiency in using thorough, rapid and user-friendly techniques for training new software users
Skills	• Possesses excellent communication skills (reading comprehension, instructing, technical writing, and listening) • Proficient in using all Microsoft Office software • Trained in using proven instructional technology in training design, delivery, and evaluation
Aptitude	• Has capability to adapt the MS Project training to the special needs of each participant • Has worked well in a team environment that is subject to frequent changes. Fast learner
Attitude	• Enjoys imparting his/her knowledge and skills to new software users • Measures his/her success on the improved performance of those trained by him/her • Believes that MS Project is the best selection of Project Management software, at this time and place • Exhibits "What can we do to make this happen?" demeanor

Additional comments:

_____

_____

_____

_____

Prepared by: Anna Lyst   Date: June 30, 2004

Figure 5.3   Project staffing—KESAA requisites analysis.

In the field of training, much is written about the need for performing a detailed needs analysis of the task requirements for which the trainees are to be qualified. That's fine, but that's for instructing existing performers in how to do a new task or enhance their present skill level. Where is effort being made to reasonably ensure that candidates for hire or reassignment are assessed for the best fit to the organization's needs? If done at all, this assessment is usually left up to the functional manager to do during an interview. Some experienced managers are capable of making good intuitive judgments or guesses. Most managers are less experienced in the hiring and assignment process and may make unsubstantiated choices.

As a quality professional, what can you do about making an informed decision in the selection of people for a project team? Do a KESAA analysis (see description of KESAA factors earlier in this chapter). Describe the criteria (the KESAA factors) that are critical to choosing the best person for the project assignment.

The analysis is a very inexpensive task. And, once the analysis is done it should remain valid for some time. Also, as a database of KESAA analyses builds there should be a decreasing need for new analyses.

Some of the advantages you may be able to document in support of the use of the KESAA factors are:

- Candidate selected is better equipped for the work to be done; the candidate:
  - Best fits the organization and the work assignment
  - Is satisfied in doing the work he or she is assigned to do
  - Demonstrates potential for further growth and development
- Higher productivity; candidate:
  - "Hits the pavement running" (gets up to speed rapidly)
  - Experiences shorter learning curve
- Lower costs; approach:
  - Develops less waste (e.g., time and errors)
  - Takes management less time to make selection
  - Decreases likelihood of making wrong selection
  - Requires less investment in assimilation and training
- Improved employee satisfaction; results in:
  - Ultimately influencing improved customer satisfaction
  - Self-motivated employees who are easier to manage
  - Facilitating transition to employee empowerment practices

Other Considerations

Résumés of candidates and records of past performance are reviewed and interviews of potential project members are conducted. Tests may augment member selection. One instrument used is the Myers-Briggs Type Indicator (MBTI®), which is based on Carl Jung's theory of personality preferences. The test results, analyzed by a trained practitioner, can aid in recruiting either the diversity or the similarity desired in potential project team members.

In addition to the composition of the team, another key factor for its success is whether the project team will function as an autonomous parallel organization or as an adjunct to the daily operation of the organization. The dedicated project team is often located away from the parent organization and is sometimes exempt from some of the restrictive rules of the parent organization. Members of such a team are typically on temporary assignment to the team and do not carry their former daily responsibilities with them while participating in the new assignment. When the project team members retain day-to-day responsibilities, conflicts can arise over which activity takes precedence. If such conflicts are not carefully handled, team effectiveness can be compromised.

> Pills-Are-Us, a cross-functional process improvement team in a small community hospital, was established to find ways to reduce the time it took to obtain medications from the hospital's pharmacy. A nine-person team was to meet for one hour once a week "until they found a way to substantially reduce the cycle time." The team consisted of seven nurses from each of the larger departments, one pharmacist and one internal delivery-service person.
>
> From the outset, the team was plagued with absences and late arrivals. Each absent or tardy member had legitimate reasons. Regardless, team effectiveness suffered and the project dragged on without an end in sight. Repeatedly, the team leader attempted to get department heads to help resolve the conflict, but their concerns were elsewhere.
>
> Finally, the team's sponsor, a vice president, stepped up to his responsibility and convened a meeting of department heads to reaffirm their commitment and reach agreement as to how their employees' participation would be handled. Priorities were established, resource-sharing agreements were reached, and supervisors were advised of the decisions. Project team participation now had its assigned priority and management commitment to back it up. The team members were relieved of having to decide which "master" to serve first and under what conditions.

Project Team Meetings

The structure of team meetings depends on the project team's objectives, its size, its duration, its projected outcomes, the competency of its members, and the degree of urgency of results required. Project teams may range from having no formal meetings to frequently scheduled meetings with extensive agenda and formal minutes. Certain rules and regulations, as well as client requirements, may specify the extent of meetings to be held. For example:

A company whose quality management system is certified under the QS-9000 or TS16949 automotive standard is expected to conduct periodic design reviews (meetings) as a product is being developed. Evidence that such reviews have been conducted and documented is examined. Failure to comply could result in suspension or withdrawal of the certification.

In a typical formal project team meeting, the team leader would arrange for an agenda to be prepared and sent to all project team members. The agenda would state the time, place, and intent of the meeting. Additional material may be attached as premeeting reading for participants to prepare themselves for discussion. In some cases the role of each team member pertinent to the topic(s) of the meeting, including why their input is needed, and decisions that will have to be made, may be spelled out in advance. The logistics of obtaining the meeting venue and equipping the meeting room is the responsibility of the leader, but the task is often delegated to an assistant.

All project team members have a responsibility to assist the project team in reaching consensus when differences of opinion arise, yet challenge assumptions that could endanger the project outcomes or the effectiveness of the team. Further, each member must respect and cooperate with others on the team.

Inasmuch as a project team should function as a process, a Team Meeting Process Self-Assessment (Figure 5.4) can be a useful tool to critique the overall effectiveness of a project team meeting. The value lies in having each team member and the facilitator, just before adjourning, complete the assessment, discuss the results, reach consensus, and set one or more meeting improvement objectives for the next project meeting.

Groupthink

In the project team selection process, as well as when the project team is functioning day-to-day, care must be taken to avoid groupthink. Groupthink occurs when most or all of the team members coalesce in supporting an idea or a decision that hasn't been fully explored, or when some members may secretly disagree. The members are more concerned with maintaining friendly relations and avoiding conflict than in becoming engrossed in a controversial discussion.

Actions to forestall groupthink may include:

- Brainstorming alternatives before selecting an approach

- Encouraging members to express their concerns

- Ensuring that ample time is given to surface, examine, and comprehend all ideas and suggestions

- Developing rules for examining each alternative

- Appointing an "objector" to challenge proposed actions

Circle a number to represent your perception of the team's process in this meeting.

We had no agenda or did not follow the agenda we had.	**TEAM ON-TRACK** 1 2 3 4 5 6 7 8 9 10	An agenda was distributed in advance of the meeting and we followed it exactly.
Members who were supposed to attend didn't show. Others straggled in late.	**ATTENDANCE & PROMPTNESS** 1 2 3 4 5 6 7 8 9 10	All expected members attended and on time. The meeting started at the scheduled time.
Some members tended to dominate and others did not participate.	**PARTICIPATION** 1 2 3 4 5 6 7 8 9 10	Member participation was evenly balanced; everyone contributed to decisions, and openly discussed ideas.
More than one person talked at a time; disruptive remarks were made; side conversations occurred. Overall disrespect of person speaking was evident.	**LISTENING** 1 2 3 4 5 6 7 8 9 10	One person talked at a time; others helped clarify and build on ideas; all were attentive to person speaking. Respect for one another was evident.
No attempt was made to redirect the team to the agenda or to encourage balanced participation.	**SHARED LEADERSHIP** 1 2 3 4 5 6 7 8 9 10	Both the team leader and team members intervened to keep the team focused on agenda and to stimulate participation when needed.
When conflicts arose chaos resulted. Differences of opinion were allowed to escalate to inappropriate behavior and lack of adequate resolution.	**CONFLICT MANAGEMENT** 1 2 3 4 5 6 7 8 9 10	The energies involved with differing opinions were directed toward understanding conflicting views and seeking consensus.
Team decisions were inferior to what individuals would have produced. There was no attempt to summarize main ideas/ decisions and/or future actions/ responsibilities.	**RESULTS** 1 2 3 4 5 6 7 8 9 10	Team expertise and decisions were superior to individual judgments. Main ideas/decisions were summarized, and action assignments made at end of meeting.
Team was totally ineffective in achieving its purpose for this meeting.	**OVERALL RATING** 1 2 3 4 5 6 7 8 9 10	Team was totally effective in achieving its purpose for this meeting. All agenda items were addressed or properly tabled for the next meeting.

Figure 5.4   Team meeting process self-assessment.

Source: *The Quality Improvement Handbook,* John E. Bauer, Grace L. Duffy, & Russell T. Westcott, eds., Source: Milwaukee: ASQ Quality Press, 2002. Reprinted with permission.

Team Stages

Teams move through four stages of growth as they develop maturity over time. Each stage may vary in intensity and duration. A brief summary of the stages follows.[2]

Stage 1: Forming

The cultural background, values, and personal agendas of each team member come together in an environment of uncertainty. New members wonder: "What will be expected of me? How do I or can I fit in with these people? What are we really supposed to do? What are rules of the game and where do I find out about them?" Fear is often present but frequently denied. Fear may be about personal acceptance, possible inadequacy for the task ahead, and the consequences if the team fails its mission. These fears and other concerns manifest themselves in dysfunctional behavior such as maneuvering for position of status on the team, undercutting the ideas of others, degrading another member, trying to force one's point-of-view on others, bragging about one's academic credentials, vehemently objecting to any suggestion but one's own, abstaining from participation in discussions, distracting the work by injecting unwanted comments or trying to take the team off track, and retreating to a position of complete silence.

Because of the diversity of some teams, there may be a wide variety of disciplines, experience levels, academic levels, and cultural differences among the members. This can result in confusion and misunderstanding of terminology and language difficulties.

A technique for moving the team through this stage is to clearly state and understand the purpose of the team, identify the roles of the members, and establish criteria for acceptable behavior.

Stage 2: Storming

In this stage, team members still tend to think and act mostly as individuals. They struggle to find ways they can work together, or sometimes belligerently resist. Each member's perspective appears to be formed from personal experience rather than from information from the whole team. Uncertainty still exists, defenses are still up, and collaborating is not yet the accepted mode of operation. Members may be argumentative. They frequently test the leader's authority and competence. Members often try to redefine the goal and direction of the team and act as individual competitors.

Stage 3: Norming

At this stage, true teamwork begins. Members change from dwelling on their personal agendas to addressing the objectives of the team. Competitiveness, personality clashes, and loyalty issues are sublimated, and the team moves toward willingness to cooperate and to openly discuss differences of opinion. The leader focuses on process, promoting participation and team decision making, encouraging peer support, and providing feedback. A potential danger at this stage is that team members may withhold their good ideas for fear of reintroducing conflict.

Stage 4: Performing

Functioning as a mature and integrated team, the members may understand the strengths and weaknesses of themselves and other members. The leader focuses on monitoring and feedback, letting the team take responsibility for solving problems and making decisions. The team has become satisfied with its processes, is comfortable with its working relationships and in resolving team problems. The team is achieving its goals and objectives. However, reaching this stage does not presage smooth waters indefinitely.

Typically a team moves through these stages in sequence. A team may regress, however, when something disturbs its growth. The addition of a new member may take a team back to stage 1 as the new member tries to become accepted and the existing team members "test" the newcomer. Loss of a respected member may shift the apparent balance of power, and the team reverts to stage 2. A change in scope or threat of cancellation of a team's project may divert a team to an earlier stage to redefine direction. An individual team member's exposed manipulation of the team can cause anger, retrenchment to silence, or a push to reject the offending member, and a jump back to stage 1.

Some teams find difficulty in sustaining stage 4 and oscillate between stages 3 and 4. This may be a matter of inept team leadership, unsupportive sponsorship, less than competent team members, external factors threatening the life of the team's project, or a host of other factors.

Following is an example of an effective project team:

Big Risk Inc., an insurer of off-road construction and sport utility vehicles, has a strategic plan to reduce administrative expenses by 30 percent over the next three years. In support of this goal, the VP of administration sponsors a project, the Claim-Processing Team (CPT). The objective of the CPT is to reduce claim-processing cycle time from three weeks to four days, within one year. A team leader is selected. She gathers data and budgets savings of $250,000 per year, as well as an estimated project cost of $25,000.

The CPT members are selected from functions affected by any potential change. A facilitator is retained to conduct team-building training and to guide the team through its formative stages until it reaches a smooth functioning level of maturity. The CPT prepares a project plan, including monthly measurement of progress, time usage, and costs. The vice president (sponsor) approves the plan. The CPT fine-tunes its objectives, determines ground rules, and allocates the tasks to be performed. The project is launched.

The CPT reviews its progress weekly, making necessary adjustments. The CPT presents a monthly summary review to the VP of administration, giving the status of time usage, costs, and overall progress toward the goal. Any problems requiring the VP's intervention or approval are discussed (e.g., need for more cooperation from the manager of field claims adjusters or a need to contract for the services of a computer systems consultant).

The CPT completes the process improvement and implements the changes. A formal report is presented to the senior management. The outcomes of the CPT are publicized (recognition). The project is documented and the CPT is disbanded.

Team Conflict

Conflict among team members can occur at any of the stages, but it is more likely to surface during the Forming and Storming stages. Conflict can occur in cooperative as well as competitive relationships. Conflict is neither good nor bad. It is a part of human life. The effort should not be to try to eliminate conflict but to focus it as a productive force. Conflict can be a vital, energizing force in any team. Conflict is inevitable—make it work for the team.

Project team leaders, with guidance from a facilitator, if needed, can help transform a conflict into a problem-solving event by:

- Welcoming differences among team members

- Listening attentively with understanding rather than evaluation

- Helping to clarify the nature of the conflict

- Acknowledging and accepting the feelings of the individuals involved

- Indicating who will make the final decision

- Offering process and ground-rule suggestions for resolving the differences

- Paying attention to sustaining relationships between the disputants

- Creating appropriate means for communication between the persons involved in the conflict

Active listening is a key attribute for team leaders in managing conflict. Active listening involves two steps:

- Accept what the individual is saying (doing so does not imply agreement) and their right to say it.

- Feed back your understanding of both the content of what was said (paraphrase) as well as your feelings about what you observe or hear, and give no unsolicited advice.

Team Leader as Coach

To lead people more effectively, a project team leader needs to become an effective coach. Coaching is an ongoing process, but it doesn't have to be a burden. Following these action steps to shape behavior will help a project team leader become an effective, quality-driven coach:

- Catch team members doing something right and positively reinforce the good behavior.

- Use mistakes as learning opportunities.

- Reward team members who take risks in changing, even if they sometimes fail.

- When discussing situations, sit next to the team member. Respond with "I see/understand."

- Acknowledge the team member's reason for action, but don't agree to it if it's inappropriate.

- When giving performance feedback, reveal reactions after describing the behavior needing change, not before it.

- Encourage members to make suggestions for improving. Always give credit to the member making the suggestion.

- Treat team members with even more care than other business assets.

What Can Go Wrong?

- Objectives of project team are not linked to the organization's strategic direction.

- Lack of or insufficient management commitment and personal involvement.

- Hostile or indifferent environment for the team.

- Assigned members lack the needed competence (knowledge, experience, skills, aptitude, and attitude).

- Team leader lacks the technical expertise to adequately assess potential as well as performing members who claim to have the technical expertise—and no provision has been made for such team members to be properly evaluated.

- Training for team members is nonexistent or is inadequate for the tasks to be done.

- Team leadership is inadequate to lead the team in meeting its objectives.

- Team facilitation is nonexistent or inadequate.

- Team ground rules are nonexistent or inadequate.

- Members are not behaving as a team.

- Team members are unsure of what's expected of them.

- Recognition and reward for work done well is nonexistent or inadequate.

- Adequate resources are not provided, such as support personnel, facilities, tools, materials, information access, and funding.

- Conflicts between day-to-day work and work on the team have not been resolved.

- The team cannot seem to move beyond "storming" stage.

- Team members need to be constantly replaced.

- Team members show little respect for one another's competency.

- Team leader is reluctant to give up absolute control and unquestioned authority.

- Day-to-day operations personnel perceive the project team as a potential threat.

- A union resists the project team's formation.

- The team, if self-directed, lacks training and knowledge to handle situations that may be off-limits, such as hiring and firing or compensation.

- Planning the process and managing the process by which the team will operate has been done poorly, if at all.

- The team is allowed to continue beyond the time when it should have been disbanded.

- Team members have been selected involuntarily.

- The basis for team member selection was not consistent with the goals, objectives, and expected outcomes of the project.

- Team members' roles and organizational levels in the day-to-day operations were carried into the team activities, upsetting the "all are equal" environment desired.

- The team assumes an unauthorized life of its own.

- The team fails to keep the rest of the organization apprised of what it's doing and why.

- Team members are cut off from their former day-to-day functions, losing opportunities for professional development, promotions, and pay raises.

- The size of the team is inappropriate for the intended outcome, for example, too limited or too large.

- The team's actions violate either a contract with the union or labor laws and practices.

What Helps a Project Team Function Well?

- All team members agree on the expected outputs and outcomes of the project.

- Each member clearly is committed to the goals and objectives of the project and understands why he or she is on the team.

- Each member fully accepts the responsibilities assigned as well as an overall commitment to help with whatever needs to be done to ensure the project's success.

- Members agree to freely ask questions and openly share their opinions and feelings, with no hidden agendas, and with respect for other team members.

- Information is not hoarded or restricted. Each member has access to what is needed when it is needed to get the work accomplished.

- Building and maintaining trust is of paramount importance to the team's successful achievement of its objectives.

- All of the members feel they can make a difference with their contribution.

- Management is committed to support the team's decisions, as does each team member.

- Conflict within the team, when properly managed, produces a win-win outcome.

- The team maintains a dual focus: its effectiveness as a team and the project's anticipated outcomes

- Serving on the team can increase a member's expertise and reputation but should never be a detriment to a member's personal development (e.g., promotional opportunities, compensation increases, or training to maintain job skills).

More on project team leadership can be found among many of the resources listed at the end of this book. The increasing use of virtual teams should be studied further if the need applies to your project responsibilities.

Notes

1. Portions of this "Project Teams" section are adapted from "Team Structure and Function," Chapter 3 of *The Quality Improvement Handbook,* John E. Bauer, Grace L. Duffy, and Russell T. Westcott, eds. 2002. ASQ Quality Press.
2. Adapted from "Management of Differences," by Warren Schmidt and Robert Tannenbaum, *Harvard Business Review,* November–December 1960.

QUICK QUIZ
NUMBER 5

1. In what significant ways does a Project Team differ from a functional work unit?
2. As a potential project leader, what are some of the ways you would use to select a Project Team?
3. What are the advantages and possible disadvantages for each of the following team structures:
   —Natural team?
   —Cross-functional team?
   —Dedicated (solely to the project)?
   —Self-directed team?
   —Virtual team?
4. What purpose(s) does a Linear Responsibility Chart serve?
5. What factors should be considered in choosing the size of the Project Team?
6. Give one or more examples for each of the KESAA Factors.
7. When and for what purpose is it appropriate to hold a team meeting? Why?
8. Under what circumstance might a team fall back to an earlier stage in its development?
9 What are the responsibilities and roles of a Project Team leader?
10. Under what circumstances might the plans fleshed out by the Project Team be turned over to another team for implementation/installation?

6

Planning Projects—Additional Considerations

Moving Up

Chapter 4 provided sufficient techniques and tools for planning the majority of small, short-term, low-budget, noncomplex projects. The chapter emphasized a balance between keeping it simple and providing enough structure to adequately control the project process. Caution was given to weigh the time and cost of producing the plans and managing the project against the size of the project and the value of the outcomes to be obtained. "Not too little and not too much structure" was the charge given the project leader.

In this chapter, we will explore additional considerations for expanding the use of planning techniques and tools to accommodate projects of longer duration (perhaps 10 to 18 months) and embody greater complexity (multiple interfaces with other functions, a larger project team, reaching a value in the high five figures or six figures, and strategically critical). Following the book's intent, we will not address the really big-dollar, multiyear projects, such as a major reengineering of the organization's processes, acquisitions and mergers, replacing or introducing a whole product family, building a facility, or instituting a Six Sigma–based culture.

More about Work Breakdown Structures

The development of the Work Breakdown Structures (WBS) can emphasize different project orientations, depending on stakeholders' needs and projected outcomes. For example, the objective of the layout of work in the WBS can be oriented to:

• Designing, building, testing, and launching a new product or process: the stages from concept to product launch or process implementation. Examples include implementing a quality management system and certification to the ISO 9001 standard, converting a product line to cellular manufacturing, establishing an in-house instrument calibration process, and designing and installing devices to reduce machine setup cycle time.

• Researching, investigating, and studying approaches to loss prevention: the steps involved in uncovering data, analyzing the data, and providing information for informed decision making. Examples include a feasibility study examining methods to reduce scrap, a benchmarking study of lost-time accident prevention practices; and an analysis of root cause investigations in search for patterns of best practices.

A person should ultimately be named responsible for every box on the WBS. In many organizations, this person is assigned based upon competency, not job title or position within the organization. It is not unusual to have persons of higher organization rank assigned to a lower level project task than an organizational subordinate. Remember, this is a breakdown of work to be done, not an organization chart.

It is not unusual to assign one person to several responsibilities, at various levels, on the WBS. Ensuring that any conflicts in time allocations are resolved is the purpose of resource leveling.

Include Project Management as a subproject within the WBS because it is work that consumes time and money. The only rational time for omitting some or all of the activities associated with project management is when the project is a very small project or when some other function outside the project includes some of the work of managing the project, such as if the regular biweekly Quality Council meeting includes advance preparation of status reports and detailed progress reviews of the ISO 9001 QMS implementation project.

Estimating

One noted author suggests that no work activity should have a duration much longer than four to six weeks; that number is shortened for knowledge work to one to three weeks because such work is more difficult to monitor and measure. Another author suggests activities of 1 to 10 days' duration.

If project progress reports and reviews are done at the Work Package level, then it is useful to limit the duration of Work Packages to the frequency of the reviews. For example, if progress reviews are held once every two weeks, the Work Package durations are of two weeks or less.

Certain types of projects may call for breaking work down into very small increments, perhaps one hour each. Preventive maintenance is a situation when tight plans and schedules involving many people are called for in order to limit the amount of downtime. For example:

> A plant that produces continuous copper wire has a policy that when a breakdown in the process requires shutting down the operation, the workforce immediately transforms itself into a preventive maintenance team. The continuous process machinery is immediately opened up and cleaned, worn parts are replaced, and the machinery is inspected by operators stationed at assigned positions along the huge machine, which occupies nearly the entire length of the plant. The objective is to completely service the machine and return it to full operation within a prescribed period. It is as carefully orchestrated and performed as an intricate ballet.

Smaller activities are easier to estimate. When a Work Package requires two or more types of expertise not normally available in one category of performer in your organization, consider breaking the one Work Package into two. Balance the ease in estimating with the added complexity of additional activities. For this example:

A Work Package states "Implement project management software," where implementation consists of a combination of installing the software on desktop computers and training people to use the software. Your performers are skilled in one or the other of the two types of work (installing computer software or training operators) but not both. Break the work into two Work Packages and estimate each separately. This will help in resource scheduling and will also facilitate outsourcing either or both activities if in-house resources are not available. This type of division of work is also applicable in estimating costs where there is a significant difference in the compensation paid for the different levels of expertise.

A common fault is not including the time and cost of people and other factors because they are "being paid anyway." This omission distorts the estimating. It also provides no basis for determining the feasibility of outsourcing work. Three examples bring out this point:

Exempt employees typically receive a fixed salary. They are usually not eligible for overtime. They are the professional and managerial "workers" most often involved as project team members. Inasmuch as they may be assigned project activities to work on without regard as to when they will do the work (normal work hours versus after-hours work) but are paid a fixed salary regardless of when and how they get the work done, some project managers feel the compensation costs for time working on the project should not be included in the estimates. "They will just have to fit the project work into their schedule. Besides, they are getting paid anyway." Not including these compensation costs can result in:

- Improper or lower estimates, which in turn affects:
  - Possibly approving of a project that should have been rejected.
  - Squeezing project work into a daily work schedule without knowing the costs of trade-offs and postponed daily work.
  - Deflating the individual's perceived value of his or her importance to the project.
  - Providing a misguided basis for investigating the feasibility of outsourcing project work. (If the project work is treated as "free," any outsourcing cost considered will be exorbitant.)
- Improperly deflated actual costs, which affects
  - Giving false praise for meeting an improperly computed budget
  - Distorting return-on-investment measures
  - Computing improper project payback period
  - Distorting project documentation in the project knowledge base (which could misinform future project managers)

A generous chapter board member of a professional association declined to budget for and submit expenses incurred in attending association division meetings as the chapter's representative. When it became necessary to replace that individual, there were no funds budgeted for the replacement. The new person needed the reimbursement. Also, there was no documentation of past actual costs by which to estimate future expenditures.

A former newsletter editor for the above chapter "donated" the reproduction and mailing services for the newsletter (paid for by his company). When he moved on, the new editor was not able to commit his employer to providing free copying and postage. The chapter was nearly bankrupted because the high newsletter expenses had never been planned for. Also, when looking into the feasibility of outsourcing the reproduction and mailing, there were no actual costs by which to compare with outside vendors' proposed charges.

More on Estimating

Document the details of what data you used, from where you located the data, why they were chosen, and how you computed each estimate. Include notes about assumptions made, percentage tolerance for errors and omissions, and the time frame of the data used to compute the estimate. The basis for your estimates should be traceable for the following reasons:

- To aid in reestimating when the schedule needs to be leveled for better resource allocation or when the project is deviating from plan

- To assist in the postproject review of lessons learned

- To provide a source (database) of documented methods used for the purpose of future training of project managers

- To contribute to the development of estimating standards for the organization

A useful method for developing estimates for complex or never-been-done-before tasks is to have three knowledgeable people provide an estimate, independent of one another. Then the three meet, discuss, and reach consensus on the best estimate.

For smaller projects, labor estimates are usually in hours. If a Work Package requires more than one type of skilled performer, subdivide the Work Package and estimate each skill type separately. Don't mix time units, that is, hours, days, and weeks.

Equipment costs usually are estimated in hours of usage. Materials and supplies are typically estimated from process and product specifications. Outsourced costs are based on contractual specifications.

Be careful that ballpark estimates are clearly stated as such. Add the caution that such estimates *will* change as more clarity and granularity is developed in the planning stage. Ballpark estimates given offhandedly to a senior official may, if you are not careful, be the estimate to which the project team is held accountable.

More on Gantt Charts

Using additional symbols can enhance the Gantt chart, discussed in Chapter 4. For example:

- Planned milestone dates can be indicated with inverted "blank" triangles.

- Actual milestone dates met can be indicated with inverted "filled-in" triangles.

- "Blank" horizontal bars can be used to indicate planned durations.

- "Filled-in" bars can be used to indicate actual time spent.

- "Cross-hatched" bars can be used to indicate critical tasks.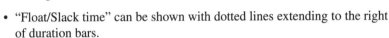

- Task dependency arrows can be drawn connecting the bars to show finish-to-start relationships.

- "Summary" bars, such as for the duration of a component level containing several Work Packages, can be inserted above the Work Package bars.

- "Float/Slack time" can be shown with dotted lines extending to the right of duration bars.

Keep these notes in mind when working on Gantt charts:

- Color should be avoided if the chart will be photocopied, as the distinctions may not be evident when reproduced in black and white.

- A Gantt chart is usually inadequate for depicting the critical path of any but the simplest projects. However, the Gantt chart should not be overlooked as a good visual method for showing the status of "summary" levels (subproject, component level, or even Work Package level) of work, at progress reviews.

- The more complicated the chart becomes the greater the time and cost to create and maintain it, and the greater the likelihood of it not being kept up to date.

- A milestone can be a significant event, a review meeting, a progress report, or the completion of a project stage (stage-gate).

Network Diagramming, the Critical Path, and Scheduling

The Activity Network Diagram

The Activity Network Diagram (AND) is a precedence diagram depicting task inter-relationships. It is a "goes-into" diagram showing what tasks precede other tasks. Drawn from left to right (usually), it shows each task in labeled circles or boxes with a line or lines indicating the linkage to the next logical task(s).

Assembling the data for an AND requires a predecessor table or list. Note the "Depends on" columns shown in Chapter 4, Figure 4.5, and in Chapter 8, Figure 8.2 (back).

Figure 6.1 shows a simplistic AND, prepared from the data shown on the Action Plan from Figure 8.2 (back). Typically, for such simple project interrelationships the

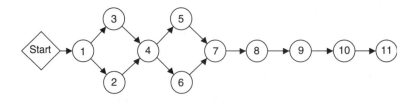

Figure 6.1 Activity network diagram.

AND would be unnecessary. For a more complex project, an AND is a useful preliminary step in preparing for a CPM or PERT network diagramming session.

Critical Path Method

A Critical Path Method (CPM) diagram is usually introduced for complex, medium-size projects and for very large projects of long duration. CPM, as the name implies, is used in computing the critical path. The critical path is the longest path through the interrelated tasks and is the path that has no "slack" (also called "float"). "Critical" means that if you fail to meet the time estimated for the work along the critical path, the entire project will be late finishing. Figure 6.2a shows a table used to record the

ISO 9001 QUALITY MANAGEMENT SYSTEM PROJECT				
#	WORK PACKAGE (WP)	START IN	DEPENDS ON WP #	WEEKS TO COMPLETE
1	Select consultant	Wk 01		3
2	Conduct ISO 9000 briefing	Wk 04	1	1
3	Conduct gap analysis	Wk 05	3	1
4	Form steering committee	Wk 06	3	1
5	Prepare QSP's	Wk 07	4	57
6	Prepare Q. policy and objectives	Wk 09	4	1
7	Prepare work instructions	Wk 14	4	39
8	Employee kickoff meeting	Wk 15	6	1
9	Evaluate registrars	Wk 26	4	1
10	Train internal auditors	Wk 26	6	2
11	Implement QSP's	Wk 29	5	35
12	Select and schedule registrar	Wk 33	9	1
13	Conduct internal audits	Wk 39	10	37
14	Prepare quality system manual	Wk 42	6	13
15	Conduct audit behavior meeting	Wk 64	11	1
16	Conduct pre-assessment	Wk 65	15	1
17	Take corrective/preventive Action	Wk 66	16	12
18	Conduct final assessment	Wk 76	17	1
19	Registration notice—celebrate	Wk 78	18	1

Figure 6.2a CPM data table.

Critical Path: 1, 2, 3, 4, 5, 15, 16, 17, 18, 19 = 78 wks.

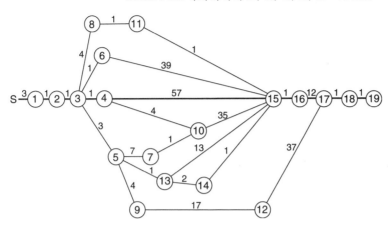

Figure 6.2b Network diagram (activity on node).

task interrelationships and estimates of task durations for a medium-size project. Figure 6.2b is the chart derived from the data. CPM charts may be developed with one of two orientations:

- Activity-oriented diagram ("arrow diagram")
  - "Activity-on-line" (AOL); also called "Activity-on-arrow" (AOA).
  - Activities are the arrows; events are the nodes.
- Event-oriented diagram ("precedence diagram"), most common (Figure 6.2b)
  - "Activity-on-node" or "circle network."
  - Activities are the nodes; events are the ends of the arrows.
  - Easier of the two to draw.
  - Most commonly used.

CPM uses one time estimate for each Work Package. Build the CPM chart using estimates from the lowest level in the Work Breakdown Structure. Estimates are based on duration of the total time to complete the Work Package (elapsed time from start to finish). For example, a Work Package "Review & edit instruction manual" could require only four hours of total effort but be interspersed over 10 days if it consists of conducting the interim reviews of segments of what will ultimately become the whole instruction manual.

Program Evaluation and Review Technique Diagram

Program Evaluation and Review Technique (PERT) estimating is done with three time estimates: "optimistic," "most likely," and "pessimistic." There are significant differences between the CPM and PERT approaches, as shown in Table 6.1. Many project management software programs tend to blend aspects of CPM and PERT. Because PERT technology is most applicable to the huge, highly complex, and (often) never-been-done-before type of project, we will not discuss it further. Table 6.1 lists some of

Table 6.1 Comparison of some of the differences between CPM and PERT.

Discriminator	CPM	PERT
Focus	Time and cost	Time
Time estimates	One best estimate	Three estimates: optimistic, most likely, pessimistic
Orientation	Activity-oriented	Event-oriented
Prevalent uses	• Industries involving well-defined projects, within one organization, e.g., construction, process industries, and in single-project industrial applications that are resource-dependent and based on reasonably accurate time estimates • Projects with relatively small uncertainties	• R&D projects and developmental projects where the risks in estimating time durations have a high variability • Projects where lack of historical information exists
Advantages	• Because it uses a reasonably accurate single-time estimate, provides better overall accurate estimate • Uses both time and cost to analyze elements directly influencing the success of the project • Especially useful for resource-dependent projects based on accurate time estimates • Can be used for projects where the percentage completed can be determined with reasonable accuracy and customer billing can be based on percent completed • Somewhat less complex (less data) and can be less expensive to maintain	• Especially useful for projects where the risks in computing time duration have a high variability • Can reveal interdependencies that are not obvious • Can determine probability of meeting specific deadlines by development of alternate plans • Has ability to evaluate effect of changes in the program, e.g., a shift of resources from a less critical activity to a more critical activity • Useful for R&D type projects where percentage complete is almost impossible to determine, because of nature of the work, except at completed milestones • Allows calculation of risk in completing a project
Disadvantages	• Because it is based on a single time estimate, it cannot calculate the risk in completing the project • Depends on reasonably accurate estimates, based on historical data	• Unless modifications are made, uses only time to analyze elements directly influencing the success of the project • Complex and expensive to maintain

Source: *The Certified Quality Manager Handbook,* 2nd ed., Duke Okes & Russell T. Westcott, eds., ASQ Quality Press, 2001. Reprinted with permission.

the differences between CPM and PERT. Several resources listed at the end of this book discuss PERT in greater detail.

Outsourced Services, Suppliers, Subcontractors, and Consultants

Outsourced Services

The term "vendor" is disappearing from use. But the everyday use of people outside the organization is rapidly increasing, especially under the umbrella of "outsourcing." Because of this trend, project managers face a dual dilemma.

First, in selecting project team members the project manager may find that some of the basic functions that need to be represented on the team are now performed by outsource service firms. This situation can raise issues of confidentiality, proprietary design issues, and exposure to organizational strategies, information that the outsource service firm would normally be prohibited from knowing.

Second, the contractual arrangement with the outsource service firm will typically not include its being involved in an additional new project. "Inviting" that firm's participation on a project team could require renegotiation or amendment to the contract as well as pose some control and reporting relationship concerns. Also, if the deliverables from a project involve changes to the services or products the outsource firm is currently providing, there may be an issue of conflict of interest if the present outsource service firm actively participates in the new project.

As more and more of the organization's basic functions are outsourced, such as information technology, routine accounting functions, maintenance activities, and recruiting, the project manager may be forced to create new protocols and safeguards. Risk assessment and contingency planning will need to be expanded to address a range of "what if" conditions that may arise in the relationships with outsourced services. Negotiating for personnel resources will be more difficult when the functions you need represented on the project team are to be performed by an outsource service firm.

Suppliers

With the advent of supply-chain management, supplier-buyer partnerships, and marketing alliances, getting supplier participation on a project team may be easier than in times past (that is, the days of the adversarial relationship between buyer and seller). The issue of conflict of interest may still be a concern, however.

When the relationship between the project and the supplier is strictly one of purchasing equipment, supplies, or one-time services, the organization's policies, procedures, protocols, and practices prevail. As a project manager in the smaller organization, you may be expected to make your own purchasing decisions directly with the supplier. However, in most organizations there is a purchasing function you may need to work with. In the latter situation, it is extremely important that detailed specifications of tangible materials or supplies are provided to the supplier, along with the intended use. Typically, a purchasing function is charged with making the best deal possible, and that could undercut your project's intentions unless the specifications are stated clearly and completely. If services, such as a training program or a customer satisfaction survey, are to be purchased, the selection criteria must be carefully spelled out or the sole-source supplier designated.

Subcontractors

Subcontractors essentially are temporary employees retained for specific tasks for a specific period; examples include computer programmer, data-entry clerk, and product-design engineer. Contractual matters are typically handled through the personnel function of the organization. These "temps," depending upon their role in the project, may be absorbed into the project activities much as full-time employees are. However, some issues do need to be addressed, such as control of work hours (especially any overtime), ongoing performance evaluation (especially relative to retention or replacement of the temp), security issues (access to proprietary information), and reporting relationships. It is imperative that the temp be provided a statement of the work he or she is to perform, the quality level expected, and the basis for measuring the contribution.

Consultants

It is not unusual for medium-size projects to retain the services of one or more consultants, depending upon the project's scope. The roles consultants may be expected to fulfill include one or more of the following:

- Review tentative project plans with recommendations for acceptance or improvement.
- Advise about a specific topic or planned action based on the consultant's known competency.
- Guide and/or coach in the application of a specific techniques, technology, or practice.
- Educate and/or train in a topical area.
- Advise the organization's "change agent" on ways to implement organizational change.
- Conduct assessments or audits (e.g., organizational diagnosis, employee surveys, or gap analysis vis-à-vis compliance to standards).
- Facilitate the meeting process at project team meetings.
- Provide subject-matter expertise (SME) for project meetings.

Consultants should not be retained as:

- *The* project manager
- *The* organizational change agent
- A full working participant on the project team, with task assignment(s)
- A "hand-holder" to an inadequate manager
- A person to blame if project is unsuccessful
- One whose advice is never challenged
- A spy or informant to top management
- A person from whom to extract information about competitors

The categories—outsourcing firms, suppliers, subcontractors, and consultants—do appear to overlap. Distinctions, as noted for each, should be considered. One piece of advice that pertains to each category is the need to detail what you expect each to do, how each will be measured, the controls (e.g., status reporting) that will be applied, and the consequences for behavior (e.g., retention, performance bonus or penalties, or termination).

Lewis provides a chapter on managing vendors in projects.[1]

Scheduling

Knowing the work to be done (from the WBS), the sequence in which the work is to be performed, and the planned start and finish time of each Work Package (durations on the Gantt chart and/or network diagram), you have the preliminary data for scheduling. Scheduling also involves the resources you will need and the availability and cost of such resources. Most organizations have limited resources, both in quantity and in the specific categories needed. A schedule can be unworkable if resource allocations are unrealistic and ineffectively planned.

Scheduling involves a juggling act. It usually means major modifications to the first-pass plans. It means looking for tasks that can be done concurrently. It involves leveling the schedule to accommodate the resources that can be available, often through determining where there is slack and where the resources can be shifted to a more critical task. As a last resort it may mean requesting more time and funding. Modifications must be made to the WBS, the Gantt and/or network charts, the resource requirement allocations, and even the budget if the changes include changed fund levels or a changed cash flow.

Your first pass at compiling the work schedule will not be your final schedule. You will unearth myriad conflicts and barriers. Producing a realistic schedule that still allows the project team to meet its objectives is referred to as "leveling." One approach is to deal with the following conditions sequentially:

- Adjust for conflicted activities that require the same personnel resources by:

    –Moving such conflicted activities to a later or earlier time period. (This will not work for Work Packages on the critical path because there is no slack time.)

    –Examining the network diagram and resource requirements to uncover any opportunities to resequence certain Work Packages to eliminate conflicts in the schedule.

    –Subdividing Work Packages to make scheduling more flexible.

    –Negotiating for additional resources. (If in adding more personnel the time to complete a conflicted Work Package does not increase the total time required for that type of expertise, this move may not increase costs. If it does increase costs, it affects the proposed or mandated budget.)

- Decrease costs to meet your proposed budget or contain costs within a mandated budget by:

    –Subdividing Work Packages to use lower-cost personnel (or equipment, facilities, or material) for some portion of the divided Work Package, such as subdividing "design" into "conceptual design," "specification preparation," "outsourcing purchase order," and "inspection and test of delivered tool." In this example, each subdivided Work Package calls for a different level of expertise, for different compensation, and for completion at different times.

    –Substituting less costly personnel, products, and services.

—Lessening the impact of cash flow in critical time periods by extending the completion date of certain Work Packages. (If this action results in extending the total project time and/or the critical path, it may not be advisable.)

Although the scheduling computations can be done manually, popular computer programs provide not only fast computation but also the ability to make estimate and interrelationship adjustments, as well as leveling trade-off modifications to improve the scheduling (testing "what ifs"). Relief from the tedium of multiple computations pretty much dictates the use of a computer program for all but a very small, simple project plan.

The purpose of this book is to discuss techniques and tools useful to the novice or infrequent project leader for use in planning and managing small projects and medium-size projects with minimum complexity. For this reason the inquisitive reader is directed to the references provided in the Resources section when circumstances suggest the use of computers for estimating time and costs, scheduling, and leveling task resources.

Managing Plan Changes

Some method for managing and controlling plan changes must be instituted. Redlining original plans with the changes, authoring initials and date may be sufficient for very small projects. However, when a number of people are involved and the changes are more than simple, a change control procedure is recommended. Everyone working on the project must work off the same set of planning documents. This involves carefully managing changes to documents, the distribution of the changed documents, the collection of the obsolete documents, and maintenance of files of successive revisions. A simple Change Control Log should show:

- Date of change

- Document(s) changed

- Person initiating change

- Brief description of change, including identification of Work Package, time and cost estimates, and so forth

- Brief answer to "Why?" change was necessary

- Date of distribution of changed document(s)

- To whom changed document(s) were distributed

- Indication that obsolete document(s) were collected and properly dispositioned

More on Budgets

As your plans go through multiple iterations before submission, changes to the initial budget are usually required. The only figure that may not change is the cap that the approving authority placed on the project—the total time and funds that can be committed.

Planning for Contingencies

Your first concern may be how to cover your ash (the residue that can result from getting burned). Do you pad the estimates to cover the uncertainties that may arise? Or do you create a slush fund that you can dip into when things go wrong? Differences of opinion abound. Those whose recommendation it is to build into the estimates a contingency allowance overlook the consequences of so overestimating a project that it gets rejected or severely reduced in scope. Those who propose a "general" fund that can freely be tapped when trouble looms face the dilemma of how much to set aside, and how might its presence and potentially uncontrolled usage affect project plan approval.

Padding estimates of tasks and Work Packages is not recommended. This approach has two major negatives:

- The creeping inflation of estimates could cause the project to be rejected because of its total cost.

- Building on the concept that work tends to expand to fit the available time, a corollary is that dollars expended tend to meet (or exceed) the dollars estimated. An estimate that has been padded for contingencies will tend to be spent.

A better approach is to estimate a realistic time and cost for each Work Package without contingency factors. Then identify and assess the potential risks to the project in terms of the probability of these risks occurring and cost of covering the contingency. These risks can be categorized by "musts" (contingencies that must be anticipated and covered, such as the loss of key personnel or equipment failure); "should haves" (set aside some contingency coverage, such as for frequently occurring weather-related events and pending regulatory and legislative changes), and "unlikely" (such as sabotage, natural disasters, theft). The dollar amount to set aside as a contingency can then be decided for each potential risk A designated contingency fund is then budgeted separately. Approval authority to tap this fund is specified in the project charter. The fund may not be accessed for performance deficiencies, such as estimating errors, failure to perform assigned work effectively and correctly, or failure to detect potential slippage in time to take appropriate corrective action.

Establishing a carefully controlled contingency fund in the budget is, in my opinion, a preferred method, provided:

- The project may draw upon the fund for only those contingencies that result from true unknowns at the time of estimating. Funds are not available for tangible or intangible things that should have been known during estimating but were overlooked, or for errors in estimating.

- The percentage of funds drawn from the contingency fund are no greater than percentage of the work already done.

- Anticipated project changes attributable to "scope creep" are tightly controlled and needed budget modifications documented and approved.

Indirect Costs

Failing to include indirect costs in the estimates severely affects the budget. Some indirect costs are:

- So-called fringe benefits that need to be added to base salaries or wages. These benefits often differ from one organizational level to another and between exempt and nonexempt personnel.

- Overhead costs (e.g., heat, light, power, facility maintenance, and security) that are allocated to work units or departments on some predetermined basis, such as:
  - Number of square feet occupied
  - Number of employees in a work area
  - Percentage of direct labor costs
  - Miles traveled
  - Dollars of sales generated
  - Potential power usage of machinery installed

- Handling, shipping, temporary storage, installation costs and taxes on purchased materials, equipment and supplies.

- Facilities, equipment, material, and supplies not allocated directly to the project.

- Interest on financed purchases, rental, leases, loans, etc.

- Equipment service contracts.

- Brokers and agents fees.

- Account service fees.

- License and permit fees.

- Legal fees.

- Transportation and living expenses for personnel working or in training offsite.

Caution: When estimating the costs of a process improvement project, don't overlook the temporary costs involved in the transition from the present process to the improved process, such as:

- Decrease in production due to learning curve

- Parallel processing to ensure the new process produces desired results while maintaining the old process

- Addition of temporary workers and/or machines to compensate for the productivity decline during transition or fill-in for people working on the improvement project

- Cost of temporary business closure (loss of revenue) during transition to new process

- Communication costs involved in informing customers and other stakeholders about process delays and ultimate improvement

- Potential costs associated with risks, such as lost customers, legal ramifications, new process errors, omissions and other waste, disoriented and/or dissatisfied employees, and so forth

- Cost of delays in other pending or ongoing projects due to a drain on resources by the process improvement project

The Cash-Flow Schedule

Some budgeted funds will be spent as a lump sum at the startup of the project, such as the purchase of a copy machine. Most funds, however, will be spent at different times during the life of the project. For good financial management, it is essential to plan when these disbursements will occur and in what dollar amount. Preparing for a Cash-Flow Schedule (CFS) starts with a Gantt chart showing the scheduled task durations. A Resource Requirements Matrix (RRM) is added, listing the major personnel resources required and spreading the days or hours horizontally across the matrix, with the requirements corresponding to the scheduled task durations in the Gantt chart. Next, the expenditures planned for each type of resource are spread across the months (or weeks) in which the expenditures are planned. The result is three-part schedule. The Gantt chart is at the top, followed by the RRM, and ending with the CFS. All three parts use the same matrix format, time periods across the top and category identifiers in a vertical list in the lefthand column. Figure 6.3 is an example of how a CFS can be developed.

Table 6.2 shows another example of how a budget may be developed.

When sizable expenditures are anticipated in a medium-size project, the CFS is vital for the financial arm of the organization to be able to anticipate the impact of cash outlays on the whole organization. An organization can't spend what it won't have or can't reasonably obtain through loans or other means. Seeing the projected cash flow could easily affect project approval or cause a major replanning effort to lessen the financial impact in certain periods.

Return on Project Investment

A ballpark estimate of the Return on Project Investment (ROPI) may have been done in preparing the initial proposal and request for planning funds (see Chapter 3). For many projects a ROPI estimate submitted with the request for project plan approval will be a key factor.

The objectives of a ROPI estimate are to:

- Cost-justify the project.

- Enable the project team to demonstrate a measurable outcome and dollar payoff from implementing the project.

- Establish a basis for measuring project results.

- Provide a basis for reinforcing management's decision to approve the project.

- Make available the means for evaluating the project team's effectiveness.

- Furnish a basis for team recognition and reward for results attained.

- Develop an awareness and importance of the project's economic effect among all stakeholders involved.

The basic concepts underlying ROPI are:

- If the analysis indicates that the project cannot produce a potential dollar payoff, then the project is probably not worth doing—unless a customer or regulatory agency mandates the project.

- Actions have measurable outcomes, although some actions appear more difficult to measure. However, means can usually be found.

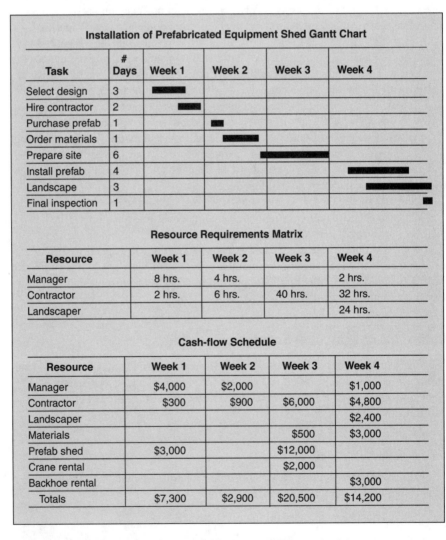

Installation of Prefabricated Equipment Shed Gantt Chart

Task	# Days	Week 1	Week 2	Week 3	Week 4
Select design	3	■			
Hire contractor	2	■			
Purchase prefab	1		■		
Order materials	1		■		
Prepare site	6			■	
Install prefab	4				■
Landscape	3				■
Final inspection	1				■

Resource Requirements Matrix

Resource	Week 1	Week 2	Week 3	Week 4
Manager	8 hrs.	4 hrs.		2 hrs.
Contractor	2 hrs.	6 hrs.	40 hrs.	32 hrs.
Landscaper				24 hrs.

Cash-flow Schedule

Resource	Week 1	Week 2	Week 3	Week 4
Manager	$4,000	$2,000		$1,000
Contractor	$300	$900	$6,000	$4,800
Landscaper				$2,400
Materials			$500	$3,000
Prefab shed	$3,000		$12,000	
Crane rental			$2,000	
Backhoe rental				$3,000
Totals	$7,300	$2,900	$20,500	$14,200

Figure 6.3 Combination Gantt chart, RRM, and cash-flow schedule.

Table 6.2 Budget example.

Assume a project has four stages and five team members.
Prepare budget for each stage.

Member	Planned hours per stage				$ per hour
	1	2	3	4	
Beth Esda	10	15	15	25	$20
Anna Lyst	8	8	6	12	$15
Ed Ifye	0	15	25	20	$18
Jule Ly	0	20	20	25	$9
Ali Ghator	10	5	10	15	$10
Total	28	63	76	97	

Labor hours budgeted per stage

Stage	Hours	%	Cum %
1	28	10	10
2	63	24	34
3	76	29	63
4	97	37	100
Total	264	100	

Labor dollars budgeted per stage

Member	Hourly $	Stage 1	Stage 2	Stage 3	Stage 4
Beth Esda	$20	$200	$300	$300	$500
Anna Lyst	$15	$120	$120	$90	$180
Ed Ifye	$18	$0	$270	$450	$360
Jule Ly	$9	$0	$180	$180	$225
Ali Ghator	$10	$100	$50	$100	$150
Total		$420	$920	$1,120	$1,415

Non-labor expenses = $2,800

Stage	%	Dollars
1	10	$280
2	24	$672
3	29	$812
4	37	$1,036
Total	100	$2,800

Project budget

Stage	Labor	Nonlabor	Total
1	$420	$280	$700
2	$920	$672	$1,592
3	$1,120	$812	$1,932
4	$1,415	$1,036	$2,451
Total	$3,455	$2,520	$5,975

- Outputs are not outcomes. Outputs are deliverable events, products, or processes produced by the project and are always measurable.

- Outcomes are the effects the project results have on the stakeholders affected. Outcomes are usually strategically critical, such as profitability, customer satisfaction, and competitive position in marketplace.

Project Name: Reference No:
                                                                Project No.:

A	Target outcome	1. [ ] increase 2. [ ] decrease	What?
B	Target population	[ ] individual [ ] group size( )	Who?
C	Desired Process Performance Level	Standard/Goal/Expectation? Percent of ( )? By when ( )?	
D	Basic for measurement (Choose one best way to measure)	[ ] Rate (qty/time) [ ] Accuracy (#per) [ ] Quality [ ] Completeness [ ] Timeliness/speed [ ] Cost	Formula?
E	Baseline (present process performance level, expressed in terms comparable to C above)	Data derived from: [ ] available records [ ] observation/interviews [ ] estimated from external source	Quantity or percent?
F	Potential for improvement process performance	A1√, then C–E=F A2√, then E–C=F	
G	Annual gross value of PIP (F) Show details of each computation, state assumptions, unit rates used. Use back of form or attachments, as needed. More detail is better than less.		$ /yr.
H	POPS (Cost total from Sheet 2B)		$
I	Potential Net Payoff for first year (G-H=I)		$

Is this project worthy of consideration?   [ ] YES [ ] NO

Prepared by:	Title:	Date:

Figure 6.4   Analysis of potential for improved process (APIP).

Project No.: _____		Sheet 2A		

?	**Relative to Target Outcome (Sheet 1, line A)**			
1	Does there appear to be a value to improving process performance?			
2	How long has this opportunity existed?			
3	Where does the opportunity occur (location)?			
4	When does the opportunity occur (situation, time period)?			
5	How often does it occur?			
6	What inconsistencies exist between: location, situation, time period, volume, frequency?			
7	Is it worth analyzing beyond this point? [ ] Yes [ ] No			

	Relative to Target Population (TP) (Sheet 1, line B) (circle applicable X)*	T	K	F	C
8	Does TP have time to do job well?	X	X		
9	Does TP have proper facilities in which to work?	X			
10	Does TP have the proper tools to do the work?	X			
11	Does TP have proper procedures, instructions, job aids?	X			
12	Does TP know what they are supposed to do?		X	X	
13	Has TP ever done the job correctly?		X	X	
14	Could TP do the job properly if their lives depended upon it?		X		X
15	If TP could do the job in an exemplary way, would they?				X
16	Are there more negative than positive consequences in doing the job?				X
17	Does TP know when they are not performing as supervisor expects?			X	
18	Do supervisors of TP have requisite knowledge/skills?		X	X	X

	Potential Areas for Solution	**Estimate of 1st Year Costs**
T*	**Task Considerations**	
	Redesign work/tasks	$
	Add, replace, rearrange facilities	$
	Add, replace, modify tools	$
	Add, delete, rewrite procedures, guides, job aids	$
	Other:	$
K*	**Knowledge Considerations**	
	Needs analysis	$
	Determine competencies required of TP	$
	Assess knowledge/skill level of TP	$
	Provide training for TP (course design, materials, instructor costs, trainee costs, travel, facilities, equipment)	$
	Other	$

Figure 6.5a Probable opportunities for process solution (POPS).

	Potential Areas for Solution	Estimate of 1st Year Costs
		Sheet 2B
	Project No.: _____	
F*	**Feedback Considerations**	
	Analyze feedback requirements	$
	Modify present feedback system	$
	Design new feedback system	$
	Implement new/modified feedback system (training, forms, data collection and analysis, communications, documentation)	$
	Other:	$
C*	**Consequences/Antecedents—Considerations**	
	Functional analysis of behavior	$
	Add, remove, rearrange consequences/antecedents	$
	Provide behavior management training (instructor costs, trainee costs, travel, facilities, equipment, printing/copying, taxes)	$
	Other:	$
	Additional Considerations	
	Building a staff (temporary, permanent)	$
	Facilities for staff	$
	Travel and living expenses of staff	$
	Running parallel systems (old and new)	$
	Additional maintenance of systems, facilities	$
	Consulting services	$
	Other	$
	Total Estimated Costs for First Year (copy to line H on Sheet 1)	$

Prepared by: Title: Date:

Figure 6.5b Probable opportunities for process solution (POPS).

Refer to two sample forms, Figures 6.4 and 6.5a–b. These forms are adaptable to almost any type of improvement project. The steps involved in computing a ROPI are:

A. Define the outcome desired (not activities). Choose one key outcome.

B. Identify the targeted population (stakeholders to be affected).

C. Select/establish the standard by which the outcome will be measured.

D. Determine the basis of measurement.

E. Determine the baseline (present level of performance).

F. Compute the value of the potential improvement (difference between baseline and standard).

G. Identify the cause of the present level of performance/problem/ deficiency and select an appropriate action/solution. Estimate the gross value of the improvement/solution.

H. Determine the cost of the solution. Use optional form, POPS (Figures 6.5a and 6.5b), to aid in selecting the solution and estimating the cost.

I. Compute the net payoff (line G minus line H, annualized).

Decide if the project is worth implementing.

Project Charter

The project charter is a means of notifying all stakeholders that the project has commenced and is supported by the organization's management. Figure 6.6 is a sample Project Charter. The use of this form presumes that a funding request was made before the project planning stage began. Used in this context, the Project Charter is the approval to launch the project represented by the plans submitted. It is recommended that this form, filled in, be available for signatures at the time the detailed plans are presented and accepted. It is important that some form of formal authorization be circulated to communicate the launch of the project to others in the organization. The formal approval also authorizes the project manager to begin the detailed work described in the plans, including obtaining the resources needed.

Implementation Planning

Planning to initiate a new project has been discussed in Chapter 3. The basic planning for the project launch was discussed in Chapter 4. Planning for launching a larger, more complex project has been discussed throughout this chapter. There is a third planning stage that may be necessary for some types of projects, especially those involving time-released type implementation.

The design and execution of implementation plans may be separated from the design stage by considerations such as time, resources, funds availability, type of product or service to be implemented, and customer needs. While the implementation stage may overlap the design stage, the implementation stage most likely will tend to be carried out by a different team.

Implementation/installation planning may include most of the techniques and tools discussed so far:

- Statement of Work—outlines the scope and type of work to be performed, including the linkage with the design stage

- Work Breakdown Structure—for example, a process change involving gradual replacement of older equipment while maintaining the production schedule:

  –Project management of implementation/installation project

  –Purchase and delivery of equipment

  –Computer program modifications or new program implementation

  –Engineer training

  –Site preparation

  –Operator training

  –Installation of equipment

PROJECT CHARTER

Project name: _____ Project No.:_____

Overall project purpose and justification:

_____

_____

Projected project start date: _____ Projected project completion date: _____

Key project objectives and success criteria:

_____

_____

_____

Major stakeholders' requirements:

_____

_____

_____

Projected organizational outcomes when project Is successfully completed:

_____

_____

_____

Proposed project budget:

_____

_____

_____

Conditions, constraints and risks to be considered:

_____

_____

_____

Project manager's name:

_____

A P P R O V A L S*

Role	Signatures	Date signed
Project manager:		
Key customer:		
Key customer:		
Key customer:		
Other key stakeholder:		
Other key stakeholder:		
Final approving authority:		

*Approvals above constitute authority to launch the project and for communicating the project launch news within the organization.

Figure 6.6 Project charter.

   –Module testing, parallel processing, and modifications

   –Procedure and work instruction changes

   –Transition to production operations

   –Implementation/installation project close-out

   –Evaluation of implementation

 • Timelines/schedule—phased implementation

   –Gantt chart—with milestones

   –Network Diagram, critical path

   –Resource Requirements Matrices

   –Measures

   –Budget/cash flow

 • Implementation Plan approval process

   –Charter for implementation stage

Communications Plan

As project manager, you need to constantly ask yourself, "Who needs to know?" After you have identified the "who," then ask, "What do they need to know?" "Why do they need to know it?" "When do they need to know it?" "Where do they need to know it?" and "How will the information affect them and how will it be delivered?" One of the largest challenges in a project-oriented organization is keeping people informed. Obviously, the first consideration is the project team itself. Is each team member completely up to date on what other team members are working on and the impact of other members' work on their own work?

Are all the directly involved stakeholders being kept informed? What about stakeholders indirectly involved, including other project teams?

When you have more than a handful of people who need to be kept informed it may be best to prepare a plan. Start with the list of stakeholders you created earlier in the planning stage. Add on indirectly involved contacts (e.g., the press, government entities, other concerned outside organizations, and the public). For any questions of whom to include or exclude, ask: "If they learn about this project from an unofficial source, what is the potential risk to my organization if the information learned is misleading, inaccurate or incomplete?"

Determine the means, frequency, and type of communication you will use with each identified contact. Integrate your communication plans with other activities and events in your planning and scheduling documents to ensure that you are constantly reminded of communication requirements.

Caution: Special plans are needed if you are involved in a sensitive project, such as those subject to strict security measures, the development of a proprietary process or product, or a politically controversial study. Take appropriate precautions to ensure that communication to those outside the project team is handled only by a trained and competent spokesperson.

Planner Accountability

You and your organization's management may be held accountable for how you account for project expenditures. The Sarbanes-Oxley Act is a congressional act that focuses on protecting investors by improving the accuracy and reliability of corporate disclosures made pursuant to the securities laws. Beginning in 2004, compliance is mandatory for most public companies. It means that controlling and accounting for project expenditures is not just good business sense, it is the law. Failing to comply means large fines, possibly jail time. The Sarbanes-Oxley Act holds CEOs and CFOs personally responsible for any discrepancies between reported data and different data that might be discovered by auditors.

In many organizations, projects constitute a sizable percentage of the business being conducted, 100 percent in some cases. The aggregated numbers are large enough to attract the attention of the shareholders and accountants. The act's goal is to minimize sloppy and intentionally inaccurate accounting.

The aim in bringing this added risk to your attention is to alert you to the consequences of inadequate or inappropriate handling of expenditures. When planning the project, check with your legal advisor on how best to comply with the act.

Reality Check

It pays to do a reality check before you submit the team's project plans for approval. Ask yourself and your team members the following questions:

- Has a project similar to this one been successful and can we reasonably draw a parallel conclusion about this project?
- What is the "big picture" for this organization? How does this project's outcome fit strategically within that context?
- What external forces and constraints could prevent this project from being successful?
- What political barriers must be overcome for this project to be approved?
- Is our organizational culture conducive to the success of this type of project?
- Can we reasonably expect to obtain the resources needed within the time frames needed?
- Will the project benefits, as the project team perceives them, be accepted as benefits by the project's stakeholders?
- Will the disruptions, inconvenience, time delays, and costs incurred be acceptable and worth it to the stakeholders affected?
- Do we have the core competencies required for staffing the project team in-house? If not, how much of the project work will have to be outsourced, and will that be acceptable?
- Does the planned outcome from the project correlate with at least one measure by which the approving authority is evaluated? (Management's "hot button.")
- Has the team discussed the plans with some of the stakeholders to gain their support and feedback?

- Has the team explored all the possible points at which the project could fail, and has it determined that the risk in moving ahead is acceptable?

Either go back to the drawing board or submit your plans for approval. Stand ready to modify the plans to satisfy the approving authority.

Project Plan Approval

The project plan you submit may include the following:

- Brief Executive Overview

- Overall Work Breakdown Structure (at the level whereby the WBS can fit on one by 8½" by 11" sheet and in an easily readable font size)

- Overall Gantt chart showing only the Work Package level, or levels 1, 2 and 3 (again, on one sheet of 8½" by 11" paper)

- Overall Resource Requirements matrix (e.g., major categories of personnel)

- Budget
  –Cash flow
  –Return-on-project-investment overview
- Draft of Project Charter for approval

Depending upon your organization's policies, procedures, protocols, and practices, additional documentation may be required. Customer and regulatory mandates may call for additional data.

Assume you'll be expected to formally present your team's project plan for official approval, either in print alone or accompanied by an oral presentation. Keep in mind the following pointers:

- You and your team have been living with the development of the project plan. You know what all the charts and figures mean, and how you created them. Chances are your approving authority will not be familiar with the plan details. This means you should prepare a brief overview of the plan (two pages at the most, but one page is even better), listing all the supporting documents being submitted.

  –Emphasize the organizational benefits (the outcomes), preferably in dollars, and how soon the benefits will begin. Be sure what you are emphasizing is what is important to the approving authority.

  –Mention one or two key examples of what your successful project will do in supporting the organization's strategies.

  –Recognize the contributions made by stakeholders in the planning process.

  –Boil down your supporting documents so as not to overburden the approving authority with all the details. However, be sure to have the full-blown planning documents as backup if they are requested.

–Clearly state the resources you will need to launch the project, including funding. Briefly mention any work that will have to be outsourced, including consulting services.

–Be prepared to respond to questions about what you did to assess the risks involved, and your conclusions.

–If any part of the project work is subject to regulations or standards, discuss how you plan to conform to these requirements.

–If possible, make a meeting appointment to hand deliver the project plan and respond to questions.

- If a formal presentation is expected, or you feel it would be advantageous, then:

–In advance of the meeting:

  * Learn who the attendees will be.

  * Attempt to schedule a one-to-one meeting with all or most of the invited attendees (not the approving authority) to:

    ○ Go through a rough draft of your plans.

    ○ Gather insight, critique, suggestions, cautions, and hopefully, support for your plan.

  * Review the data gathered and make any adjustments to the plan and/or presentation that you deem beneficial.

  * Try to obtain a second individual meeting with as many of the attendees as possible to do a "dress rehearsal" of what you plan to present, and:

    ○ Point out where you made use of their previous input.

    ○ Ask for their support when you make your presentation to the approving authority.

–At the meeting where you will seek approval:

  * Present a copy of the plan to all attending the meeting.

  * Orally (with or without visual aids depending on your organization's customs) present the highlights of the plan.

  * Indicate where you have received valuable input from other attendees, including paraphrasing supporters' statements where you're sure you have support.

  * Be prepared to answer all questions.

  * Ask the approving authority for his/her approval.

  * Have the Project Charter or other sign-off document available for approval signature (if custom permits).

–After the meeting:

  * Contact all attendees and thank each for their participation and/or support.

  * Publish a brief summary of the meeting to all who attended

  * Include items discussed.

  * Decisions made.

  * Actions to be taken, by whom, and when.

To summarize: the very small project may require simple plans and, perhaps, just one pass for approval. More complex, medium-size projects may require the two-stage approval process: (1) approval of concept and of funds to commence developing the formal project plans, and (2) approval of the more extensive project plans.

The Project Management Office

Although you may be working on a small- to medium-size project, and one that will not use many resources or cost a heap of money, you may still be subject to an intermediate approving authority—the project management office. In many organizations, a Project Management Office (PMO) may have responsibility for:

- Overseeing all projects planned and ongoing—the project portfolio.
  - –Recommending priorities
  - –Facilitating resource allocations
  - –Serving as a third-party facilitator/arbitrator in interorganizational conflicts relating to projects
  - –Ensuring that projects proposed have been scrutinized for their impact on the organization's strategies, financial stability, legal and regulatory compliance, and interaction with other projects being considered and ongoing—as well as the impact on ongoing operations
- Training project managers in project management techniques and tools.
  - –Establishing the organization's standard project management practices and guidelines
  - –Coaching project managers in the planning, implementing, evaluation and close-out phases of their projects
  - –Maintaining the databank of completed projects for:
    - * Use as training material (lessons learned)
    - * References to aid in estimating future project resources required (funding, personnel, facilities, equipment, material, outsourced services, etc.)
    - * Baseline for comparing future plans with past performance
- Carry on continual research on project management best practices in order to assist the organization in employing the most appropriate methodology. This activity may involve:
  - –Researching print material, online information services, the World Wide Web
  - –Benchmarking with other external organizations known to be leaders in project management

If a PMO exists in your organization, establish contact before you start to produce your plans. The PMO is there to help you plan a successful project, and its recommendation will probably be required before top management approves your plan.

If there is no PMO, you and your project team may have some additional issues to deal with:

- Ensuring your project ties into the organization's strategies

- Interfacing and negotiating with suppliers, suppliers, contractors, consultants, and outsourced services; that may mean:
  –Working with such contacts at arm's length (strictly on a buyer-seller basis)
  –Integrating such contacts into your project team (as full participants or as "subject-matter experts on-call")
  –Establishing a quasi-partnership or an alliance

- Interfacing with the organization's external customers (if they are team participants or on an on-call basis)

- Working out agreements with the stakeholders affected by the project to clarify what your team will do and how they will do it and to clearly state the stakeholders' roles and commitments needed to ensure on-time, within-budget deliverables and organizational outcomes
  –Clarifying differences between "must haves," "wants," and "nice to haves"
  –Differentiating between primary and secondary stakeholders, and the needs of each

Proven Points to Keep in Mind

- Scope changes may be necessary because you have forgotten something. To alleviate the potential embarrassment, invest sufficient time upfront in defining the scope, including stakeholder requirements.

- Understand and respect the cultural differences that are present among the stakeholders you will serve as well as the project team you will manage—both the people and the organizational entities.
  –To obtain top management support, one vital practice is to be sure your project is planned so as to enhance the results by which top management is measured.
  –Remember Parkinson's Law: "Work expands to fill the time available for its completion."
  –Beware of analysis leading to paralysis—know when to stop gathering and analyzing data and when to start using the information derived from the data.
  –Learn the basics of project planning and management before jumping into using project management software. The most costly aspect of software is not the purchase price of the software, nor is it the computer's cost. It is the cost of the untrained, uninformed person in a trial-and-error approach, and his or her failure to learn any but the rudimentary features of the program.

Comments about Six Sigma Projects

Six Sigma Lite—The 80/20 Rule[2]

As with many organizational improvement technologies, Six Sigma has been hyped as an absolute necessity for organizations that want to survive in today's business environment. Of course the ones creating the hype are often those who have something to gain, such as the $40,000 that used to be charged to train a Black Belt, or the minimum $1 million contract required by some consulting firms to help an organization launch a Six Sigma initiative. The reality, however, is that most of the impact of Six Sigma can be attained by applying just a few core components of the technology.

What are the most important factors for achieving significant gains? The first is a rigorous project selection process carried out by top management, which includes evaluation of the real potential impact on the bottom line. That is, if revenues do not increase or expenditures do not decrease, there will be no real financial impact. Looking at the potential impact on customers, as well as cost of poor quality, will help this evaluation. Projects should also be organization-wide in scope (as opposed to working on one part of a process). The actual causes of defects are likely to be many, located anywhere in the process, and interrelated, and if the scope is too narrow the effect will be to work on a link in the chain that is not the weakest. The result is then no real impact on organization performance.

The second factor for ensuring significant gains is the use of highly skilled project managers who guide improvement projects. They must be highly analytical and good at project management and at working with others, and they must understand how to apply the multitude of process improvement tools. One of the parallels between Six Sigma and lean manufacturing projects (when the latter are carried out using the blitz approach) is that in both cases the individuals who guide improvement projects have a high level of authority to steer the team in the right direction.

This authority must be based on competence, rather than just appointed power. While putting other team members through a Green Belt–type course will help to reduce resistance to the project manager's direction (since team members will have greater knowledge about the tools), this is not a necessary component for success. Nor is whether or not the project manager is assigned to projects full time or part time, although of course making it full time indicates that the projects are highly important and will accelerate the rate at which improvement will occur.

Related to the second factor is a third one—the steps used to execute projects. The Design-Measure-Analyze-Improve-Control (DMAIC) approach has been well validated and greatly increases the likelihood of success. DMAIC pulls together many of the tools that have been used somewhat ad hoc in the past and integrates them in a logical sequence that ensures that causes of defects are correctly identified and resolved.

In organizations where systems thinking is not yet prevalent, one additional success factor will be needed—the identification of a top management sponsor or champion for each project. Such an individual can run interference when members of the organization try to block progress.

In summary, working on the right projects, having them led by highly skilled project managers, and executing them using the DMAIC model nearly guarantees that improvement projects will significantly affect an organization. If a broader change is desired in organizational mindset, then other aspects of the Six Sigma approach may also be useful. But in today's business environment organizations must ensure that efforts are carried out in ways that do not waste resources. The 80/20 rule indicates that most of the gains from Six Sigma can be achieved with just some of the key factors.

Notes

1. Lewis, James P., *Mastering Project Management: Applying Advanced Concepts of Systems Thinking, Control and Evaluation, Resource Allocation.* 1998. New York: McGraw-Hill. Chapter 20, "Managing Vendors in Projects."
2. Reprinted with permission from "APLOMETrics," December 2003, a newsletter from *APLOMET,* written by Duke Okes, Blountville, Tennessee.

QUICK QUIZ
NUMBER 6

1. Under what circumstances might it be advisable to subdivide a Work Package?

2. How would you estimate a task that had never been done before?

3. What is the major concern when adding more detail to planning charts and matrixes?

4. What is the benefit in knowing where there is float in the schedule?

5. What are the potential advantages and disadvantages for an organization to outsource some of the project work?

6. Given that lack of the right resources at the right time is the primary obstacle in scheduling project work, what are ways to reduce or eliminate this problem?

7. What are the reasons why change control is needed for larger, more complex projects? How is change control typically handled by an effective project team?

8. What negative effects can "padding" task estimates to allow for contingencies have on the project?

9. What are the reasons why computing a ROPI is an important project planning step?

10. What is the purpose of a Project Charter, and what types of information should be included?

11. For what reasons might a project be subdivided into a "design" phase and an "implementation/installation" phase?

12. Why is it important to have plans to communicate information about the project and to whom should such communication be directed?

13. What are some of the factors that should be considered in presenting a project plan for approval?

14. Why is a Project Management Office important to organizations having to initiate, plan, and manage multiple projects?

15. In what ways are project management techniques and tools applicable to Six Sigma–type projects?

7

Implementing, Tracking, Evaluating, and Closing Projects: The Project Plan Is Approved; What's Next?

Depending upon the size and complexity of the project, you will need some systematic approach for tracking (monitoring) the ongoing project, measuring results, reporting progress, making changes, and correcting the plans, and if necessary, aborting the project. You will also need a methodology for documenting the project and closing out the completed project.

Keep in mind you are working at two levels: the management of the project itself and the development of the deliverables and results derived from the project—the execution activities.

Managing the Project Activities

Performance Measures

In measuring and assessing a project, consider:

- Is the project producing results?
- Are the project objectives being accomplished?
- Is the project on time?
- Is the project within budget?
- Are the allocated resources adequate?
- Is the project team functioning effectively?

Frequency of Measurement

There are two primary times to measure a project:

- At appropriate intervals while the project is still in process
- At the end of the project

Measuring the Ongoing Project

Typical measures used while the project is in progress are:

- Project on schedule.
- Milestones met.
- Appropriate Stage-Gate[1] decisions made.
- Project within budget.
  –Variances of actual vs. budgeted amounts.
  –Return on project investment still viable.
  –Cash expenditures occurring as planned.
- Assessment of barriers affecting project success and how effectively these barriers are being addressed.
- Project is following its critical path.
  –Corrective action plans initiated to get the project back on track (if the project is off track).
- Opportunities to positively reinforce good progress or good effort recognized and acted upon.
- Progress reports on the project made at appropriate intervals.
- Potential problem/opportunity analysis performed at reasonable intervals.
- Assessment of potential impact of risks on project success performed at reasonable intervals.

End-of-Project Measures

The measures of project success should be directly linked to the project's scope, objectives, charter, and schedule. Examples of typical end-of-project measures include:

- Project objectives accomplished.
- Project deliverables achieved.
- Project deadline met.
- Project within budget.
- Projected outcomes are achieved or remain viable.

Examples of additional measures are:

- ROPI (return on project investment) ratio of 3:1 minimum (unless project mandated).
- Desired project payback period achieved.
- Annual cost savings (savings per year) realized.
- Earned value analysis[2] favorable.

- Response time improvement.
- Waste reduced.
- Process capability improved.
- Plant start-up at projected start-up efficiencies and rates.
- Lessons learned captured, documented, and accessible for subsequent projects.

Project Schedule

It's a fact: the estimating you have done and the resulting schedule you have created will be subject to change—many changes if it is a medium-size, longer duration project. You will need to track actual project performance against the approved plans (the baseline) in order to detect when and where changes may be necessary. The occurrence of any of the following will cause schedule changes or even total project termination:

- Customer's requirements change.
- "Scope creep" (small incremental changes or additions that tend to creep into the project requirements; unless absorbed within the initial parameters these changes ultimately force considering renegotiation of schedule, resources, and budget).
- Resources planned cannot be made available (especially people and money).
- Project loses support of top management.
- Organization's strategy has changed.
- Higher priority project or activity takes precedence.
- Key members of project team are no longer available.
- Organization experiences loss due to unanticipated risk.
- Technology upon which project depends is not available or fails to work.
- Outside contractors (vendors, consultants, etc.) fail to meet project requirements.
- Unplanned regulatory requirement is imposed.
- Organization is reorganized, sold, merged, or terminated.

Schedule changes may require modifications to:

- Project definition, scope, and charter
- Work breakdown
- Estimates and timelines
- Task interdependencies
- Critical path

- Milestones and Stage-Gate™ decision points
- Alignment of resources
- Budget and/or cash flow
- Conditions relevant to original approval of plans

"Crashing the schedule" is a term used to represent the actions taken when the project is not going to make its planned deadline. The project manager may compress the duration of the remaining activities (those on the critical path) by:

- Adding resources
  –More internal performers and experts
  –External contractors, suppliers and consultants
  –Outsource work
- Working overtime

- Finding ways to increase the productivity of the project team
  –Substitute more competent members for less competent members.
  –Bring in more labor-saving equipment and/or practices.
  –Introduce multitasking where appropriate.
  –Add performance incentives.

Keep in mind that crashing the schedule may create an entirely new critical path. Several of the resources previously listed discuss the steps to take, the choice of priority of tasks to crash, and the evaluation of the cost and risks of compressing the schedule. Crashing the schedule causes a tradeoff of money for time (you may complete on time but overrun the budget).

Change Control

Except for the short, simpler project, a system for controlling changes is mandatory. The Change Control Log (discussed in Chapter 6) is recommended. It is essential that document changes be assigned to a responsible person. All persons who have a need to know must be kept up to date on the changes.

It is especially important that trade-off decisions be documented. Such decisions are often made in the heat of battle in order to get the project back on track. In postproject reflection ,these decisions are key learning points in how to, or how not to, make certain decisions—lessons learned for the education of future project managers.

Tracking the Ongoing Project

The more timely the awareness that the project may go off track, the faster that corrective action can be initiated. "Milestones" are points within the project where the project team checks on whether the work is proceeding on time and within budget. The frequency of such checkpoints must be decided carefully. If too much elapsed time between milestones is allowed, there may be the risk of a serious deficiency going undetected for a long time period. If milestones are too frequent, such checks become a time and cost burden and a nuisance. Needless to say, critical activities or events (those on the critical path) need more frequent attention.

In larger projects, Stage-Gates™ may be used to trigger logical points in the schedule when a decision should be made to continue, make major modifications to the plans, or discontinue the project. Usually the Stage-Gate™ decisions are keyed to the scheduled completion date of a phase or stage in a multistage project. The decisions are sometimes referred to as go/no-go decisions.

The actual mechanism for tracking progress should be scaled to the size and complexity of the project. For a short-term, noncomplex project involving few people and a low budget, an oral check by the project manager may be sufficient (perhaps daily, for a two- or three-week project).

For depicting project status on all but the very small project, an expanded Gantt chart (showing the actual duration of Work Packages completed or in-process as horizontal time bars just below each planned duration) generally suffices. For this type of Gantt chart, hollow bars show planned durations, solid (filled-in) bars show completed durations, and cross-hatching shows the uncompleted portion of work in process. Where the time durations are very short, downward-pointing hollow triangles may be used for planned events and filled-in triangles used to indicate completion. (Upward-pointing hollow triangles may be used on top of the planned durations to indicate milestones.) Note: Some computer programs use symbols different from those suggested in this book. Adapt/adopt the graphical symbols that make most sense for your organization; just be consistent in your usage.

Cost Variance Analysis and Reporting

The concept of identifying a variance, such as planned cost versus actual cost or scheduled activities versus actual occurrence, is simple to understand. Implementing the system for collecting the right data, establishing the criteria for analyzing the data, and transforming the data into meaningful information for decision making, by the right person at the right time—this is a little more complex.

Consider the following five primary questions in establishing your control plan:

1. What is to be tracked, analyzed, measured, and reported?

   –What data are needed?

   –Where and for what purpose is the information derived from the data needed?

   –Where can the data be found?

   –Are the data readily accessible?

   –How frequently are the data available?

   –Are the data current when selected?

   –What criteria will be used in making the selection of data?

   –How will the data be selected and collected?

2. How frequently is the information derived from the data to be reported?

   –Is the information to be presented as a stand-alone report or included with other information?

   –To whom is the information directed for decision making?

   –What is the overall distribution plan for the information?

3. What methodology will be used to analyze the data collected?

   –What measurements will be used?

   –Will the data require only sorting and accumulation?

   –Will the data require further statistical analysis?

4. In what format will the information derived from the data be presented?

5. What explanations, interpretations, and recommendations will be presented in support of the information?

   –Is the information presented actionable?
   * Timely?
   * Accurate?
   * Complete?
   * Usable without further analysis or manipulation?

   –Is there provision for evaluating the recipients' satisfaction with the analysis and presentation of the information?

   –Has timely action been taken, where needed, based on the information presented?

   –How can the tracking, measuring, analyzing, and reporting process be further improved?

In organizations that formally and frequently initiate projects, the accounting system has probably been modified to accumulate costs by assigned project numbering schemes. However, as an occasional project manager you may find that there is no mechanism for capturing the detail data you need to properly control your project. In the absence of an adequate accounting system, you'll have to devise your own system. Be sure the time and cost of doing so is included in your project management planning.

In your planning (Work Breakdown Structure), you assigned cost estimates for labor, equipment and tools, and materials to the Work Packages (or lowest level of you plan). As each Work Package is completed, provide for capturing the actual costs. Be especially careful not to let this action lag until the details are forgotten. Where delayed payments for external contractors' services and/or progress payments on equipment or materials are involved be sure to devise a means for including these costs when they become known.

Insofar as possible, Work Packages should be planned for completion within the time period covered by status reviews, for example, two weeks on a medium-size project. Record actual labor hours and actual non-labor costs for each Work Package.

Work Package	Labor Hours & Costs						Suppliers' Charges			Equipment Charges		
	Pld Hrs	Act Hrs	Var	Pld $	Act $	Var $	Pld $	Act $	Var $	Pld $	Act $	Var $
Project management (QE)	25	15	10	600	375	250						
Needs analysis (QE)	24	18	6	600	450	150						
Write calibration specs (PE)	32	26	6	960	780	180						
Select suppliers (QE)	8	10	–2	200	250	–50						
Order equipment (QE)	8	8	0	200	200	0				8200	8300	1000
Order computer prog. (QE)	1	1	0	25	25	0						
Train QE (supplier)	24	7	16	600	200	400	5000	2500	2500			
Set-up system (QE, PS)	40			1000								
Calibrate tools, equip. (QE)	240			6000								
Set calibration sched. (QE)	16			400								
Write procedures (PE, PS)	30			735								
Close-out (QE, PE, PS)	24			680								
Contingency fund				1000								
Totals	472	86		13000	2280		5000	2500		8200	8300	1000

Figure 7.1 Calibration system project—sample variance report.

Figure 7.1 shows a simple variance report for a small project. The project spans three months and involves the quality engineer (project manager), production engineer, and production superintendent—all part-time. The project scope is to determine the organization's tool calibration needs and set up an in-house calibration laboratory. The project plans were approved for a maximum budget of $100,000, including equipment and training. The project status is at the point where the Quality Engineer is receiving training from the supplier. Of the budgeted dollars, $87,780 has been spent.

Another approach for tracking expenditures is to graphically display the cash outlays against the budgeted cash flow. The graph can consist of two trend lines, representing planned cash outlays and actual expenditures, displayed on a time scale. Or shaded, alternating vertical bars can show planned and actual cash expenditures, displayed for each time period. Or the trend lines can be superimposed over the bar chart more graphically displaying relative volume (the bars) with the two trend lines depicting the direction the expenditures are taking.

Project Team Responsibility

In all cases, all project team members must assume responsibility for informing the team if they detect actual or potential slippage on their assignments, as soon as they know or suspect such slippage. Where tasks are assigned to people outside the project team, such as contractors, suppliers, consultants, other employees, and stakeholders, the project manager must ensure that compliance to plan is proactively checked. Although less frequently encountered, situations where the project is underrunning the scheduled time and budget, or has the potential to do so should also be communicated throughout the project team. Learning about "why" this is occurring is a valuable lesson learned.

Longer term, more complex projects may be tracked visually by updated and posted schedules (e.g., milestone charts) or by computer-generated reports. The important points to consider are:

- Is the frequency of status reporting the most cost-effective in highlighting unplanned deviations and detecting risks in order to take timely corrective action?

- Are the right activities/events being tracked (especially those that are critical)?

- Have the best frequencies been established for assessing progress?

- Have the responsibilities for tracking progress been clearly assigned?

- For reporting and corrective action purposes, has the best balance between too little data and too much data been carefully determined?

- Do all the data reported have a purpose?

- How are the reported data going to be used in the analysis and to make informed decisions?

- Do all the project team members understand that they are responsible for informing the team of any actual or potential deviation from plan, as soon as they are aware of such a deviation?

- Have change control and corrective action procedures been established?

- Is there a protocol for communicating changes and plan deviations to stakeholders who need to know?

- Have Stage-Gate™ decision points been established whereby the project activities and results to date are evaluated and the project is either continued or terminated?

- Are the effectiveness of the project team itself and the management of the project assessed on a periodic basis during the life of the project?

The Job's Not Done until the Paperwork Is Finished

Many projects involve developing a new or changed policies, processes, or products. This implies that some types of paperwork will need to be generated or modified:

- Policy change

- Process map, procedure, and work instruction

- Engineering design/print

- Training material

- Workers' job aid, work standards manual, and safety alert

- Marketing material (advertisement, sales material, catalogs, Web site, product warranty, consumer warning and instruction)

- Accounting practice

- Customer relations protocol

These are but a few of the potential documents that may require change before the project's deliverables are ready for customers' use. Designing, drafting and producing these documents should be addressed in the work breakdown structure. Ensuring that *all* of the needed documents are ready by the deadlines for the pertinent deliverables is often a neglected control aspect of the project execution stage. This apparent neglect may be because producing many of these types of documents calls for design and production activities different from those of mainline execution activities, including special creative talent. Suffice it to say, don't find yourself ready to deliver and then find that the paperwork is missing, incomplete, or unacceptable.

Measuring Results

In the planning stage, you identified and quantified the project objectives, identified the project outputs, and quantified projected project outcomes. As an integral part of the project plans, you also established timelines, resources required, a budget, and projected cash flow. You may have also computed a potential return on project investment (ROPI). You now need to measure progress and the results against these baselines.

Mandates from regulatory agencies and customer contractual requirements concerning measures take precedence. However, absent these requirements or often in addition to the mandates, decisions have to be made as to what to measure, how to measure, when to measure, where to measure, and who will measure.

The caveat: no project shall be initiated without provision to measure progress and results. Fulfilling this caveat requires two primary actions: (1) determine the baseline (the status just before initiation of the project), and (2) determine the most effective metric to use that most accurately and completely portrays the ongoing and final results. For example:

Assume the project is to develop and deliver skill training to a work unit of 15 operatives to acquire skill in performing a specific new task. To select the most effective metric for measuring results, the following are examples of options that may be considered:

1. Number of hours of training provided to each operative

2. Number of operatives demonstrating proficiency in the skill taught, at completion of training

3. Cost to develop and deliver the skill training

4. Individual scores on multiple-choice questions pertaining to knowledge about the skill taught

5. Supervisor's assessment of operatives' post-training competency in using the learned skill

6. Evidence of operatives' use of the skill taught in the timely production of error-free products that meet specifications

The one single metric that most effectively measures the desired objective of the training is number 6. Numbers 2 and 5 come close. Number 3 may be required but is relatively meaningless without determining the cost relationship to the benefits obtained.

If the project was to produce defect-free product X and "increased customer satisfaction" was identified as an outcome, then additional metrics might be chosen from these alternatives:

7. Number of sales of product X

8. Number of product X complaints received

9. Number of product X complaints resolved to the customers' satisfaction within 3 days

10. Unconditional guarantee policy established for product X

11. Number of complaints resolved under the unconditional policy for product X

12. Number of customers continuing to purchase product X

13. Number of customers continuing to purchase product X after making a complaint

Corrective Action for the Overrunning Project

The smaller project has one disadvantage over the larger, longer-term project. The smaller project has less time to get back "on track" when a deviation from plan occurs. Furthermore, because controls over the smaller project are more likely to be less stringent than with a larger project, the occurrence of a deviation may take longer to detect. In other words, the project may reach its deadline before someone notices it's in trouble! The smaller project, while perhaps lacking the more sophisticated controls of a larger project, needs constant vigilance to ensure that estimated time and costs are being met, and the work planned is being done on schedule. Watch out for a project that for several review periods remains at 90 percent completed. The project somehow never quite gets finished.

Project process tracking should be ongoing, with periodic reviews (daily, weekly, monthly, or quarterly) appropriate to the nature of the project. There is a reason for including time estimates on the work breakdown structure, the Gantt chart, and the Personnel Resource Requirements matrix. Use the estimates to compare with actual performance. Expand the Gantt chart to plot the actual duration of each activity/task and compare with the planned duration. Check for opportunities to double up activities/tasks to enable the project to complete on time. Check again for any tasks that might be omitted or modified to reduce costs and possibly changed to compensate for overruns on other tasks.

When a project is reaching a point where targets may be missed, or that point has occurred, consider the following options for corrective action:

- Increase frequency and surveillance of project performance.

- "Borrow" resources from Work Packages not on the critical path.

- Compress the schedule ("crashing") by trading additional cost for a decrease in time.
  - –Request additional internal resources.
  - –Schedule overtime work.
  - –Hire temporary workers.
  - –Outsource work.
- Request additional time.
- Request division of the project into two or more subprojects with new delivery targets staggered to allow spreading out resource requirements.
- Request decrease in project scope.
- As a last resort and as appropriate, apply for relief from a contingency fund (see Chapter 6).

Risk Assessment

Relative to a project, there are three places when a risk assessment is called for:

1. In determining the feasibility of launching a project (discussed in Chapter 3)

2. As an integral part of the project planning stage

3. Continuing assessment of risks during an ongoing project related to:

   –Internal project conditions or events affecting the continuation or termination of the project

   –Changes in scope (increasing or decreasing)

   –Change in priorities among the portfolio of projects underway

   –Resource shortfall (quantity, competency, capacity)

   –Deficiencies (missed deadlines, wasted resources, errors, forgotten activities in the plan)

   –Factors outside the project affecting continuation or termination:

   –Change in organizational strategy

   –Change in organizational leadership structure and/or ownership

   –Developing financial crisis

   –Looming competitive crisis

   –Potential product obsolescence

   –Disaster: act of God, act of humans (intentional or unintentional)

Risk assessment and reduction activities should be included within the project management segment of the work breakdown structure. Risk identification and initial assessment of the potential impact of risks, along with actions to mitigate the risks, should be addressed in the planning stage.

In managing an ongoing project, risk assessment should be revisited at each project review meeting. The goal is to spot potential problems in time to take action to eliminate the risk or reduce the effect of the risk. Actions to deal with risks may be preventive to ensure the risk does not occur and/or dealing with contingencies if a risk occurs.

Consider adapting the reliability engineers' failure mode and effect analysis (FMEA) to your project needs. This tool enables you to identify, classify, and rate potential risks and the countermeasures to reduce or eliminate the risks. D. H. Stamatis's book, *Failure Mode and Effect Analysis,*[3] provides guidance in designing and using the tool.

Project Review Meetings

Status reports may, for the short-range and small project, be an informal, unscheduled oral report by the project manager to the project sponsor. At the opposite end of the spectrum, larger projects and organizational practices may call for a formal presentation to key stakeholders, and involve visual aids and a printed report with charts (a "dog and pony" show). Regardless of the delivery method, project status reports are reviewed by interested parties to:

- Learn where the project stands relative to earlier approved plans, including:
  - –Any variance from time, cost and resource utilization estimates
  - –Potential impact of any significant variances and/or deviations from scope
- Be made aware of barriers and potential risks, as well as opportunities that could impact project plans
  - –Monetary impacts
  - –Organizational impacts (e.g., organizational strategy, customer satisfaction, competitor threat, new opportunities)
- Be informed of actions taken or in process to mitigate the negative impacts and take advantage of positive impacts

- Review the information presented and provide continued support for the project

- Recommend amendment of the project scope, schedule or project termination

Figure 7.2 is one example of a formal Project Status Report. This form is used where Work Packages have planned durations not exceeding the time period between project reviews, for example, two weeks. The form records status of scheduled Work Packages as 0 percent (not started), 50 percent (started but not finished), and 100 percent (finished). A cost variance is documented for each scheduled Work Package. Other pertinent data are documented for presentation to the reviewing parties.

PROJECT STATUS REPORT

Project name: _____Number: _____

Period from: _____ to: _____ Prepared by: _____ Date:_____

WP #	Work Package Scheduled	0% Complete	50% Complete	100% Complete
		$	$	$
		$	$	$
		$	$	$
		$	$	$
		$	$	$
		$	$	$
		$	$	$
		$	$	$
		$	$	$
		$	$	$

$ = Cost variance (budget − actual) (negative = over budget)

Project is on schedule   ahead of schedule   behind schedule

Project is meeting budgeted cost   exceeding budgeted cost   below budgeted cost

List any changes to project scope or objectives in this period:

_____

_____

What unanticipated problems and/or risks have become apparent?

_____

_____

What actions are needed to overcome these problems/risks? Whose approval is needed?

_____

_____

Significant achievements made in this period:

_____

_____

Significant performance deficiencies noted in this period:

_____

_____

Continued

Figure 7.2   Project status report.

Continued

List corrective actions that have been taken in this period and status of each:

_____

_____

List corrective actions not completed from previous period and status of each:

_____

_____

Rating of project schedule and cost estimates for this period: scale 1 (poor),   5 (excellent)

Rating of project team effectiveness in this period: :   scale 1 (poor),   5 (excellent)

Additional comments:

_____

_____

_____

_____

_____

_____

_____

A few suggestions for making a status report at a project review meeting are:

- Be totally honest. Do not hide facts that could impact the success of the project.

- Stress the benefits (project outcomes and return on project investment).

- Be sure all your statements, oral or in print, are backed up with data.

- If corrective action is being taken, state clearly what the action is and what the expected results are.

- Remember that your report could either reinforce top management's decision to approve your project or result in top management's backing away from supporting your project. Be prepared to seek affirmation of top management's continued support.

- If you and your team really feel the project should be terminated, say so and state logical reasons for your recommendation.
  - –Be prepared for a backlash and edict that the project will be continued (possibly an attempt by management to save face). Clearly document this decision and your objections.

–Be prepared in the event that a project termination decision is made abruptly and you are given directions to immediately cease all work and disband the team. Such a quick decision could mean you may have to complete the project documentation and closeout on your own time.

Stage closing and/or deliverables approval

When Stage-Gate™ (go/no-go) decisions have been planned and/or whenever designated deliverables are achieved, an approval document may be required.

Figure 7.3 is a suggested format for interim approval of stages or designated deliverables.

Lessons Learned

When working on a medium-size project, it is useful to devote some time to exploring lessons learned at the periodic review meetings. Documenting these lessons, and the actions taken to benefit from the lessons, is critical to building project management competence.

At the very least, lessons learned should be incorporated with the project closeout process. For example:

At a previous employer, my boss met with the project team at closeout time to "reverse engineer" the project. He led us through the project working back from the project end, step by step, asking why it went well, or why it went poorly, what corrective actions were needed, and how could we improve the next time around? His intriguing name for the process was "dissecting a debacle." (He had apparently somehow learned this from his earlier days as a sales rep selling dynamite to mining companies. And he still had all his original body parts!)

The session(s) should involve the entire team and other key stakeholders. The effort is not to fix blame but to fix problems, practices, and processes—to continually improve.

The documented lessons learned, and subsequent preventive actions taken, become a valuable part of the completed project database. Successful project actions, as well as less than successful actions, should be discussed and documented.

Figure 7.4 is a sample form to trigger discussion and documentation of lessons learned.

Figure 7.5 lists "thought starters" for reviewing lessons learned.

Recording Interim Improvements

As the project work progresses, improvements are often made to the project management process itself and/or to the development of the deliverables. These often small improvements tend to go unrecorded because they were not part of the project plan. When such improvements are made, documenting the improvements is helpful for several reasons:

PROJECT STAGE/DELIVERABLES APPROVAL FORM

Project name:		Project No.:	
Stage (if applicable):		Yes [ ] No [ ]*	
Deliverable name: (1)		Yes [ ] No [ ]*	
Deliverable name: (2)		Yes [ ] No [ ]*	
Deliverable name: (3)		Yes [ ] No [ ]*	
Deliverable name: (4)		Yes [ ] No [ ]*	
Deliverable name: (5)		Yes [ ] No [ ]*	
Deliverable name: (6)		Yes [ ] No [ ]*	
Deliverable name: (7)		Yes [ ] No [ ]*	
Deliverable name: (8)		Yes [ ] No [ ]*	
Deliverable name: (9)		Yes [ ] No [ ]*	

Changes to stage required before approval can be granted (describe what change required, by whom, and by when):

_____

_____

_____

_____

_____

Deliverables requiring change before approval can be granted (describe what change, by whom, and by when):

No.	Highlights of change required (attach supporting specifications, if needed)

Complete approval of items listed (no changes):

Signature & Title _____ Date _____

Approval except for starred (*) items:

Signature & Title _____ Date _____

Note: Changes not covered by the approved Project Plans may require extension of project completion dates, additional resources and/or additional costs.

Figure 7.3 Project stage/deliverables approval.

POINTS TO DISCUSS AT A LESSONS LEARNED DEBRIEFING

Project name: _____   Project Manager: _____   Project No. _____

Debriefing meeting date(s): _____

Work Package/ Activity/Event	P*	S*	E*	What occurred?	Why?	Improvement action?	Action responsibility?	By date?	Documented?

P = Poor results   S = Satisfactory results   E = Exemplary results

Persons attending debriefing

Comments

Figure 7.4   Points to discuss at a lessons learned debriefing.

Project selection

- The stated outcomes were not worthwhile.
- Unanticipated political obstacles inhibited project implementation.
- Project idea was sound but it didn't fit the organization's overall strategy.
- Organizational functions that would be impacted by the results of the project were not adequately informed of the plans or involved in planning for the changes that would occur.

Project team

- In selecting/recruiting project team members, the project leader underestimated the competencies (knowledge, experience, skills, aptitude, attitude) needed.
- People selected to work on the project felt it was a waste of time.
- Team was formed but time was not allocated for team building.
- Team members did not get along well with one another.
- Team members needed additional training to build needed knowledge and skills.
- Project manager was not well-accepted, respected, and followed.
- Members were absorbed in working their personal agendas and satisfying their egos.
- Routine day-to-day work infringed upon team members' time and attention.
- Members' supervisors did not support their members' participation on the project.
- Team leader/members alienated people outside the project who were needed to help the project achieve its objectives.
- Team members were not empowered sufficiently.
- Team leader's management style was not supportive of intrateam or interteam collaboration and cooperation.

Resources and support

- Management support was not adequate to overcome barriers project team faced.
- Resource commitments were not honored.
- Majority of organization's employees perceived the project as unimportant.
- Little or no recognition for the project team's effort was provided.
- Because of the off-site location and lack of contact with former colleagues the team felt isolated and "off the organization's radar screen."
- Full-time team members felt penalized due to lost opportunities for new training and assignments as well as losing out on promotions and compensation increases provided their peers not on the project.

Project management

- Initial estimates were way off, the return-on-investment expectation too high, costs were estimated too low, and time to complete was underestimated.
- Breakdown of the work to be done was not carefully planned beforehand.
- Project was executed in linear mode when many tasks could have been in parallel.
- Team failed to tap into knowledge gained from previous projects.
- Team failed to call upon "subject matter experts" from outside the project.
- Inadequate problem "root cause analysis" was done when project was impacted.
- Team stalled by unresolved conflicts, griping, and pointing fingers.
- Project linkages/interfaces broke down, within the project or outside the project.
- Project progress was not tracked frequently or thoroughly enough resulting in lost time and increased costs.
- Project sponsor, as well as top management, was not regularly apprised of project status.
- Team members were reluctant to seek help before a crisis developed.
- Scope creep was allowed without renegotiating for needed resources.
- Project results were thrust upon impacted functions without advance warning or adequate preparation for the changes.

Unfulfilled project objectives

- Management failed to close a doomed project in time to minimize losses.
- Project team failed to conduct an "autopsy" on a failed or seriously off-track project to identify causes of failure and document lessons learned.

Figure 7.5   "Thought starters" for reviewing lessons learned.*

*Although the above statements are stated in "what went wrong" terms, care should be taken to document "what went right."

- Reinforces the organization's theme of continual improvement in all its endeavors.

- Provides evidence of such unplanned benefits.

- Adds to advantages for management's support of the project.

- Inspires other teams to institute process improvements.

- Basis for recognizing team's accomplishments "beyond project requirements".

Figure 7.6 is a sample log for capturing interim improvements.

Closing Out the Project

The time to close down the project occurs when:

- All planned deliverables have been completed.
- All project documentation has been completed, including:
  –A postproject summary review report has been presented to key stakeholders.
  –Assessment of key stakeholders satisfaction has been done, feedback shared, and necessary actions taken.
  –Project history (plans and decisions) has been documented.
  –"Lessons learned" have been discussed and documented.
  –Appropriate project closeout document has been approved.
  –The project team has received appropriate recognition for their accomplishments.
  –Formal documented recognition.
  –Team celebration.
  –Project team is disbanded.
- The project is terminated by the approving authority.
  –Project is no longer strategic or desirable.
  –Funds are no longer available.
  –Higher priorities prevail.

Figure 7.7 is an example of a closeout form used by one company to ensure that all bases have been covered before shutting down the project. Note: For some projects the final closeout cannot be completed until the outcomes have been evaluated. A waiting period may be needed before the actual outcomes can be validated. Also, for some types of projects, material, contract labor, and installation service charges may arrive after the project team has been disbanded. This may necessitate keeping the "books" open until all charges are recorded.

LOG OF INTERIM IMPROVEMENTS MADE WHILE WORKING ON

Project name: _____ Project Manager: _____ Project No. _____

Date	Initiated by	Process affected	Procedures/ documents affected	Description of opportunity/deficiency	What improvement made	Action responsibility	Results	Payoff ($, qty, %)

Figure 7.6 Log of interim improvements.

Instructions:
Complete this form only after all work on the project has been completed, all charges to the project have been submitted (inclusive of hours, shipping charges, materials, subcontractor charges, etc). and the project has been dormant for at least one month. If you are unsure whether all charges have been received, check with accounting. Do not file this form until the project results and outcomes have been evaluated. Enter this completed form and all project documentation in the *Projects Information Database (PID)*.

Project name: _____   Project number: _____

Project approved by: _____   Project Manager: _____

Project start date: Day _____ Month _____ Year _____

Close-out date: Day _____ Month _____ Year _____

Planned Duration: _____   Planned Benefits: $ _____   Budget Costs: $ _____

Actual Duration: _____   Actual Benefits: $ _____   Actual Costs: $ _____

Variance: _____   Variance: $ _____   Variance: $ _____

Project Summary:
(Quality of product(s) or service(s) provided, lessons learned, specific problems, reasons for variances, etc.)

_____

_____

_____

_____

_____

_____

_____

_____

_____

_____

_____

_____

_____

_____

_____

_____

_____

Customer/Project recipient sign-off: _____   Date: _____

Project sponsor sign-off: _____   Date: _____

Form completed by: _____   Data entered into **PID** by: _____   Date: _____

Continued

Figure 7.7   Project close-out.

Satisfaction level recorded from customers/project results recipient(s):
Contact person(s):

Indication was obtained:
[ ] Solicited   [ ] E-mailed   [ ] Via Letter/memo   [ ] Orally   [ ] 3rd-Party, Non-specific

Performance rating:
[ ] Outstanding [ ] Excellent   [ ] Good   [ ] Fair   [ ] Poor, Unacceptable

Specific quotes/comments (reasons for rating, problems experienced, commendations):

Supplier/sub-contractor (name and contact person):

Services/products provided:

Performance rating:
[ ] Outstanding [ ] Excellent   [ ] Good   [ ] Fair   [ ] Poor, Unacceptable
Should they be used again: [ ] Yes   [ ] No

Reasons:
Supplier/sub-contractor (name and contact person):

Services/products provided:

Performance rating:
[ ] Outstanding [ ] Excellent   [ ] Good   [ ] Fair   [ ] Poor, unacceptable
Should they be used again: [ ] Yes   [ ] No

Reasons:

Continued

Continued

Documents Attached	Check off
Project proposal	
Feasibility analysis	
Request to fund project planning	
Stakeholder analysis	
Output requirements	
Risk analysis	
Work breakdown structure	
Timelines (Gantt chart)	
Network diagram	
Resource requirements matrices: [ ] Personnel [ ] Facilities [ ] Equipment [ ] Materials [ ] Supplies [ ] Suppliers/sub-contractors [ ] Other	
Team members	
Schedule	
Budget	
Return-on-project-investment (ROPI) analysis	
Project status summary reports	
Final project report	
Customer/Project Recipient Correspondence: [ ] Complaints [ ] Commendations [ ] Other	
Other: (Specify)	

Historical Database

It is recommended that an information database be established to store completed project documentation (as hard copy and/or electronically). The objectives for this database are to:

- Archive models of project planning and management practices
  – Project definition (scope, statement of work)
  – Project approval process (project justification, charter)
  – Team formation and management
  – Use of project planning and management techniques and tools
    - Work breakdown method
    - Estimating methodology (time, costs, resources required, return on investment, budgeting, and cash-flow projections)

- Scheduling methodology (interdependencies, time lines)
- Project tracking, measurement, and evaluation methodology
- Project reporting methods (milestones, Stage-Gate™ decisions)
- Record evidence of the payoff that can be obtained from successful project planning and management, and the basis for justifying future projects.
- Catalog learning opportunities (what worked well, what worked not so well, what failed).
- Document improvements planned or made resulting from the lessons learned.
- Provide case studies to train future project initiators and managers.

Party Time

As appropriate to the success of the project team, the value the team created, the duration and intensity of the project, the difficulties faced and overcome—and the organization's policies—some level of recognition is called for. Some of the means to recognize team contributions are:

- Commendation from top-ranking company executive naming all team members and statement of team achievements:
  –Orally presented by top executive in a company-wide meeting (or a division or plant-wide meeting); photo opportunity
  –Copy of commendation given to each member
  –Copy of commendation filed in individual's personnel file
  –In-house publicity citing team and its accomplishments
  –Public (media) recognition (insofar as appropriate)
- Token rewards for team members:
  –Choice of a product from an incentive catalog
  –Education voucher for public seminars
  –"Field trip" to another company location to talk about project experience
  –Stakeholders affected by project outcomes invited to a "show and tell" meeting hosted by project team
  –Trip and/or meal for team member's family
- Brief "party" on company-time for project team members and the work units from which they were selected and to which they will return:
  –Pizza or snacks, soft drinks
  –Photo opportunity

An emotional bond has developed among the project team members as they matured, overcame barriers, and produced outputs and outcomes that generated a payoff for the project's key stakeholders. Depending upon the duration and intensity of the team's assignment, individuals may leave the team with one or more of the following feelings and concerns as they return to their prior position:

- "Will I be welcomed or treated as an outsider?"

- "Have I lost ground while I was away?" (knowledge, skill, promotability, personal relationships, pay, etc.)

- "Will I ever see and/or work with my project colleagues again?"

- "Will I like my old job now that I've been on a different assignment?" (Comparing degree of autonomy, participating in decisions, being valued for my competency and contribution while on the project team.)

- "Will my favorable record on the project contribute or detract from my status and treatment among my co-workers at the old job?"

- "Will my work relationships on the project, established with persons of higher rank than my former supervisor, affect how I'm treated when I return to the old job?"

Care should be taken in addressing each returning individual's concerns and issues. Try to understand the needs and determine how best to facilitate the individual's transition.

Postproject Checkup and Evaluation

Evaluations of projects that are planned to produce substantive outcomes after the project is closed are usually accomplished at three- to six-month intervals, for the first year or two. Examples of such project outcomes are:

- Projected increase in market share

- Improved customer retention

- Waste reduction initiatives

- Increased sales volume from successful new product launch

Figure 7.8 is a sample postproject checkup and evaluation form.

As an occasional project manager, you probably now have all you need to effectively lead a team in completing a project on time and within budget. Chapter 8 presents examples and excerpts from a variety of projects. Observe the different uses of the tools presented and the adaptations made.

POSTPROJECT CHECKUP AND EVALUATION

Project name: _____   Project Manager: _____

Project no.: _____

Actual dates   Started: _____   Ended: _____

Final close-out: _____   Last check-up: _____

No.	Projected Project Outcomes	FA+	PA*	NA*
1				
2				
3				
4				

FA+ = Fully Achieved (attach documented evidence) PA* = Partially Achieved (explain) NA* = Not Achieved (explain)

No.	PA	NA	Explanations for not fully achieving projected outcomes	What, if any, action taken?

No.	Unplanned project outcomes achieved
1	
2	

Overall outcome evaluation–by project manager   5   4   3   2   1

by primary client/customer   5   4   3   2   1   (circle rating, 5 = highest)

Project manager: _____   Date: _____

Project manager: _____   Date: _____

(Attach any supporting documentation.)

Figure 7.8   Postproject checkup and evaluation.

Notes

1. Stage-Gate is a term coined by Robert G. Cooper in "The New Product Process: A Decision Guide for Managers," *Journal of Marketing Management* 3, 3 (1988), pp. 238–255. His book, *Winning at New Products*, 3rd ed. 2001. Cambridge, MA: Perseus Publishing, devotes a substantial portion of the text to the Stage-Gate practice.

2. Earned value analysis (EVA) is a methodology used to examine the actual costs being paid versus the actual work accomplished, or did you get what you paid for? There are three questions to be answered:
   - What is the planned value of the work to be done?
   - What is the earned value of the actual work accomplished?
   - What are the actual costs incurred in achieving the earned value?

   EVA addresses the variance between the planned value of scheduled work compared with the earned value received and, secondly, with the earned value compared to actual dollars paid for the work. For example:

   > A one-year project is budgeted for a total of $300,000. At the end of the first three months the planned value was $60,000 (20%). The earned value of the actual work done was $45,000 (15%). The money expended for the same time period was $60,000 (20%). The real cost variance was $15,000. Measured the traditional way the variance would have been $0.

   EVA is beyond the intended scope of this book. However, it is good to know that for the larger, more complex projects, a methodology exists to measure the project progress and a means for predicting the project's ultimate time to complete and cost. Several of the resources listed at the end of this book address EVA in detail.

3. D. H. Stamatis, *Failure Mode and Effect Analysis: FMEA from Theory to Execution,* 2nd ed. 2003. Milwaukee: ASQ Quality Press.

QUICK QUIZ
NUMBER 7

1. When is the most appropriate time(s) to measure a project?
2. Who should be informed on project progress?
3. Why is it important to document trade-off decisions?
4. Differentiate between a milestone and a stage gate.
5. At what point in the planning stage is it most appropriate to define the measurements that will be used?
6. Differentiate between the terms "variation" and "variance."
7. Assume your organization has not been actively engaged in using project management techniques and tools. What will typically be deficient about the existing accounting system relative to controlling project costs?
8. Whose responsibility is it to detect potential slippage in the project schedule?
9. At what time in the project's life cycle is it most effective to take corrective action if the project looks as if it may not achieve its objectives?
10. Risk assessment was identified as an element in the project planning process. What role does risk assessment play in managing the project?
11. What is the purpose of a formal project closeout?
12. When should lessons learned be captured, documented, and discussed?
13. What documents should be archived after a project is completed, and for what purpose(s)?
14. If a postproject assessment is to be conducted to determine if the planned outcomes have been achieved, who should conduct the assessment and what should be done with the assessment findings?
15. What effect(s) may the disbanding of a project team that has completed a year and a half project have on its members? How can negative effects be minimized?

PART III

Examples from Actual Projects

KEY LEARNING POINTS

Chapter 8   **Small and Medium-Size Project Examples**

a. Writing a Book
b. Replace a Laser Cutting Machine
c. Upgrade a Payroll and Personnel Record Computer-Based System
d. Merchandise Processing—User Training
e. Preparation of a New Claim Processing Process
f. Office Move (the Giant Rubik's Cube)
g. Customer Response Project
h. Implementation of an ISO 9001:1994-Certified Quality Management System
i. Implementing an ISO 9001:2000-Based Quality Management System
j. Division Performance Improvement project
k. Combining "Basics of Quality Improvement" and "Project Management" Training with a Class Improvement Project

8

Small and Medium-Size Project Examples

Small Projects

Let's look at examples of techniques and tools that can be used for the simpler projects. The samples include a Task Schedule, an Action Plan, and a Work Breakdown Structure (outline format). This section also includes an example of a combined schedule, resource requirements, and a budget.

a. Project: Writing a book

Figure 8.1 is the *Task Schedule* for writing this book. The clear statement of the project's deliverables and authorization to proceed was covered in the book proposal sent to the publisher and the resulting signed contract. The 46 steps/tasks listed the work to be done. I did the work until the first manuscript was submitted. The editing process was then split between the publisher and myself. Start and finish dates and the estimated time for each task state when the work was to be done and the estimated time allowed for each task. A column is used to record actual completion dates for each task (dates not shown).

Note: I could have set up other columns for the estimated cost of my time and expenses. For example, the value of my time not available for conducting other business, lost opportunity cost, and the allocated costs of office expenses based on the percentage of time spent on the book could have been estimated. Inasmuch as office expenses would be negligible and I was not planning to monitor the project for costs, I chose not to prepare a dollar budget.

In the book project case I needed to lay out the major tasks and time lines to be sure I allocated sufficient time in my daily work to meet the added contractual deadline and achieve the project's objectives. Assuming most readers do have a similar situation, that is, project work and daily work commitments, the Task Schedule approach may be sufficient for many straightforward, simple projects.

Keep in mind when I use the word "simple" I'm referring to the planning process, not the outputs of the project. Writing a book itself is not a simple task. Neither is completing a credible book on time while performing one's regular work in

	Book Title: Simplified Project Management for the Quality Professional						
ID	Task Name	Days	Start	Finish	Dep	Comments	Actual
1	Conduct PM research	120	14-Nov-01	20-Apr-04	*	Read, Internet search, etc.	
2	Concept and colleague review	2	9-Nov-01	14-Jan-02	*	Asked D.O. to critique idea	
3	Research competition	1	2-Jan-03	2-Jan-03	*	Amazon.com	
4	Draft table of contents	1	4-Jan-03	4-Jan-03	*		
5	Draft preface	2	3-Jan-03	6-Jan-03	4		
6	Draft chapter 2	8	5-Jan-03	12-Sep-03	5		
7	Draft chapter 3	7	1-Jan-03	15-Sep-03	6		
8	Draft author bio	1	1-Jan-03	1-Jan-03	7		
9	Draft proposal	4	1-Jan-03	17-Sep-03	8		
10	Refine proposal	2	17-Sep-03	19-Sep-03	9		
11	Submit proposal	1	22-Sep-03	22-Sep-03	10		
12	Draft chapter 1	5	24-Sep-03	1-Oct-03	11		
13	Process reviews	2	10-Nov-03	18-Nov-03	*	Publisher obtains 3 reviews	
14	Review, sign contract	1	26-Nov-03	26-Nov-03	13		
15	Rework chapter 2	1	4-Dec-03	4-Dec-03	14		
16	Rework chapter 3	1	5-Dec-03	5-Dec-03	15		
17	Draft chapter 4	6	26-Sep-03	12-Dec-03	16		
18	Draft chapter 5	8	15-Dec-03	26-Dec-03	17		
19	Draft chapter 6	10	29-Dec-03	9-Jan-04	18		
20	Draft chapter 7	8	12-Jan-04	23-Jan-04	19		
21	Draft chapter 8	10	26-Jan-04	13-Feb-04	20		
22	Draft chapter 9	12	16-Feb-04	2-Apr-04	21		
23	Draft chapter 10	6	5-Apr-04	16-Apr-04	22		
24	Draft chapter 11	6	19-Apr-04	30-Apr-04	23		
25	Add maps	2	31-May-04	4-Jun-04	24	Map of each chapter	
26	Add chapter summaries	1	7-Jun-04	7-Jun-04	24	Key points at end of chapters	
27	Draft glossary	2	30-Jan-04	8-Jun-04	24		
28	Refine graphics	1	9-Jun-04	9-Jun-04	24		
29	Add "What you will learn"	1	7-Jun-04	10-Jun-04	24	Learning points for reader	
30	Draft resources	2	18-Apr-03	11-Jun-04	24	Books, articles, Web sites, etc.	
31	Add study questions	2	11-Jun-04	14-Jun-04	26,29	? for reader's further study	
32	Refine chapters	4	16-Jun-04	19-Jun-04	31	Readability check	

Continued

Figure 8.1   Task schedule.

Continued

ID	Task Name	Days	Start	Finish	Dep	Comments	Actual
33	List Figures and Tables	1	21-Jun-04	21-Jun-04	32		
34	Draft Notes to reader	1	21-Jun-04	21-Jun-04	34	Hints for using the book	
35	Draft Acknowledgments	1	22-Jun-04	22-Jun-04	34	Recognize those who helped	
36	Proofread & spellcheck MS	2	22-Jun-04	22-Jun-04	35		
37	Compile permissions	3	2-Jan-04	24-Jun-04	*	Gather as needed	
38	Compile MS to submit	2	28-Jun-04	30-Jun-04	35,37	Special formatting	
39	Submit 1st MS	1	30-Jun-04	30-Jun-04	38	Publisher obtains critiques	
40	Process review suggestions	4	1-Sep-04	6-Sep-04	39	Make desired modifications	
41	Submit MS rev.1	1	7-Sep-04	7-Sep-04	40	Publisher edits copy	
42	Process editing chages	4	1-Oct-04	7-Oct-04	41	Make desired modifications	
43	Submit MS rev. 2	1	8-Oct-04	8-Oct-04	42	Publisher "sets type"	
44	Review galley proof	3	1-Nov-04	5-Nov-04	43	Make any final adjustments	
45	Submit changes to proof	1	5-Nov-04	5-Nov-04	44		
46	Review/modify/submit index	2	15-Nov-04	16-Nov-04	45	Publisher does indexing	
47	Await publication				46	Publisher "goes to press"	

any way simple. However, planning the steps to write the book is fairly simple, especially if you work with a helpful publisher. There has to be a careful balance between overplanning and overmanaging a project versus underplanning the project and neglecting to properly manage it.

For example, the book project could have been divided into three stages or phases:

- The proposal—selling the concept and obtaining a contract

- Drafting the book

- Preparing the book for publication

More granular planning was unnecessary, in my case. I had experience in writing other books and experience with the publisher. Between the acceptance of my proposal and contract signing and up until the manuscript-editing phase, I was the only person involved. The Task Schedule was quite adequate for my purposes. It broke the tasks down to manageable Work Packages and provided me with both a time-phased plan and a means for monitoring my progress.

b. Project: Replace a Laser Cutting Machine

A typical small project planned using the Action Plan approach might have only a dozen or fewer steps or major tasks.

> A process audit revealed several deficiencies in the material cutting operation. A preventive action was initiated. In a meeting of the Quality Council, it was decided that to improve throughput and reduce breakdowns. The existing cutting machine would be replaced with an advanced laser cutting machine. RTW, the quality engineer, was designated to head the implementation. RTW's manager needed to review the plans prior to authorizing the project and committing resources.
>
> The Action Plan tool appeared adequate for RTW's planning purposes. Figure 8.2 (front and back) shows the basic planning information for implementing the replacement project.

c. Project: Upgrade a Payroll and Personnel Record Computer-Based System

The quality and cycle time of the existing PPRS (Payroll and Personnel Record System) was deteriorating because of all the "patches" that had been made to the system over the previous four years. There has also been a computer system upgrade in recent months. The old system did not use newer installed features and capabilities. The IT Council decided it was time to upgrade the PPRS to take advantage of the advanced computer capabilities and build-in a more comprehensive personnel record database.

The PAPERS (PAyroll, PErsonnel Record System) project was approved. A project team was formed with representatives from the Payroll, Personnel, and Information Technology (IT) departments, including IT's quality assurance. The first assignment was to develop a macro-level WBS as a basis for more detailed planning and scheduling.

Figure 8.3 is the macro-level WBS created by the PAPERS project team. Note that the work to be done includes planning and managing the project itself.

ACTION PLAN

Poject Title: Replace existing laser cutting machine	Plan No: *Q-5*
	Date Needed: *091004*
Description: Determine, select, purchase and install an appropriate laser cutting machine that will meet our need through 2009	Date Initiated: 032904
	Approval by: *T.B.B.*
Linked to what (strategic objective, contract, policy, procedure, process, corrective or preventive action, customer mandate, or regulatory requirement)?:	Team Leader: *R.T.W.*
	Team Member: *T.R.E.*
	Team Member: *F.P.M.*
PAR # 04-21—Resulting from 2/24/04 process audit & Quality Council decision of 3/19/04	Team Member:
Project Objectives:	Team Member:

To replace existing cutting machine with the most cost-effective laser cutting machine that meets engineering specifications, capital equipment purchase policy, and production criteria, by August 31, 2004. Must meet SMED-type setup requirements and accommodate manufacturing cell configuration changes as needed when lean thinking is applied in the plant.

Scope (Where and for whom will the solution/implementation be applied? What limitations & constraints?):

Up to ten equipment suppliers will be contacted with our Request for Proposal
Up to five vendor proposals will be evaluated in detail. Up to three vendors' machines will be subjected to a live demonstration using our materials and specifications.
Preference will be given to U.S. suppliers, if all other factors are equal.

Deliverables (include Outputs re Content, Outputs re Project Management, and Outcomes):

Evaluation criteria
Engineering specifications
Request for Proposal
Review of project status at weekly management meeting (time and costs expended)

By what criteria/measures will completion and success of project be measured?

Equipment meeting all specifications and production requirements selected, purchased, installed, tested and turned over to Production
Purchase within capital project policy parameters

Assumptions made that might affect project (resources, circumstances outside this project):

Machine selected will not require pre-delivery design modifications.

Describe the overall approach to be taken, data needed, processes to apply:

A three-person team will be formed (leader from Quality, members from Engineering and Production). Within an extended workweek (48 hours), the team will:
• Research appropriate suppliers and their equipment
• Prepare requests for proposal from selected vendors
• Evaluate proposals and select machines to subject to demonstration testing
• Select and place purchase order for equipment
• Arrange for appropriate operator and supervisor training
• Provide necessary changes to procedures and work instructions
• Install, test, accept and turn over machine to production

When should the project be started to meet the date needed/wanted? March 29, 2004

Continued

Figure 8.2a   Action plan (front).

Continued

Estimate the resources required (time, personnel, facilities, equipment, tools, materials, money):

- Quality Engineer for 16 hours per week for 22 weeks
- Production Engineer for 16 hours per week for 10 weeks
- Production Planner for 16 hours per week for 18 weeks
- T & L expenses for trips to machine demonstrations $5,000
- T & L expenses for training first operator and supervisor $3.000
- Machine replacement (transportation, rigging, etc.) $4,000
- Machine cost $850,000
- Other expenses $2,000

Is there sufficient organizational capacity and are resources sufficient to meet the objectives? Yes

Estimate the benefits versus costs value:

Annualized decrease in setup costs = $75,000. Annualized decrease in cycle time = $200,000
Salvage value of obsolete machine = $5,000
Project costs = $14,000
Annual amortized machine cost = $170,000
Total costs = $184,000
First year payoff ($280,000 – $184,000) = $96,000
Second year payoff = $110,000.

Outline the major steps and dates on page 2.
(See Figure 8.2b.)

1

ACTION PLAN—STEPS

Outline the <u>major steps</u> *to be taken, a projected* <u>start and finish date</u> *for each step and the* <u>person to be responsible</u> *for each step. Attach any backup data.*

					Plan No: Q-5
Step No.	Activity/Event Description	Depends on Step	Start Date	Finish Date	Person Responsible
1	Form project team and launch project		032904	040104	RTW
2	Prepare machine specifications and request for proposal	1	040104	041204	TRE
3	Research suppliers	1	040104	050304	RTW
4	Select suppliers and order machine	2,3	050304	051004	TRE
5	Train initial operator	4	052404	052804	FPM
6	Install machine	4	062104	062504	FPM
7	Conduct trial runs	5,6	062804	071204	FPM
8	Revise documented procedures & operator training materials	7	072604	080204	RTW
9	Train supervisor	8	080204	083104	FPM
10	Place machine in production schedule	9	082304	083104	FPM
11	Document project and disband team	10	083104	091004	RTW

2

Figure 8.2b   Action plan (back).

Work Breakdown Structure—Payroll and Personnel Record System

1 PAPERS project
1.1 Project planning and management
1.1.1 Plan project
1.1.1.1 Layout work, timelines, interrelationships, resources required, budget
1.1.1.2 Submit for approval
1.1.2 Project management
1.1.2.1 Establish project tracking, measuring and reporting system
1.1.2.2 Establish project close-out and evaluation procedures
1.1.2.3 Manage project activities
1.1.2.4 Evaluate installed system
1.1.2.5 Evaluate project teams' effectiveness, lessons learned
1.1.2.6 Close-out project
1.1.2.7 Enter project documentation into "project archives" database
1.1.2.8 Celebrate and disband team
1.2 Systems requirements analysis
1.2.1 Form SRA team
1.2.2 Identify Requirements
1.2.3 Measure present satisfaction with requirements
1.2.4 Analyze resources
1.2.5 Prioritize list of requirements
1.3 System specifications
1.3.1 Organize systems specifications
1.3.2 Design overall system
1.3.3 Prepare equipment and facilities plan
1.3.4 Prepare computer software plan
1.3.5 Prepare staffing plan
1.3.6 Prepare project cost estimate
1.3.7 Prepare and present proposal
1.4 System design and programming
1.4.1 Establish quality and design standards
1.4.2 Form system design and programming team
1.4.2.1 Select computer operating system
1.4.2.2 Design database
1.4.2.3 Design system modules
1.5 Systems integration and implementation
1.5.1 Technical integration and evaluation
1.5.1.1 Form TIE team
1.5.1.2 Design and coordinate testing program
1.5.1.3 Design and coordinate system validation and technical evaluation
1.5.1.4 Coordinate documentation
1.5.2 Implementation
1.5.2.1 Form installation team
1.5.2.2 Design and coordinate training
1.5.2.3 Perform system acceptance tests
1.6 Full system rollout
1.6.1 Customer acceptance

Figure 8.3 Work breakdown structure.

d. Project: Merchandise Processing—User Training

A consumer-goods retail chain needed to implement user training to support a major process change. Of the four subprojects identified, one was chosen to be the first phase of the user training that ultimately would include users at all 39 stores throughout the Southwest. To obtain initial approval to staff up to produce the detailed plans, representatives of the dock receiving department, an in-house instructional designer, a quality professional, and an external consultant met to create a tentative WBS.

Figure 8.4 is the preliminary WBS resulting from the initial meeting. While it does attempt to take the tasks down to the fifth level of detail, another level will probably be necessary because of mixed skills required and longer durations than are feasible for control purposes.

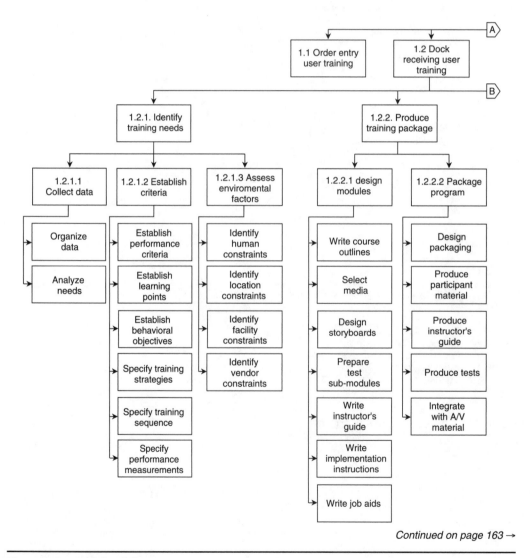

Continued on page 163 →

Figure 8.4   Work breakdown structure.

Usually this level of detail would not be required as part of the documentation to obtain initial funding authorization. However, early on the quasi-team wanted to get a better handle on what would be involved before moving further into requesting approval to launch the full-scale planning effort.

This organization had experience with this type of project. Because of that and their overall size and because the subprojects were to be done sequentially, the organization considered this a small project.

The WBS extends down to five levels. Note that the identifying numbers (for tracking time and costs) do not extend to the task level, although they may do so should that degree of control be desired. Also note that "Project Management" is included in the WBS. That probably makes sense for this phase-by-phase approach.

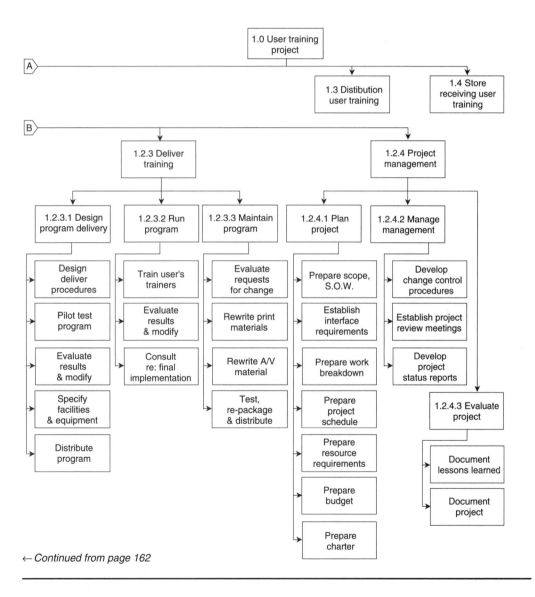

← Continued from page 162

e. Project: Preparation of a New Claim Processing Process

In the quest to keep it simple, Figure 8.5 shows a technique combining a schedule, resource requirements, and the budget on a single page using a similar matrix format. This combined form was used as part of the documentation presented to obtain

Preparation of New Claim Processing Process

Schedule (Gantt chart)

Task	Days	Week 1	Week 2	Week 3	Week 4
Determine scope deliverables and output design	3	▬			
Hire consultant	2	▬			
Purchase software	1	▬			
Order materials	1		▬		
Software training	6			▬	
Modify software and test process	4				▬
Publish and distribute process documentation	3				▬
Final evaluation and sign-off	1				▬

Resource Requirements

Resource	Week 1	Week 2	Week 3	Week 4
Manager	8 hrs.	4 hrs.		2 hrs.
Consultant	2 hrs.	6 hrs.	40 hrs.	32 hrs.
Programmer				24 hrs.

Cash Flow Schedule (Budget)

Resource	Week 1	Week 2	Week 3	Week 4
Manager	$4,000	$2,000		$1,000
Consultant	$300	$900	$6,000	$4,800
Programmer				$2,400
Claim regulations			$500	$3,000
Software	$3,000		$12,000	
Training			$2,000	
Printing & distribution				$3,000
Totals	$7,300	$2,900	$20,500	$14,200

Figure 8.5 Combined schedule, resource requirements, and cash flow/budget.

authorization to proceed with more detailed planning and implementation. Being a project of short duration and low cost, the documentation was kept simple.

f. Project: Office Move (the Giant Rubik's Cube)

This is one of those projects that may come up once in your lifetime. It's both frustrating and fun, and very satisfying when everything works out as planned.

Your objective, should you choose to accept this assignment, is to plan for and execute an office move of 150 people on the same floor of a building and within the same space presently occupied. In advance you will assess the condition of existing furniture and recommend replacement where needed, allowing sufficient time for the replacements to be purchased and to arrive.

The move will occur between 8 A.M. and 5 P.M. on a Saturday (when the office is normally closed). The rearranged office is to be fully functional Monday at 8 A.M. With the exception of the telephone provider's technicians, you will use the services of the company's maintenance people and as many of your department's people as is feasible. You may use the hallways, the building's receiving space, and elevators as staging areas for new and replaced furniture. Displaced furniture is to be loaded (by dealer personnel) into the used-furniture dealer's trucks by 5 P.M. Saturday. Safety and efficiency are your primary operational concerns.

You begin to plan using a simple Tree Diagram for a macro-level map. See Figure 8.6.

Medium-Size Projects

How an organization categorizes its project—small, medium, or large—mostly depends upon the size of the organization, the scope of the project (especially duration and cost), and the resources needed. In the section on small-size projects, the "User Training" project, while considered small by the initiating organization, would be huge to a really small company. Placing the project within a specific size category is not the essential point. Wisely choosing the techniques and tools to use for the project is the primary focus.

The examples in this section begin with a project that some smaller organizations would call large. However, we can look upon it as a borderline medium-size project encompassing less than two years and really only one process in one department.

g. Project: Customer Response Project

There is an unprecedented increase in the volume of customer complaints (2000 per month from being handled ineffectively by direct-contact customer representatives). These complaints have gone through four organizational levels to land ultimately at the CEO's office. This intolerable situation prompted the CEO to authorize a project to find the cause(s), stop the escalation and, ultimately, eliminate

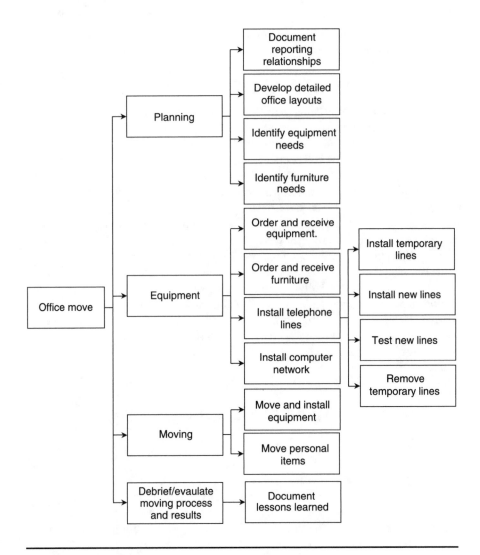

Figure 8.6 Tree diagram.

the need for customers to feel they have to appeal to the CEO for a solution to their problem.

This project used the following documents in the planning stage (the figure numbers are shown):

- 8.7.1 Authorization to Commence Planning—the CEO's authorization

- 8.7.2 Statement of Work (SOW)—detailed project scope

- 8.7.3 Stakeholder requirements—overview of requirements
- 8.7.4 Project outputs—deliverables and outcomes
- 8.7.5 Work breakdown structure—hierarchy of tasks (outline format)
- 8.7.6 Schedule —Gantt chart of primary timelines
- 8.7.7 Personnel resource requirements—matrix of personnel required
- 8.7.8 Project budget
- 8.7.9 Analysis of potential for improved process—benefits to cost analysis
- 8.7.10 Request for project plan approval—authorization to execute project plan

Note that in following this company's practices, Figure 8.7.10 is not called a charter, but serves the intent of a charter.

CUSTOMER RESPONSE PROJECT

AUTHORIZATION TO COMMENCE PLANNING

The MANAGER OF CUSTOMER SERVICE QUALITY is authorized to plan a project the outcome of which is to be the elimination of all customer complaints escalating to the CEO's office. Preliminary project plans, including team formation, task assignments, project schedule, and project budget are to be submitted for approval on or before two weeks from today. Following approval of the project plans, the project should be launched within two weeks and achieve its purpose within eight months from the start date.

June 2, 2004

Roy Dollar
Chief Executive Officer

CRP Doc 1

Figure 8.7.1 Authorization to commence planning.

CUSTOMER RESPONSE PROJECT—STATEMENT OF WORK

June 5, 2004

Purpose: The purpose of this project is to analyze the types of complaints that reach the CEO's office and identify the patterns to determine why the escalation occurs. From the analysis and a review of alternative solutions an approach will be recommended. The data to be analyzed will include all documented complaints for the 12 months prior to this date.

Scope: By the end of second year following implementation, the approved approach is to produce a return-on-project-investment ratio of at least 3:1 and the elimination of complaints escalating to the CEO level.

Responsibilities: The project responsibilities include:
• Initiating plans that incorporate, at a minimum:
  –Identifying the stakeholders and specifying the ultimate organizational outcomes to be achieved.
  –Identifying project outputs.
  –Identifying project resource requirements.
  –Identifying and evaluating risks.
  –Forming a team of qualified personnel to plan and implement an improved approach to handling customer complaints, including external consulting services as needed.
  –Identifying and assigning appropriate tasks to team members.
  –Setting a project schedule.
  –Establishing a project budget.
  –Seeking cost-effective solution alternatives and recommending one approach for approval.
  –Selecting appropriate measures for evaluating project performance and the ultimate outcomes.
  –Establishing phased implementation plans and internal communication plans.
• Establishing new or changed procedures for the approved approach (with care taken that no customer complaint directed to the CEO is arbitrarily excluded).
• Developing and delivering all training needed to implement the approved approach.
• Completing project documentation
• Conducting postimplementation evaluation

This project is not responsible for:
• Initiating any changes in organizational structure.
• Making any direct contact with customers.
• Initiating any changes to any employee's job description, position, position level, compensation, or any initiative affecting employee retention, termination, transfer, or promotion.

At a minimum, this project will deliver:
• Recommended project plans for approval.
• Once the project is approved, a recommended approach to achieve the project's purpose.
• Fully developed procedures for implementation of the approved approach.
• Targeted training for operatives affected by the new procedures.
• Two major outcomes: zero customer complaints escalated to the CEO's office achieved with an approach that reflects a ROI ratio of at least 3:1.
• Fully documented project to use for future training purposes.

Reporting relationships: The manager of customer service quality will serve as project manager, reporting directly to the vice president (serving as project sponsor). During their time assigned as project-team members, persons from other functional areas will report to the project manager, and will be relieved of their normally assigned duties and responsibilities.

CRP Doc 2

Figure 8.7.2   Statement of work.

CUSTOMER RESPONSE PROJECT—STAKEHOLDER REQUIREMENTS

Stakeholder	Requirements	Medium	Impacts
Customer	• Timely initial response • Courteous response • Timely call-back response, if needed • Satisfaction with action taken or reasonable explanation as to why no action will be taken	• Phone • Correspondence • Face-to-face	Satisfaction with complaint response & resolution process.

Customer Service Rep (CSR)	• Effective procedures, tools, and techniques for handling customer complaints.
	• Positive reinforcement for work done well.
	• Organizational objective to achieve a balance between serving volumes of customers quickly and serving customers satisfactorily.
	• Well-trained and available support/supervision.
		• CSR training:
		  −Customers' needs
		  −Complaint handling
		  −Tact
		• Responsive systems (phone & computer)
			Productivity loss due to overload of inadequately handled customer complaints.
			
			Customers' mood and satisfaction with responses.
			
			CSRs' demeanor and satisfaction in serving customers.
			
			CSRs' morale and motivation.

Complaint investigators (experienced CSRs removed from customer contact duties)	• Reduction in number of complaints to investigate. • Reassignment of CSRs to customer contact duties.	• Tracing activities involving manual and computer data analysis to resolve complaints	Elimination of complaints escalated to CEO's office. (Average = 2,000/month with investigation cost of 20 CSRs/month)
Customer Service Management	• Senior management commitment to customer satisfaction as top priority. • Revised measurements that reflect more appropriate balance between achieving customer satisfaction and productivity.	• Organization's mission, strategic objectives and plans. • Balanced scorecard.	More satisfied customers. Lower operating costs. Less employee turnover, fewer grievances and disciplinary actions. Time better spent on preventive actions.
CEO	• No poorly handled customer complaints to deal with.		Time better spent on future planning, attracting and retaining investors.

CRP Doc 3

Figure 8.7.3 Stakeholder requirements.

CUSTOMER RESPONSE PROJECT—PROJECT OUTPUTS			
Output	**Format**	**Recipients**	**Frequency**
Project plans	• Statement of work • Stakeholder list • Output list • Work breakdown Structure • Gantt/milestone chart • Resource requirements matrix • Budget	Project members Project sponsor President	As many iterations as it takes to obtain approval
Project status	• Updated milestone chart • Expenditure report (time, resources, cost vs. budget) • Summary of positive and negative highlights	Project members Project sponsor	Fridays every second week during project
Project implementation plans	• Gantt/milestone chart for phased implementation • Implementation Resource requirements matrix	Project members Project sponsor Affected unit management	Three weeks before scheduled implementation for unit
Implementation status	• Updated milestone chart • Expenditure report (time, resources, cost vs. budget) • Summary of positive and negative highlights	Unit management Project sponsor	Every Friday during implementation period
Project completion & evaluation	• Executive summary • Final milestone chart • Budget variance & ROI report • Project management evaluation, lessons learned	Project members Project sponsor Unit management President	One week after implementation completed
Project documentation	• All plans, status reports, evaluations, lessons learned	Project archives	Within three weeks after implementation
Project follow-up	• Outcomes achieved	Project members Project sponsor President Project archives	Three month and six month point following project completion

CRP Doc 4

Figure 8.7.4   Project outputs.

CUSTOMER RESPONSE PROJECT—WORK BREAKDOWN STRUCTURE

1.0 Project Plans
   1.1 Statement of Work
   1.2 Stakeholder List
   1.3 Output List
   1.4 Tasks
      1.4.1 WBS
   1.5 Schedule
      1.5.1 Gantt/Milestone Chart
   1.6 Resource Requirements
      1.6.1 Personnel Matrix
   1.7 Budget
      1.7.1 Project Development
      1.7.2 Project Implementation
      1.7.3 ROI Projections
   1.8 Approval Request
2.0 Project Team
   2.1 Selection
      2.1.1 Criteria
      2.1.2 Authorization
   2.2 Structure
      2.2.1 In-house personnel
      2.2.2 External consultants
      2.2.3 Reporting relationships
   2.3 Training
      2.3.1 Team Building
      2.3.2 Project Tools
3.0 Data Processing
   3.1 Complaints to CEO-past year
      3.1.1 Data retrieval
         3.1.1.1 Categorization
         3.1.1.2 Tabulation
      3.1.2 Analyses
         3.1.2.1 Types of complaints
         3.1.2.2 Reasons for escalation
         3.1.2.3 Customer impact
         3.1.2.4 Resolution costs
4.0 Solution targeting
   4.1 Identifying potential solutions
   4.2 Grouping potential solutions
   4.3 Prioritizing potential solutions
   4.4 Selecting solution alternative

5.0 Assessing feasibility of alternatives
   5.1 Form, fit and function analyses
   5.2 Benefits-to-cost analyses
   5.3 Risk analyses
   5.4 Outcomes analyses
   5.5 Recommend solution
      5.5.1 Resources required
      5.5.2 Projected outcomes
6.0 Design solution
   6.1 Prepare interim procedures
   6.2 Establish measurements
   6.3 Establish communications protocols
7.0 Test solution (one unit)
   7.1 Select test unit
   7.2 Deliver interim training for unit
   7.3 Conduct test
   7.4 Evaluate test results
      7.4.1 (No-go) Close project
      7.4.2 (Go) Make any needed changes
           to solution
8.0 Prepare phased rollout schedule
9.0 Publish procedures
10.0 Rollout solution to all units
   10.1 Deliver training just-in-time
   10.2 Monitor implementation
11.0 Close project
   11.1 Evaluate solution implementation
   11.2 Evaluate project management
   11.3 Document project
      11.3.1 All plans
      11.3.2 All key decisions
      11.3.3 Lessons learned
   11.4 Recognize success
      11.4.1 Team recognition
      11.4.2 Celebration
12.0 Postimplementation follow-up (3 months, 9 months)
   12.1 Assess outcomes achieved

CRP Doc 5

Figure 8.7.5 Work breakdown structure (outline).

Task No.	Task	Start	Finish	June	July	August	September	October	November	December	January
1.0	Project plans	Jun 3	Jun 16	▮							
2.0	Project team	Jun 6	Jun 30	▮							
3.0	Data processing	Jul 1	Aug 16		▮						
4.0	Solution seeking	Aug 2	Aug 31			▮					
5.0	Feasibility	Aug 23	Sep 6				▮				
6.0	Design solution	Sep 1	Sep 16				▮				
7.0	Test solution	Sep 17	Sep 30					▮			
8.0	Prepare rollout	Oct 1	Oct 11					▮			
9.0	Issue procedures	Oct 1	Nov 1					▮			
10.0	Phased rollout	Oct 25	Dec 16						▮		
11.0	Close project	Dec 16	Jan 4							▮	
12.0	Follow up	T/b/d	T/b/d								

CRP Doc 6

Note: Only major tasks are depicted. A more comprehensive schedule would include most, if not all, of the tasks shown on the WBS with the person responsible.

Figure 8.7.6 Schedule (Gantt chart).

CUSTOMER RESPONSE PROJECT

Personnel Resource Requirements

(Estimates shown in days.)

Tasks	Project Manager	Customer Service Rep.	Data Analyst	Systems Analyst	Computer Programmer	Consultant	Totals
Project plans	23.0	46.0	0	15.0	0	8.0	92
Project team	12.0	20.0	5.0	5.0	0	10.0	52
Data processing	32.0	20.0	30.0	16.0	0	0	98
Solution targeting	23.0	20.0	0	23.0	0	12.0	78
Feasibility assessment	15.0	30.0	0	15.0	0	5.0	65
Solution design	22.0	44.0	0	22.0	10.0	10.0	108
Test solution	28.0	56.0	8.0	28.0	5.0	2.0	127
Rollout schedule	1.0	1.0	0	0	0	0	2
Publish procedures	15.0	30.0	0	15.0	0	0	60
Phased rollout	50.0	50.0	0	0	0	25.0	125
Close project	18.0	36.0	2.0	2.0	.5	2.0	60.5
							867.5
Totals	239	353	45	141	15.5	74	867.5

Note 1: A more comprehensive resource requirements matrix would show estimates for each subtask.
Note 2: Project manager also works on some tasks.
Note 3: Consultant delivers the training.

CRP Doc 7

Figure 8.7.7 Resource requirements matrix.

CUSTOMER RESPONSE PROJECT			
BUDGET			
Category	**Quantity**	**Rate**	**Total**
Personnel (days):			
• Project Manager	239	$312	$74,568
• Customer Service Reps.	353	$130	$45,890
• Data analyst	45	$109	$4,905
• Systems analyst	141	$234	$32,994
• Computer programmer	15.5	$182	$2,821
• Consultant	74	$800	$59,200
Computer time (hours)	16	$25	$400
Telephone (hours)	50	$15	$750
Internet/e-mail (month)	8	$20	$160
Copying/printing (document)	3500	$.05	$175
Equipment rental (month)	1	$750	$6,000
Miscellaneous supplies			$200
Total			$228,063

Note: For projects extending over six months the budget is often broken down by month.

CRP Doc 8

Figure 8.7.8 Budget.

Project name:

Reference No:
Project No:

A	Target outcome	1. [ ] increase 2. [√] decrease	What? Number of customer complaints reaching CEO's office.
B	Target population	[ ] individual [√] group size(4)	Who? Four customer service locations
C	Desired process performance level	Standard/Goal/Expectation? Percent of ( )? By when (January 4, 2005)?	Quantity or Percent? Reduce to zero complaints at zero cost.
D	Basic for measurement (choose one best way to measure)	[ ] Rate (qty/time) [ ] Accuracy (#per) [ ] Quality [ ] Completeness [ ] Timeliness/speed [√] Cost	Formula? Average cost to investigate and resolve one CEO-level complaint is $260. (2 days @ $130/day)
E	Baseline (present process performance level, expressed in terms comparable to C above)	Data derived from: [√] available records [ ] observation/interviews [ ] estimated from external source	Quantity or Percent? An average of 2,000 CEO-level complaints are received each month. 2,000 x $260 = $520,000 (annualized)
F	Potential for improvement process performance	A1√, then C – E=F A2√, then E – C=F	$520,000
G	Annual gross value of PIP (F) Show details of each computation, state assumptions, unit rates used. Use back of form or attachments, as needed. More detail is better than less.	When CEO-level complaints are reduced to zero, no investigation costs will be incurred. Full $520,000 in gross value. $520,000/yr.	
H	Budgeted project costs		$228,063/yr.
I	Potential Net Payoff for first year (G – H = I)		$291,937

Potential Net Payoff for first two years ($1,040,000 – $228,063 = $811,937 = 3.6:1 ROI)
Is the project worthy of consideration?   [√] YES [ ] NO

Prepared by: Able Bodi	Title: Project Manager	Date: June 9, 2004

CRP Doc 9

Figure 8.7.9 Analysis of potential for improved process (APIP).

To: Roy Dollar
       Division Vice President

From: Able Bodi
          Customer Response Project Manager

Date: June 16, 2004

Subject: Elimination of CEO-level Customer Complaints

Attached are the following documents supporting a request for project plan approval:

Document title

1 Project charter
2 Statement of work
3 Stakeholders
4 Project outputs
5 Work breakdown structure
6 Project schedule
7 Personnel resource requirements
8 Budget
9 Payoff/ROI rrojection

Please note that with improved training and procedures implemented customer complaints be handled more effectively at the customer service level. Customers will no longer feel a need to write directly to the CEO expressing dissatisfaction.

The measurement of the potential improvement is based on the tangible cost to investigate a CEO-level complaint ($260) rather than the real but intangible measure of improved satisfaction. The estimated payoff ratio is 3.6:1, that is, $3.60 return for every dollar expended.

Commencement of the project is targeted for June 17, 2004, with the project completed by January 4, 2005, assuming you approve the plans as submitted.

I look forward to the opportunity to lead this very worthwhile project and await your approval.

Able Bodi

CRP Doc 10

Figure 8.7.10   Request for project plan approval.

h. Project: Implementation of an ISO 9001:1994-Certified Quality Management System

This project took place in a 50-person sheet metal fabrication plant. In this case the project team consisted of representatives of each major function (except Finance) and was led by a vice president, also serving as the ISO 9001 management representative. An external consultant coached the team throughout the project. There were four reasons for the project length: (1) project work had to be fit around the daily production schedule, (2) no prior procedural documentation existed, (3) training of process owners, internal auditors, and workers had to be squeezed into the time allowed, without overtime, and (4) there was a cash-flow constraint.

Three documents, selected from the project files, are:

- Figure 8.8   Overall schedule (Gantt chart)

- Figure 8.9.1   Network data table—data for constructing the network

- Figure 8.9.2   Network chart—activity-on-node chart, single time estimates

This project could also be categorized as a small project inasmuch as it involved simple project planning and low overall costs. The reason it appears in this section is that the project involved almost all of top management, it was to be done on a part-time basis, it had to be executed over a long time period, and it represented a substantial effort for the company.

78-Week ISO 9001 Quality Management System Implementation Project

#	Task	Weeks 1–13	Weeks 14–26	Weeks 27–39	Weeks 40–52	Weeks 53–65	Weeks 66–78
1	Select consultant	▽					
2	Conduct ISO 9000 briefing	▽					
3	Conduct gap analysis	▽					
4	Form steering committee	▽					
5	Prep. Q. sys procedures	████	████	████	███		
6	Prep. Q. policy, objectives	▽					
7	Prep. work instructions		███	████	███		
8	Employee kickoff meeting		▽				
9	Evaluate registrars			▽			
10	Train internal auditors			▽		▽	
11	Implement QSPs			███	████	███	
12	Select, schedule registrar			▽			
13	Conduct internal audits				████	███	
14	Pre. Q. system manual				███		
15	Conduct audit behav. mtg					▽	
16	Conduct pre-assessment					▽	
17	Take corr./prevent. action					███	██
18	Conduct final assessment						▽
19	Registration—celebrate						▽

Figure 8.8   Gantt chart.

	TASKS	START IN	AFTER TASK #	BEFORE TASK #	WEEKS TO COMPLETE
	ISO 9001 QUALITY MANAGEMENT SYSTEM PROJECT				
1	Select consultant	Wk 01		2	3
2	Conduct ISO 9000 briefing	Wk 04	1	3	1
3	Conduct gap analysis	Wk 05	3	4	1
4	Form steering committee	Wk 06	3	5	1
5	Prepare QSPs	Wk 07	4	16	57
6	Prepare Q. policy & objectives	Wk 09	4	8	1
7	Prepare work instructions	Wk 14	4	16	39
8	Employee kickoff meeting	Wk 15	6	11	1
9	Evaluate registrars	Wk 26	4	12	1
10	Train internal auditors	Wk 26	6	13	2
11	Implement QSPs	Wk 29	5	16	35
12	Select & schedule registrar	Wk 33	9	16	1
13	Conduct internal audits	Wk 39	10	18	37
14	Prepare quality system manual	Wk 42	6	16	13
15	Conduct audit behavior meeting	Wk 64	11	16	1
16	Conduct pre-assessment	Wk 65	15	17	1
17	Take corrective/preventive action	Wk 66	16	18	12
18	Conduct final assessment	Wk 76	17	19	1
19	Registration notice—celebrate	Wk 78	18		2

Figure 8.9.1   Network data table.

78-WEEK QUALITY MANAGEMENT SYSTEM PROJECT

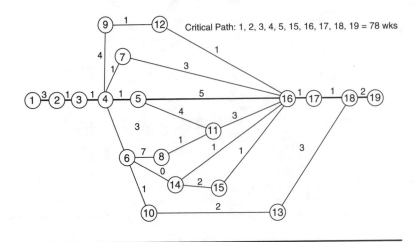

Critical Path: 1, 2, 3, 4, 5, 15, 16, 17, 18, 19 = 78 wks

Figure 8.9.2   Network chart.

In spite of starting with nothing, experiencing horrendous time conflicts, and the loss of two key people, the project was completed on time and within budget. The outcome, obtaining ISO 9001 certification of the system, was achieved on the first pass.

i. Project: Implementing an ISO 9001:2000–Based Quality Management System

Under the guidance of an external consultant, an ISO 9001 QMS Project team sketched a preliminary Work Breakdown Structure as a basis for developing estimates of the time and money the project would take. This WBS is shown in Figure 8.10. It is an example of how a project can be decomposed into logical units of work (further analysis will be necessary to bring the WBS to a Work Package level to allow for meaningful assignments and estimates).

j. Project: Division Performance Improvement

This project is an example of a medium-size project that eventually grew to become a very large project. Initially identified as a project aimed at improving the organization's performance (effectiveness and efficiency), the project contained a hidden agenda—to transform the culture of a 2000-person division of a major corporation.

The setting was in a rapidly worsening work environment where the external customers were universally dissatisfied with the service they were receiving and fighting mad about the huge jump in rates they had to pay. (This was a large urban electric utility company.) Employees, mostly long-service people with vested retirement funds, were frustrated and depressed and felt management didn't care about them. A moderately militant union represented the hourly workers. The company's reputation was spiraling downward, morale was at an all-time low, mistakes were commonplace, maintenance was neglected because of financial difficulties, and local political entities were making noises about a hostile takeover of the division. Many employees dreaded going to work each day—customers literally threw garbage at crews and managers heaped punishments on employees for real as well as unsubstantiated error incidents. Internal "spy networks" developed. Supervisors were drafted into "rat patrols" to roam the streets looking for poor-performing employees. Suffice it to say, something had to be done.

The director of Human Resources prepared and presented a plan to the division vice president. The plan was simple in concept. As an experiment, the director would choose 12 supervisors (from field operations and back office operations). He would provide the 12 with training in Applied Behavior Management and project planning for four hours every week for eight weeks. Each participant would assess the performance of his (they were all men) work unit and select a process where performance could be improved. With their manager's approval, this process became the participant's project.

The training would provide each participant with techniques and tools to select from and apply to their projects. The director, as trainer, would meet with participants to assist them in applying the lessons learned. These meetings would be once a week during each of the seven intervening weeks in the training period. The director-trainer would take as his special project the training and transforma-

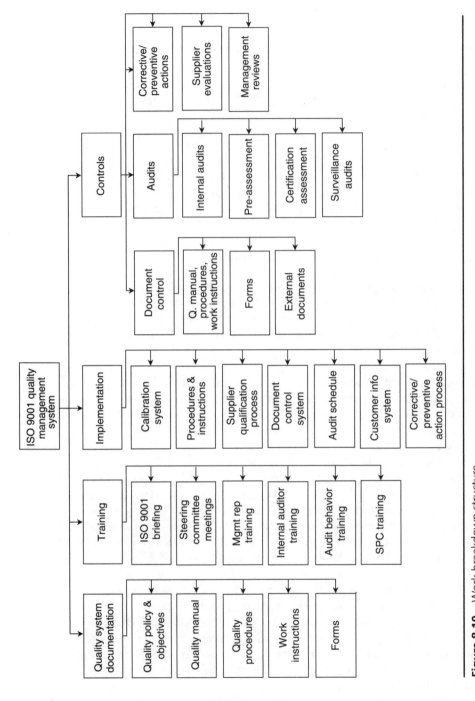

Figure 8.10 Work breakdown structure.

tion of the division's top management from a punishment-oriented managing style to a positive-reinforcing style.

The director "sold" the experiment on the following premises:

1. The director would get to choose the participants, who could accept or reject the offer (none did).

2. The vice president would approve the cost of training materials ($8500).

3. The director-trainer would guarantee a return on investment of a minimum total $20,000 net payoff from the 12 projects combined.

4. The director would be relieved of his day-to-day responsibilities.

5. The vice president could fire the director if he failed.

The vice president approved the plan, except for item 4. The director could not be freed from his Human Resources director responsibilities. The vice president "accepted" item 5 with enthusiasm.

The experiment succeeded so well the vice president approved the program for the entire division. The experimental group launched 12 improvement projects and aggregated $72,000 in first-year net payoffs (1976 money). The director, now Project Office overseer, was successful in modifying the behavior of top management (and eventually revealed the hidden agenda—the culture change—after the first year of successes).

Over the three-year duration of the project, all 200 management personnel participated in the training. All 2000 division personnel were involved in the program. One hundred seventy-three individual projects were completed. The project outcomes were achieved:

- Reduced customer complaints to nearly zero.

- Moved division from last to first place on all indicators by which divisions were measured.

- Changed the organization culture:

  –Reoriented management to looking for employees doing something right.
  –Vastly improved employee morale and self-esteem.
  –Created a collaborative relationship with union.
  –Provided a motivational environment in which employees embraced process improvement and error-free performance.
- Documented $1,078,000 total payoff, less $216,000 in project costs, a 5:1 benefits-to-cost ratio, and a net payoff of $862,000 (1979 money).

Due to the time elapsed and several organizational realignments, the project documentation is no longer available. However, here are excerpts from published material, recollections, and saved summary notes:

- For the first experimental group of 12, what is now called a Task Schedule and an early version of the Analysis of Potential for Improved

Performance were used by both the director/trainer and by each of the 12 participants for their individual work unit projects.

- As the program was gradually deployed throughout the division, a master schedule (Gantt chart) was maintained by the director/trainer.

- With the number of individual projects rapidly expanding, each at different stages of planning and execution, the role of the director/trainer changed to what is today referred to as a Project Office. All training was done by the Project Office, as was the tracking and reporting of the aggregated progress of the projects (status and costs). (Note: Every project had to demonstrate *real* return on investment.) The Project Office periodically audited the ongoing projects and postproject evaluations.

- Monitoring and support of individual participants' projects was turned over to the individuals' supervisors once the training was completed. The Project Office maintained continual oversight of all projects until implementation and evaluation was complete.

Table 8.1 lists examples of the types of projects undertaken by the participants. Extracts of this project have been published in several books and articles.[1]

k. Project: Combining "Basics of Quality Improvement" and "Project Management" Training with a Class Improvement Project

As part of its efforts to improve the quality of its operations and patron satisfaction, Yale University Library[2] (YUL) designated a cross-functional project team to receive education in the Basics of Quality Improvement[3] and Basic Project Management.[4] The team was assigned to plan and manage a project to improve internal book delivery cycle time and optimize delivery schedules.

The situation, as the project was launched, was this: patrons of the libraries (students, researchers, and faculty) as well as library staff were expressing dissatisfaction with the delivery schedules during peak periods of withdrawals and returns. The library needed to seek approval for purchase of an additional delivery van. The university was in a budget crunch and curtailments in expenditures were in place.

The activities began with a three-hour alignment meeting facilitated by the external project advisor and coach. In this meeting, participants identified YUL's organization structure, the varying procedures for handling patrons' requests, and the key issues indicating a need for improvement. The significant outputs of this exploratory analysis consisted of:

- An organization chart showing the key reporting relationships

- A process map depicting the flow of library materials from and to the individual libraries holding the collections

- An affinity diagram showing the issues and types of problems needing to be addressed

Following the alignment meeting, 10 combination training and project team sessions were scheduled for the eight-person team, spanning eight months (interrupted by

Table 8.1   Examples of types of projects implemented.

Project Category	Project Goal
Cost savings	Reduce tool and supplies expenses Increase reuse of material formerly scrapped Reduce auto mileage expenses Increase timely collection of accounts receivable
Cost avoidance	Restock service trucks at end of each day to reduce time lost in the field when parts not on the truck Decrease visits to medical department
Productivity	Increase number of consumer contacts Increase contacts with commercial accounts Improve productivity of maintenance crews
Service quality	Increase accuracy of meter reading Decrease number and severity of customer complaints Increase availability of vehicles with more reliable repair and maintenance practices Improve response time for customer complaints Improve new-customer follow-up to ensure customer satisfaction Increase timely response to new service requests

a strike). The cross-functional team[5] consisted of long-service librarians from the larger libraries, the facility manager, and one of his direct reports, a delivery van driver.

During the early sessions, the project team was exposed to a "toolbox" of proven quality improvement techniques and tools as well as basic tools for planning and managing a project. The team showed great potential for achieving its objective as exhibited by cooperation, collaboration, and willingness to contribute personal time to the tasks. (Each team member held full-time duties within the library system.) However, the team's focus was frequently distracted by two common conditions: (1) frequent interruptions to introduce "quick solutions" to problems that had been tabled earlier or were outside the scope mutually agreed to, and (2) confusing the planning and managing of the project itself with the execution activities called for in the project plans. Considerable time was spent in the first couple of meetings in pinpointing the specific scope of the work the team was to accomplish.

"Low-hanging fruit" was identified and corrective action was immediately initiated. Another unforeseen advantage arose when the university was involved in a strike. Certain team members were able to experiment with schedule and delivery route changes by actually driving the delivery van. (The university is spread throughout downtown New Haven, CT. The streets are narrow and continually congested, and many are one-way streets. It is a maze.) These experiments resulted in improved schedules and routes.

Information Technology, while not represented on the project team, was brought into the team process when communication with the patrons was being examined. IT's involvement and cooperation resulted in changing to a more patron-oriented book availability notification schedule and improved process cycle time.

Team members, many whom were not used to a structured way of documenting plans, had some initial difficulty generating the planning documentation at a meaningful level for the type of project they were working on. Perhaps the first justification for their planning efforts occurred when the team found that its project plan was easily understood and readily accepted by higher management. (A similar improvement effort had been unsuccessfully tried a few years earlier.)

The final project plans as submitted for approval by the team are reproduced with the permission of Yale University Library, Eli Express Quality Improvement Team. Many other documents consisting of tables, matrices, and schedules were created and used by the team during the project. Such documents are not relevant to the purpose of this chapter. The team's plans consisted of:

- Figure 8.11.1 Charter
- Figure 8.11.2 Statement of work
- Figure 8.11.3 Stakeholders
- Figure 8.11.4 Project outputs
- Figure 8.11.5 Work breakdown structure
- Figure 8.11.6 Gantt chart
- Figure 8.11.7 Analysis of potential for improved process

Following the successful completion of the project, the project's sponsor, Danuta Nitecki, associate university librarian, had this to say:

> You should be proud to learn that the Eli Express Improvement Team was awarded one of this year's 10 Service Quality Improvement Awards! Very nice tribute to your coaching.

ELI EXPRESS QUALITY IMPROVEMENT PROJECT CHARTER

The office of the AUL for Public Services establishes a quality improvement initiative to seek ways in which Eli Express, the university's intralibrary delivery service, might be improved. The members of the team assembled for this purpose will receive instruction in quality improvement techniques, collect pertinent data about the service, and identify areas for possible enhancement. Preliminary project plans will be submitted to the sponsor no later than the conclusion of the formal training period.

Figure 8.11.1 Charter.

Reprinted with permission of Yale University Library, Eli Express Quality Improvement Team.

ELI EXPRESS QUALITY IMPROVEMENT PROJECT—STATEMENT OF WORK

July 7, 2003

Purpose: The purpose of this project is to analyze and define Eli Express, the intralibrary delivery service, and identify ways in which the efficiency and quality of the service may be improved. The project team will analyze all available data pertaining to the intralibrary paging and transport of materials. From the analysis of the service and a review of alternative recommendations for enhancement, a specific approach for improvement will be recommended.

Scope: By the end of the first year following implementation, the approved approach is to decrease turnaround time for the delivery of intralibrary materials by 30%.

Responsibilities: This project is responsible for:
- Initiating plans that incorporate, at a minimum:
  - Forming a team of qualified personnel to plan and implement the recommended improvements.
  - Identifying and assigning appropriate tasks to team members.
  - Identifying the stakeholders and specifying the ultimate organizational outcomes to be achieved.
  - Identifying project outputs.
  - Setting a project schedule.
  - Seeking cost-effective solution alternatives and recommending one approach for approval.
  - Selecting appropriate measures for evaluating project performance and the ultimate outcomes.
- Establishing phased implementation.
- Completing project documentation
- Conducting post-implementation evaluation

At a minimum, this project will deliver:
- Recommended project plans for approval.
- Once the project is approved, a recommended approach to achieve the project's purpose.
- Fully developed procedures for implementation of the approved approach.
- Fully documented project to use for future training purposes.

Reporting relationships: The Associate University Librarian will serve as project sponsor. Findings and recommendations for action will be presented to the AUL and under her auspices presented to the Library Management Council for approval.

Figure 8.11.2 Statement of work.

Reprinted with permission of Yale University Library, Eli Express Quality Improvement Team.

ELI EXPRESS QUALITY IMPROVEMENT PROJECT—STAKEHOLDERS

Stakeholder	Requirements	Medium	Impacts
Patron	• Simple procedures for requesting intralibrary delivery of material • Notification of status of request (fill/no fill) • Timely delivery of requested materials • Convenient pickup locations • Timely notification of item availability at designated pickup location	• OPAC • E-mail • Face-to-face	• Satisfaction with paging procedures and outcomes. • Decrease in customer complaints • Increase in utilization of YUL materials
Circulation staff	• Tools for analyzing patterns in paging requests • Effective schedule/procedures for paging requests • Reliable schedule for pickups/deliveries • More frequent pickups/deliveries of paged items • Timely and accurate procedures for receiving and charging paged items • Timely and accurate patron notification of item availability at pickup location	• Creation of necessary reports • Appropriate scheduling of paging routines • Staff training	• Better management of paging service • Increased productivity in paging • Timely retrieval of paged items. • Decreased turnaround time for delivery of paged material. • Decrease in customer complaints • Increased customer satisfaction.
SML shipping	• Materials prepared for pickup at designated stops in a timely manner. • Pre-sorting of materials to be delivered by designated units • Elimination of nonessential stops • Flexible Delivery to low-volume stops • Efficient routing for transport • Creation of reports to monitor/manage Service	• Formulate criteria to identify nonessential/low volume stops • Reroute truck • Formulate criteria to identify stops for pre-sorting • Identify reporting needs of stops made per day.	• Reduction in mileage driven • Reduction in driving time • Reduction in sorting time • Increase in the number of stops made per day • Reduction in Service turnaround time.
Library system office	• Create report for tracking/managing Eli Express Service	• Placement on LSO's strategic plan.	• Allow intelligent management of the Eli Express Service
ITS	• Reschedule/augment scheduling of notification batch jobs	• Adjustment of schedule for running Circjob 5 (batch for "Hold Recall Available Notices").	• Decrease the time elapsed between the delivery of an item to the requested drop-off point and patron notification of availability

Figure 8.11.3 Stakeholders.

Reprinted with permission of Yale University Library, Eli Express Quality Improvement Team.

ELI EXPRESS QUALITY IMPROVEMENT PROJECT—PROJECT OUTPUTS			
Output	**Format**	**Recipients**	**Frequency**
Project plans	• Charter • Statement of Work • Stakeholder list • Output list • Work Breakdown Structure • Gantt/Milestone Chart	Project members Project sponsor	As many iterations as it takes to obtain approval
Project status	• Updated Milestone chart • Summary of positive and negative highlights	Project members Project sponsor	Every Friday during project
Project implementation plans	• Gantt/Milestone chart for phased implementation	Project members Project sponsor Affected unit management	One month before scheduled implementation
Implementation status	• Updated Milestone Chart • Summary of positive and negative highlights	Unit management Project sponsor	Every Friday during implementation period
Project completion & evaluation	• Executive summary/ Report to LMC • Final milestone chart • ROI report • Project management evaluation, lessons learned	Project members Project sponsor Unit	One week after implementation completed
Project documentation	• All plans, status reports, evaluations, lessons learned	Project archives	Within three weeks after implementation
Project follow-up	• Outcomes achieved	Project members Project sponsor Project archives	Three month and six month point following project completion

Figure 8.11.4   Project outputs.

Reprinted with permission of Yale University Library, Eli Express Quality Improvement Team

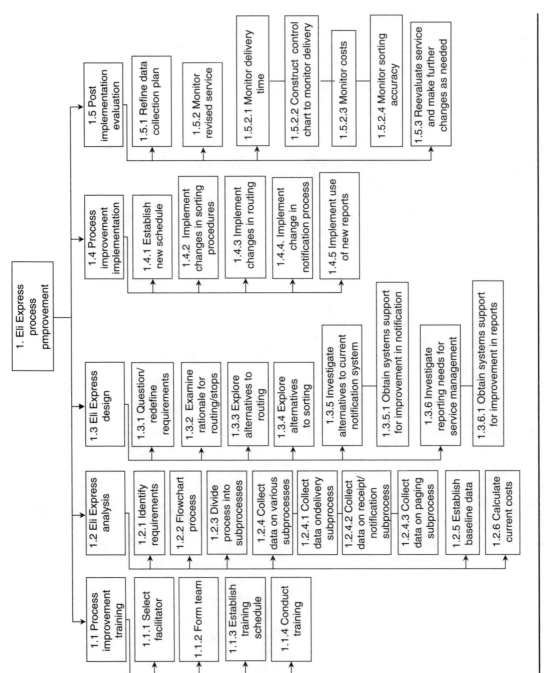

Figure 8.11.5 Work breakdown structure.

Reprinted with permission of Yale University Library, Eli Express Quality Improvement Team.

Task		Week 1-2 Apr28-May9	Week 3-4 May12-May23	Week 5-6 May26-June6	Week 7-8 June9-June20	Week 9-10 June23-July4	Week 11-12 July7-July18	Week 13-14 July21-Aug1	Week 15-16 Aug4-Aug15	Week 17-18 Aug18-Aug29	Week 19-20 Sept1-Sept12	Week 21-22 Sept15-Sept26	Week 23-24 Sept29-Oct10	Week 25-26 Oct13-Oct24	Week 26-27 Oct27-Nov10
Select facilitator	1.1.1	▶													
Form team	1.1.2	▶													
Establish training schedule	1.1.3	▶													
Conduct training	1.1.4	■													
Identify requirements	1.2.1		▶												
Flow chart process	1.2.2		▶												
Sub-divide process	1.2.3		▶												
Collect data on various taks	1.2.4					■									
Establish baseline data	1.2.5			▶											
Calculate current costs	1.2.6			▶											
Question/redefine requirements	1.3.1					■									
Examine rational for routing/stops	1.3.2					▶									
Explore alternatives to routing	1.3.3						▶								
Explore alternatives to sorting	1.3.4							▶							
Investigate alternatives to current notification system	1.3.5							■							
Obtain systems support of improvement in notification	1.3.5.1							▶							
Investigate reporting needs for service management	1.3.6							▶							
Obtain systems support for improvement in reports	1.3.6.1							▶							
Establish new schedule	1.4.1							■							
Implement changes in sorting/prep procedures	1.4.2								▶						
Implement routing changes	1.4.3								▶						
Implement changes in notification	1.4.4											▶			
Implement use of new reports	1.4.5											▶			
Refine data collection plan	1.5.1								■						
Monitor revised delivery process	1.5.2								▶						
Monitor delivery time	1.5.2.1									■					
Construct control chart to monitor delivery	1.5.2.2									▶					
Monitor costs	1.5.2.3									▶					
Monitor sorting accuracy	1.5.2.4									▶					
Reevaluate service/make further changes as needed	1.5.3														■

Figure 8.11.6 Gantt chart.

Project Name: ELI EXPRESS QUALITY   Reference No: 1
                 IMPROVEMENT PROJECT   Project No:

A	Target outcome	1. [ ] increase 2. [√] decrease	Turnaround time in the intralibrary delivery of paged materials
B	Target population	[ ] individual [√] group size(14)	14 Participating Circulation Units
C	Desired quality/ performance level	For 100% of items transported via the Eli Express service	Reduce turnaround time to 24 hrs. (M-F)
D	Basic for measurement (choose one best way to measure)	[ ] Rate (qty/time) [ ] Accuracy (#per) [ ] Quality [ ] Completeness [√] Timeliness/speed [ ] Cost	The average turnaround time for all items is 38.4 hours
E	Baseline (present process performance level, expressed in terms comparable to C above)	Data derived from: [√] available records [ ] observation/interviews [ ] estimated from external source	Approximately 10% of all items transported have a turnaround time of 72 hrs, while 40% of all items transported have a turnaround time of 48 hours.
F	Potential for improvement process performance	A1√, then C − E = F A2√, then E − C = F	Decrease turnaround time for all items by an average of 37%
G	Annual gross value of PIP (F) show details of each computation, state assumptions, unit rates used. Use back of form or attachments, as needed. More detail is better than less.	Service will improve 37% at no additional cost. If current cost to transport an item via the Eli Express Service is 0.23, suggested improvements would in effect reduce the per item cost to 0.15 per item. On a projected volume of 200K, first year savings = $18,000. $ /yr.	
H	POPS (Cost total from Sheet 2B)	$ 0.00	
I	Potential net payoff for first year (G-H=I)	$ 18,000	

Is this project worthy of consideration?   [√] YES [ ] NO

Prepared by:
Eli Express Quality Improvement Team
	Title:
	     Project Manager
		Date:
		    7/14/03

Figure 8.11.7   Analysis of potential for improved process (APIP).

Reprinted with permission of Yale University Library, Eli Express Quality Improvement Team.

Notes

1. R. T. Westcott & Associates (Russell T. Westcott) has published the following material relating to return on training investment and return on quality investment:
   - "Behavior Management Training," *Human Resources Management & Development Handbook.* 1985. New York: AMACOM.
   - "Return-On-Quality-Investment: The Overlooked Quality Tool," *The Quality Management Forum* (Quality Management Division, American Society for Quality Control). 1993, Fall. Milwaukee: ASQ.
   - "Behavior Management Training (Revised)," *Human Resources Management & Development Handbook,* 2nd ed. 1994. New York: AMACOM.
   - "Applied Behavior Management Training: Case Study: North County Electric & Gas," in *In Action: Measuring Return on Investment.* 1994. American Society for Training and Development.
   - "ROQI: Overlooked Quality Tool" *The Total Quality Review,* November–December 1994.
   - "Has Your Quality Initiative Overlooked ROQI?" (chapter), *Essence of Quality Management Anthology Series, Volume 3.* Milwaukee: American Society for Quality Control, Quality Management Division, 1999.
2. The Yale University's Library system consists of 23 individual libraries located throughout the New Haven area. Each library "specializes" in acquiring and maintaining books and other materials on specific topical areas pertinent to the school they serve. The library system employs approximately 600 people. Through its checkout process, students are able to requisition a book or document from any of the libraries at any of the libraries or even by computer from their room on campus. Returns may be made to any library, regardless of the book's shelving location. This flexibility is made possible through Yale's interlibrary delivery service called *Eli Express.*
3. A course based on *The Quality Improvement Handbook*, J. E. Bauer, G. Duffy, and R.T. Westcott, eds. 2002. Milwaukee: ASQ Quality Press.
4. A course based on a draft of this book.
5. The Eli Express Quality Improvement Project Team: Michael V. DiMassa (project team leader), Susan E. Burdick, John Gallagher, Linnard Inabinet, Carol Jones, Michelle A. Rubino, Alan Solomon, and John Vincenti.

QUICK QUIZ
NUMBER 8

1. Choose the most recent project (whether you called it a project or not) you worked on, either as a team member or team leader. Write a brief summary of the project planning, management, and results. Critique the project: what went well, what could be improved if done again, what were the key lessons learned from your experience on the project?

2. From your daily activities as a quality professional, choose a real-life process, product, or service you feel could be improved. Assume you are going to propose a project to address the deficiency and/or improvement opportunity. Lay out your plans to demonstrate feasibility and sell the project idea to management. Assume you obtain approval to head this project; lay out your plans as you would present them for approval. Self-critique what you have done. Refine your planning.

3. Give it a shot! Go for it!

PART IV

Project Management as Leverage

KEY LEARNING POINTS

CHAPTER 9 Developing Personal Competency in Project Management

■ Project management skills, knowledge, and attributes you need as a project manager

■ Pursuing a career in project management

CHAPTER 10 Promoting Project Management as an Organization's Core Competency

■ Organizational core competency in project management—a strategy

■ New product/service development and launch

9

Developing Personal Competency in Project Management

Look to the Future

Given the trend set by so many organizations—that is, they are structured and operated to manage a series of ongoing and pending projects—the paramount need of employees is to enhance their project management competency.

In days past it used to be customary for a person being groomed for a high-level management position to be rotated through three to five of the major business units of the organization. These rotational assignments, sometimes lasting a year or two, provided the incumbent with an overall working knowledge of the total business.

In present times, a substantial number of the middle management positions are no longer in existence because of:

- Technology changes

- Organizational structural changes (moving toward a more horizontal structure)

- Managing style changes (empowering employees to make a broader range of decisions)

- Outsourcing of support functions and even major line operations

Further, the speed of operations has so drastically increased that there is literally no time to "season" future executives through rotational assignments. So, you ask: Where, when, and how does one learn what one needs to know to manage a total organization? One answer is the *project management route*.

Participating first as a member of a cross-functional project team exposes you to some of the other functions in the organization. If you learn quickly and perform your assignment excellently, ask to be assigned to a larger project to build added competence. Then ask to head a small or medium-size project (or sell and initiate your own project). Continually strive for further challenging project assignments. If you're so inclined to do so, try to position yourself to be included in the organization's strategy-making process. Leverage your project management competency to becoming the resident expert—and consequently a much-sought-after person for your advice and counsel. If the presidency or CEO position looks right for you, go for it.

Project Management Skills, Knowledge, and Attributes You Need as a Project Manager

Interpersonal Skills

- Communicating (listening, speaking, writing)
- Getting work done when you're not in charge
- Providing a motivating work environment
- Managing conflict
- Negotiating
- Creativity, innovative thinking
- Team building and leadership
- Managing behavior: providing effective performance feedback and reinforcement

Project Management-Related Skills

- Planning project work
- Scheduling project work
- Expediting project work
- Tracking project work
- Measuring project work
- Reporting project work status
- Problem solving
- Decision making (under stressful conditions)
- Managing change
- Conducting effective meetings
- Administrating (handling the project paperwork)

Figure 9.1 is a Project Management Self-Assessment tool to assist you in evaluating your level of expertise in understanding and applying project management techniques and tools. The tool's focus is on identifying areas for improvement.

Name _____

Technique/Tool	(1) I do not understand the technique/ tool at all	(2) I do understand the purpose of the technique/ tool but cannot use it	(3) I believe I can use the technique/ tool to a limited degree	(4) I have some experience using the technique/ tool	(5) I have used the technique/ tool successfully many times
Selling your project to your boss					
Defining project objectives					
Identifying project constraints and risks					
Identifying contractual requirements					
Identifying project deliverables					
Defining outcomes expected from project					
Selecting & building an effective project team					
Building a Work Breakdown Structure					
Creating a Gantt chart, schedule					
Creating a Network diagram					
Preparing a resource requirements matrix					
Developing a project budget					
Tracking & measuring project progress					
Assessing ongoing risks					
Reporting project progress and results					
Documenting lessons learned					
Closing out a project and evaluating outcomes					

I need specific help in these areas:

_____

_____

Specific barriers I face in planning and managing a successful project:

_____

_____

Figure 9.1 Project management self-assessment.

Knowledge

- Working knowledge of the work to be done by the project team
- Working understanding of the organizational context in which the project work is to be done (e.g., strategic plans, other projects, financial and competitive status)
- Good grasp of the risks that could affect the fulfillment of the project's objectives
- What, why, when, where, and how to apply techniques and tools pertinent to managing the project (e.g., planning, estimating, scheduling, tracking, measuring, reporting, intrateam and interteam interfaces)
- What, why, when, where, and how techniques and tools applicable to the delivery of the project's outputs and outcomes are best used
- When and how to resolve conflicts and setbacks and make decisions affecting the project schedule, resources, and costs
- How to identify and act upon opportunities for improvement
- How to aid the development of project team members' competence
- How to build and manage supplier relations

Attributes

You are:

- Visibly and personally involved in supporting team members
- Goal oriented
- Very organized
- Open in acknowledging your own competency and capability limits
- Businesslike
- Perceived as having a sense of humor
- A follow-up and follow-through type of person
- Willing to share your experience and expertise with others
- Fair, firm, and flexible in managing others
- Open to suggestions and critique
- A wise delegator
- Honest beyond question
- One who engenders trust
- A buffer between the team and other internal and external entities
- One who creates a motivating environment for team members

- A person who strives to learn about the strengths and weaknesses of each team member
- Respected as a leader

Trends

More and more, projects are becoming cross-functional and related to improving processes. Project teams need to bring to the table a broader exposure to business functions, systems thinking, marketplace savvy, and financial exigencies. In addition, team members should be well-versed in the available and emerging practices, processes, equipment, and tools pertinent to their industry.

There is a growing expectation (not always openly expressed) that organizational members add value to their employers' products and services and increase customer satisfaction. The smart quality professional develops a portfolio of value-added achievements (including projects), preferably showing a return on investment for each achievement. Successful project management experiences add significantly to your portfolio.

Some years ago, Ferdinand Fournies wrote about the concept that organizations do not "buy" you but "rent" your behavior.[1] With the almost total disappearance of the loyalty factor, from both the employer's and the employee's perspective, Fournies's premise has become a reality. With the advent of more outsourcing, more independent contractors, constant churning through acquisitions and mergers, and layoffs it is evident that the traditional role of "employee" is tenuous. Gone are the days when your employer was the leading force in your growth and development. Today, you are the primary person in charge of your career and, if you're fortunate, your employer provides some support for your career development.

Chances are you will start your career in project management as a part-time member of a project team. You will have been selected because of your availability, because you are a respected representative of a stakeholder function to be affected by the project, because you have expertise in the work to be done, or applicable academic achievements, or some combination of these and other factors. Presuming you make a noticeable contribution to a successful project you may be assigned a larger role as a full-time project team member of a larger, longer duration project. These two assignments gave you an inside look of some of the issues, concerns, tribulations, and satisfaction that can be derived from managing a project. You decide whether the role of project manager is for you. If it is, make your aspirations known to those who make such assignments.

Either an opportunity arises for you to propose your own project or you are asked to head a full-time project to meet a strategic or mandated organizational need. You have now joined the "big leagues." You will now get to experience the more hidden aspects of project management, such as:

- Committing, or being committed by a superior, to produce outcomes from project activities that are very frequently underfunded, short of the time and other resources required, and subjected to internal and external pressures that will test your competency, patience, and perseverance to the extreme.
- Interacting with people at higher organizational levels, with suppliers and contractors, with consultants, even with external customers—interactions that will

require a variety of responses depending upon the delicate nature of the contact and the potential impact on the organization, the project, and on you.

• Taking on a responsibility whereby you will have to "bet your job" that you can pull it off.

• Needing to become immediately expert at negotiating: getting cooperation and work out of people over whom you have no direct control (project team members, their supervisors, higher management, suppliers, and subcontractors); pleading for and cajoling others for needed resources; building and sustaining alliances and partnerships; working near-miraculous trade-offs when project scope is changed.

• Managing conflicts of every kind and at every level, ranging from minor differences of opinion to major interorganizational boundary-type disputes.

• Leading a team of big egos in pursuit of a high-profile project outcome that impacts the very existence of the sponsoring organization—an awesome responsibility.

• Being subject to the same policies, procedures, practices, and rules that apply to the mainline organization when many such structures may be dysfunctional relative to the activities of the project team.

• And, often being expected to manage a mainline function while serving as a project manager.

Should You Pursue a Career in Project Management?

Wysocki and Lewis[2] explain how to use the six levels (Knowledge, Comprehension, Application, Analysis, Synthesis, and Evaluation) of Bloom's Taxonomy[3] to self-assess against 54 project management skills. Further, they identify four project types from the very simple to mission critical. They then apply the Bloom levels to the 54 skills for each of the four project types.

Wysocki and Lewis explore seven other tools for gaining insights into what you are and what you want to become, including the Myers-Briggs Personality Type Indicator (MBTI®). In exploring the use of the MBTI to understand and position oneself for the best career fit, the Tiegers[4] build on the concept of "do what you are." They assert that knowing the strengths and hidden areas of your personality type can be an advantage in advancing your career.

As to the type of organizational structure that best fits you, consider the alternatives. Working in a fully developed matrix organization means that as a project manager, you have at least two bosses: a functional manager and the head of all projects. The functional manager usually is in charge of persons possessing a common expertise or discipline and is responsible for the training, development, and deployment of those individuals to projects where their competency is needed. The project czar oversees all projects, assists project managers in obtaining resources, and is concerned with the effective performance of the project managers assigned. When an individual is assigned to work on more than one project team, that individual reports to more than one project manager, hence multiple bosses. What's exciting and challenging for one person is anathema to another person. The balancing act that is required to remain effective in multiple assignments for multiple bosses is troubling and too stressful for many people.

More frequently found is the organization where project assignments are either added to the routine management of a function or the individual is temporarily detached from routine duties to serve on or to manage a project team. In the former situation, reporting relationships remain the same as before the added project responsibility. In the latter situation, the detached person may have a new temporary boss.

The temporarily detached person, in the absence of a functional manager (as in the fully developed matrix organization), may have difficulty transitioning back into his or her former position. Some of this difficulty may have been caused by lack of time to maintain his or her skill set while on the temporary assignment. Problems could also arise due to being "forgotten" (e.g., not included in the budget) by the former boss or because an organizational change happened while on the project assignment. Compensation inequities, as well as missed promotional opportunities, can be troublesome.

Some project managers may find that they are constantly in the spotlight. They are working on a strategically critical and perhaps sensitive project subject to controversy and adverse reactions—or subject to positive publicity that overwhelms. The focus on the project manager requires time, energy, and expertise in responding to public criticism or acclaim. The added effort detracts from the project work and can cause the project manager to be less than effective. Added to that frustration is the possibility the project manager's self-esteem can be deflated by the potential negative outcomes of the project or inflated by the perceived importance of the project.

Suffice it to say, navigating the perilous waters confronting a project manager can be either the best opportunity you could wish for or the worst experience in your work life. You can learn the techniques and tools of project management, build your career from membership in a small project team to taking on larger and more critical projects as the project manager. Success is largely up to you. You decide on whether you want to pilot the boat through the rapids or seek another career.

Certification

The Project Management Institute (PMI) provides an "official" project management body of knowledge and books for sale. PMI also offers the opportunity to become certified as a project management professional (PMP). See the Resources section at the end of this book for how to contact PMI about the certification examination application and applicant eligibility requirements. Numerous independent training organizations offer courses and workshops aimed at preparing the PMP applicant.

Observations

Stewart[5] writes about organizations becoming project-oriented and project managers replacing the old middle management tier. In newer organizations the power stems from the competencies of the individuals, not their positions. Organizations are increasingly defined by their portfolio of projects and processes, not by their functional departments. Disappearing are the days when being assigned to work on a project equated with a doomed career. Today working on a project means being chosen to do important work. It's an opportunity to rise above the mundane administrivia and make a name for oneself. And, one primary advantage is if you do an exemplary job you'll usually be rewarded with a new and challenging role.

There are fewer and fewer opportunities available, due to the abolishment of middle-management roles, for the competent and ambitious person to interact with all levels within the organization and with outside stakeholders. Where else could you gain the generalized knowledge and experience in the fields of marketing, engineering, production/service, finance, and human resources—knowledge and experience needed to become an effective CEO? Where else but as a project manager?

Kerzner[6] explores the excellent project management practices used by 26 of the most successful corporations. His research recognizes six categories: training and education, behavior, process integration, culture, informal management, and management support. His observations can serve as the basis for developing your career plans.

How better to outfit yourself for the ultimate position of CEO than moving up along the project management pathway? Most organizations in the future will be heavily project-oriented. And, keep in mind that project management competency is portable!

In his frequent television ads, Lee Iacocca, former CEO of Chrysler Corporation, said: "Lead, follow, or get out of the way." Is project management for you? Could you lead a project, could you make a contribution to a project as a team member, or would you prefer to not be involved in a project? It's your choice. Take the following quiz to help you sort out your direction.

Notes

1. Fournies, Ferdinand F., *Coaching for Improved Work Performance*. 1978. New York: Van Nostrand Reinhold.
2. Wysocki, Robert K., and James P. Lewis, *The World Class Project Manager: A Professional Development Guide*. 2001. Cambridge, MA: Perseus Publishing.
3. Bloom, Benjamin S., *Taxonomy of Educational Objectives Book I: Cognitive Domain*. 1956. Longman.
4. Tieger, Paul D., and Barbara Barron-Tieger, *Do What You Are: Discover the Perfect Career for You Through the Secrets of Personality Type*. 1995. Boston: Little, Brown.
5. Stewart, Thomas A., *Intellectual Capital: The New Wealth of Organizations*. 1997. New York: Doubleday/Currency, pp. 207–209.
6. Kerzner, Harold, *In Search of Excellence in Project Management*. 1998. New York: Van Nostrand Reinhold.

QUICK QUIZ
NUMBER 9

1. In what ways does managing a project differ from managing a work unit?
2. If a project opportunity arises, what could you bring to the table?
3. What project management knowledge and skills would you be willing to learn in order to participate in a project?

10

Promoting Project Management as an Organization's Core Competency

Chapter 9 points you to a way in which you can develop and grow profession-ally, having gained competency in the field of project management. This chapter will address ways in which your organization can develop and grow competitively with successful project management as one of its core competencies.

Organizational Core Competency

An organization's core competencies consist of specific attributes that distinguish the organization, for example, exceptional workforce skills, innovative applications of state-of-the-art processes, research and development expertise, extraordinary cus-tomer service, award-winning designs, and value-creating capability. These core competencies enable the organizations possessing them to attract customers to their products and/or services, build and retain a highly satisfied customer base, and attract the most capable people as employees.

Underlying an organization's recognized successes is its competence in select-ing, planning for, launching, and managing projects that further the organization's mission and strategies. To leverage the core competencies of the organization, Pra-halad and Hamel[1] speak to two actions that are needed:

1. Identify the core competencies that provide possible access to a wide range of markets and that contribute to benefits the customers derive from the products or services, as well as the competencies that competitors would find hard to replicate.

2. Organizations must acquire competence in forming alliances and focus on their internal development.

Kerzner[2] provides two questionnaires. One is useful in identifying whether or not your organization has reached project management maturity. The other assesses the degree of excellence your organization has achieved. Peters[3] writes about core competencies that are represented by an "affinity group," a critical mass for knowledge development, including subcontractors and university affiliations.

Assume a strategic objective is to exemplify your organization's core competence in project management as a competitive advantage. This would mean effectively using most, if not all, of the techniques and tools of project management. But, most important, your organization would focus on its ability to capitalize on adding value that is meaningful to the customers by applying project management competence. To thwart early duplication by competitors, it will be critical to identify one or more innovative uses of this competence that no competitor is presently close to applying. Considerations (hypothetical) could include:

• Development and use of a proprietary computer-based estimating methodology. The computer program statistically analyzes the organization's database of hundreds of past projects (successfully completed, completed but less than successful, aborted projects). The output is a continually revised table of estimates for a wide selection of project activities, under a broad range of conditions and parameters. The objective of the process is continual refinement of estimates. As new projects are initiated, the work to be done (activities) is processed against the database of refined estimates. Up to 95 percent of all estimating is now achieved through this semi-automated process. Computer-generated estimates are running within plus or minus 2.5 percent of actual performance, and the percentage is continuing to drop. Advantages of possessing this competence are:

- Can respond much faster to customers' (internal and external) requests for proposals
- Time and cost estimates are more reliable, resulting in:

    –Meeting nearly all milestones and project completion targets

    –Improving resource management

    –Lowering cash reserves needed for contingencies

    –Being able to reduce price to external customers or budget charge-backs to internal customers

    –Being able to quote more accurate costs when scope changes need to be negotiated

    –Improving morale of project members by removing much of the risk and fear of making a mistake and facing blame for a project failure

• For years manufacturers have touted "building quality into their products." A few manufacturers have advertised the training provided their employees. Few, if any, have given public notice of what they do to hire the appropriate people to enable the organization to build quality into their products and services. There is a whole other virtually untapped facet of quality improvement in project management that screams for attention: the concept of hiring/assigning high-quality people. Chapter 5 discussed use of the KESAA factors in selecting the best people for performing the work outlined in the project plans. The unique process your organization uses to staff project teams, and the demonstrated success of those teams is a marketable core competency.

• When your organization's present and proposed clientele are project oriented and your organization can cite numerous project successes, your organization can assure clients that you understand the project management milieu and have earned high marks for project competence. The marketing of your organization's core competency builds on the statement: "Our project managers talk with your project managers during the whole project life cycle. They speak the same language. The resulting synergy between two collaborating experts produces extraordinary project outcomes."

• By developing and sharing its competency in project management, your organization can strengthen partnerships with suppliers. Suppliers with project management knowledge and skills enhanced by guidance, and training from the buying organization can be more valuable contributors on mutually beneficial projects.

• Alliances with other product or service providers can be facilitated. Your organization provides the project management know-how. Working together the alliance offers turnkey delivery and implementation of the product/service in support of the customer's project team.

• A core competency in project management attracts presently competent project managers to your organization, as well as project manager aspirants. Realizing that organizations are rapidly becoming project oriented your organization's advertised core competency in project management acts as a magnet.

New Product/Service Development and Launch

Cooper[4] provides extensive explanations and examples of the use of the Stage-Gate™ system as a means for defining the stages of product development and launch. Each "gate" is the point where a decision is made to go forward or terminate the effort. Stage-Gate™ incorporates all of the methodology of project management. The process culls the poor projects early to divert limited resources to the potentially more beneficial projects. Typical stages may include:

1. Assessment of opportunity and scoping the project

2. Investigations, research and building a business case for developing the product

3. Planning the development and building a tested prototype

4. Validation of the project, the product, the process, customer acceptance, and the projected financial outcomes

5. Implementation of the marketing and production plans—the product launch

6. Postintroduction assessment and review (from six to 18 months later) to evaluate the strengths and weaknesses and lessons learned

Over time, the Stage-Gate™ system has evolved from a measurement and control orientation to a more flexible and fluid approach that is continually improving the product development and launch process. If in your role as a project manager you have a responsibility to design, develop, and launch a new product or service, Cooper's book is recommended as a guide.

An advantage to the new-product project is it usually is totally cross-functional. Virtually every function in the organization is involved, and often so are representatives of the customer base and suppliers. An organization that has honed its product development and launch capability, and continually refines it, demonstrates a very marketable core competency.

Notes

1. Prahalad, C. K., and Gary Hamel, "The Core Competence of the Corporation," *Harvard Business Review,* May 1, 1990.
2. Kerzner, Harold, *In Search of Excellence in Project Management.* 1998. New York: Van Nostrand Reinhold.
3. Peters, Tom, *Liberation Management.* 1992. New York: Alfred A. Knopf.
4. Cooper, Robert G., *Winning at New Products: Accelerating the Process from Idea to Launch,* 3rd ed. 2001. Cambridge, MA: Perseus Publishing.

QUICK QUIZ
NUMBER 10

1. What is an organization's core competency?
2. Why would an organization wish to publicize its competency in project management?
3. In what ways would a new product or service launch differ from a process improvement project?
4. What leverage does an organization having a notable core competency in project management have over organizations not having (or not promoting) this competence?
5. In what ways does leveraging an organization's core competency in project management parallel an individual's leveraging his or her core competency in project management?

Final Thoughts

If you've read the book to this point, you know why organizations need project managers and quality professionals need project management skills. Within the context of small and medium-size projects, you have been exposed to strategies for visualizing, selling, and initiating a project. You have learned the basics of project planning and the formation and leadership of a project team. Adding to that knowledge, you have enhanced your repertoire with more sophisticated techniques and tools applicable to the medium-size projects. You have added knowledge and skills in implementing, tracking project progress, evaluating the completed project, and closing a project. You've seen application examples of very small projects up through 18-month projects.

Lastly, you've learned ways to further develop your personal competency in project management and ways to promote project management as one of your organization's core competencies.

Some caveats that have emerged are:

• KISS (Keep It Simple, Silly). Don't break down tasks to the point where the maintenance of controls tends toward a negative benefit-cost ratio.

• Set the duration of work packages to be no more than the span of time between project reviews. This leads to fewer incomplete work packages at the progress review and places a focus on work packages that may be in trouble.

• Estimate as carefully as humanly possible. Do not pad estimates for contingencies.

• Don't forget risk assessment (in the feasibility stage and during the ongoing execution of the project).

• Faithfully and thoroughly debrief completed projects for "lessons learned."

• Don't continually reinvent the wheel. Maintain a database of previous projects as a reference when planning new projects.

• Don't use a project management technique or tool just because it seems like the right thing to do. Have a solid rationale for selecting the techniques and tools to use.

• Don't use a project planning and management software program unless you understand the basics of project management. And, unless you're familiar with such a computer program, don't use it if you have a very small project or only rarely get involved with projects. A lot of time and money can be spent learning how to efficiently use the software.

 • Do use project management software if you are frequently involved in planning and managing medium or larger projects. Use the software if you have a good knowledge of project management techniques and tools, and if you have experience with the software or have received sufficient training. Remember, the adequacy and quality of the computer output are only as good as the accuracy and completeness of the estimates, the availability of resources, and the timeliness of reviews and corrective actions.

 • Except for the very small project, consider the planning sequence outlined in this book, namely: preparing preliminary macro-level planning. Such planning for the purpose of seeking authorization (and funding) to proceed with setting up the project team and preparing micro-level plans. This sequence places the preparing of the Project Charter as the last step before presenting the detailed plans for final approval. This sequence focuses the approving authority on the feasibility of the project and if he or she approves the initial overall plan you have management buy-in and funds to do the detailed planning. Other authors draw up the charter first and often appear to make no provision for funding the costly planning process. This often causes the project leader to have to beg for "free" resources from functional organizations in order to draw up the plans for approval.

 • Whenever possible, the project manager should have approval to seek and identify the desired project team members. While still requiring cooperation of the releasing-manager, the project manager does have approved project-planning funds and can at least offer budget relief to the releasing manager.

 • You should be able to link each project's outcomes to one or more strategic objectives of the organization. You should also be able to show a positive benefits-to-cost ratio for each project (except for some projects that may emanate from mandated regulations, laws, or contractual requirements).

 • Your organization should respect the role of project manager and position the role on a parallel with functional managers for purposes of promotional opportunities and compensation.

 • Excelling in managing projects can be publicized as an organization's leading core competency.

 • Your developing competency in project management is a portable and very salable feature, and much in demand. What are you doing about it?

Go forth and produce successful projects.

Glossary

Action Plan—A tool used to aid in planning the achievement of a specific project's objectives. Usually used for small projects. It is a simpler version of a project plan.

Activity—A discrete piece of work performed as part of a project. Typically an activity has an estimated duration, cost, and resource requirements. An activity can be partially complete.

Activity-on-arrow—A network diagram where the arrow represents a specific work activity and has a time estimate to complete and where the circles or boxes to which the arrows connect represent the activity completion (and have no time estimate). Also called "activity-on-line (AOL)," "activity-oriented diagram," or just "arrow diagram."

Activity-on-node—A network diagram where the arrow merely represents connectivity and the circles or boxes represent the activity, with a time estimate. Also called "event-oriented diagram," "precedence diagram," or "circle network." AON diagrams are considered easier to draw than the AOA, and are more commonly used.

Affinity diagram—A team tool used to organize information (usually gathered during a brainstorming session) into categories. The organization process continues until consensus is reached.

Alignment meeting—A meeting, usually between project team members and the stakeholders to be affected by the project's outcomes, to ensure that the project will be planned in support of the stakeholder's needs as well as the organization's overall strategy.

AND—Activity Network Diagram. An arrow diagram used to display sequentially interconnected activities. A preliminary step to creating a CPM chart.

APIP—Analysis of Potential for Improved Process. A document used to compute the potential net payoff from a process improvement.

Arrow Diagram—See "AND."

Backward pass—The computation of late finish dates and late start dates by working backward through the network's logic from the project's end date.

Benefit-cost analysis—Estimated or actual aggregated dollar value of benefits derived from a project and the estimated or actual associated costs and computing the ratio of benefits to cost.

Cash-flow schedule—A matrix-type budget presentation displaying the planned project expenditures by type and allocated to the time period in which the money will be spent.

Change control—A system whereby all changes to project documentation are recorded and persons needing to know about the changes are notified in a timely manner. The objective is to ensure that all persons involved with the project are working from the same updated information.

Charter—See "project charter."

Competence—The totality of an individual's knowledge, experience, skills, aptitude, and attitude (the KESAA factors).

Consensus—A state in which all the team members support an action or decision, even if some of them don't fully agree with it.

Contingency fund—A reserve fund set aside to assist in covering unforeseen major events that could impair the project team's capability to complete the project on time and within budget. Tightly controlled by higher management, the fund is usually not available to cover estimation errors nor for occurrences that the project planners should have considered but overlooked.

Core competency—Pertains to the unique features and characteristics of an organization's overall capability.

Cost of quality—Costs incurred in assuring quality of a product or service.

Cost-benefit analysis—See "benefit-cost analysis."

CPM—Critical Path Method. An activity-oriented project management technique that uses arrow diagramming to display both the time and cost required to complete a project. It employs one time estimate per activity.

Crashing the schedule—A corrective action to decrease the duration of an activity or project by accelerating the pace and increasing the expenditure of resources.

Critical path—Refers to the sequence of tasks that takes the longest time and determines a project's earliest completion date.

Cross-functional team—A formal team, consisting of members from more than one function and/or discipline, organized to execute a specific project.

Culture—The values, beliefs, behaviors, and artifacts unique to a given organization.

Customer value—The accumulated dollars spent by a representative customer over a specified time period. Usually associated with an analysis of the losses incurred from lost customers and causes of the losses.

Cycle time—Refers to the time that it takes to complete a process from beginning to end.

Deliverables—The tangible products, services, processes, reports, and so forth that are produced by the project and delivered to one or more stakeholders. Deliverables include tangible project outputs and may also include intangible, but measurable, outcomes derived from the project.

Discount rate—The interest rate used by the organization when computing the present value of an investment's future cash flow.

DMAIC—Pertains to methodology used in the Six Sigma approach: define, measure, analyze, improve, control.

Dummy—Used in a network diagram; an activity that requires no work and no expenditure of resources, but merely indicates a precedence condition. Dummies may be shown on the network diagram as a dashed line headed by an arrow.

Duration—The period of work, excluding holidays and other nonworking periods, required to finish an activity; measured in workdays or workweeks.

EVA—Earned value analysis. A methodology used to measure project performance by comparing planned work with actual work accomplished to determine if performance is adhering to plan.

Event—A point in time. An event does or does not occur. An event may start or finish an activity.

Failure Mode and Effect Analysis—A tool used to identify, classify, and rate potential risks and the countermeasures to reduce or eliminate the risk.

Float—See "slack."

Forward pass—The computation of the early start and early finish dates. Also see "backward pass."

Functional manager—A person responsible for activities in a department or function performing a specific type of work and/or employing persons having a common skill-set or discipline. In a matrix-type organization, the person having responsibility for hiring, training, developing and deploying available individuals to projects as needed.

Gantt chart—A type of bar chart used in project management to display planned work and finished work in relation to time. May also be called a "milestone chart."

Groupthink—A situation in which critical information is withheld from the team because individual members censor or restrain themselves, either because they believe their concerns are not worth discussing or because they are afraid of confrontation.

IRR—Internal rate of return. A discount rate that causes net present value to equal zero. The true annual rate of earnings on an investment.

KESAA factors—The knowledge, experience, skills, aptitude and attitude that comprise an individual's competence.

KESAA Requisites Analysis—Documenting the KESAA factors applicable to a stated project task or occupational role.

Lessons learned—The process of debriefing project team members (could also include key stakeholders) following a completed project for the purpose of discussing and documenting what went well and why and what did not go well and why. Often the debriefing is done by tracing backward from project end to project start. The objectives are continual improvement and not reinventing the wheel when similar projects are encountered in the future. Documented lessons learned may be used in training new project teams.

LRM—Linear Responsibility Matrix. A matrix providing a three-dimensional view of project tasks, responsible person, and level of relationship.

Matrix—A planning tool for displaying the relationships among various data sets. Also, an organizational structure in which designated individuals report to both a functional manager (for assignment and training) and a project manager (to perform project activities).

MBTI®—Myers-Briggs Type Indicator (MBTI®). A methodology and an instrument used for identifying an individual's personality type, based on Carl Jung's theory of personality preferences.

Milestones—The points in time when a critical event is to occur; symbols placed on a Gantt chart to indicate when critical events are due.

Mitigation—Actions taken to lower the probability, incidence, and magnitude of a risk event occurring or reducing the effect if it occurs.

Natural team—A team composed of individuals drawn from a single work group, not cross-functional.

NPV—Net present value. A method for determining whether the anticipated financial performance of a proposed project investment appears to meet the organization's criteria.

Objective—A quantitative statement of expectations and an indication of when the expectations should be achieved; it flows from goals and clarifies what people must accomplish. (See "S.M.A.R.T. W.A.Y."©)

Outcomes—The tangible or nontangible planned or ultimate effect on stakeholders resulting from the project's activities, usually stated in monetary terms when measurable.

Outputs—Tangible products, materials, services, events, or information provided by the project to stakeholders, including project team members.

Outsourcing—A strategy to relieve an organization of processes and tasks in order to reduce costs, improve quality, reduce cycle time, reduce the need for specialized skills, and increase efficiency.

Payback period—The number of years it will take the results of a project or capital investment to recover the investment from net cash flows.

PDCA cycle—Plan-Do-Check-Act cycle (Shewhart/Deming). A chart laid out in quadrants showing the steps for planning and managing projects.

PERT—Program Evaluation and Review Technique. An event-oriented project management planning and measurement technique that uses an arrow diagram to identify all major project events and demonstrates the amount of time (critical path) needed to complete a project. It uses three time estimates: optimistic, most likely, and pessimistic.

PMP—Project management professional. The certification received by an individual when meeting the qualifications specified by the Project Management Institute and passing the requisite examination.

POPS—Probable Opportunities for Process Solution. A document supporting the APIP that is used to define the target(s) for process improvement and summarize the costs of solution within five possible considerations: task, knowledge, feedback, consequences/antecedents, and additional considerations.

Portfolio analysis—A process of comparing the value of proposed projects relative to the financial impacts on current projects as well as the potential impact of resources of the proposed project.

Postproject evaluation—An audit or assessment of the ultimate effect of a project's outcomes on the stakeholders that should have been or are affected. Depending on the anticipated time before results can logically be discerned, the evaluation may be done (e.g., in three months) or at stated time intervals into the future (e.g., every six months for first three years).

Precedence relationships—The relationship between the start and finish dates of activities displayed on a network diagram, which include:

- Finish to finish—suspending the finish until the finish of a subsequent activity.
- Finish to start—allowing an activity to start as soon as another is finished.
- Start to finish—suspending the finish of an activity before another can start.
- Start to start—suspending the start of an activity until a proceeding activity has started.

Process improvement team—A team with a specific objective to improve an organizational process.

Project advocate—See "project champion."

Project champion—A person, usually a member of management, who advocates a concept or idea for making a change or improvement.

Project charter—A documented statement officially initiating a project with a clearly stated purpose and for which approval is conferred.

Project closeout—The action taken after all project activities have been completed. The formal documentation and closing of the project and disbanding of the project team.

Project life cycle—Refers to five sequential phases of project management: concept, planning, design, implementation, and evaluation.

Project management—The process involved in planning, implementing, managing, and controlling a project throughout its life cycle.

Project manager—See "project team leader."

Project office—An individual or group of individuals with responsibility for overseeing all ongoing projects, reviewing new project proposals, recommending projects to senior management, providing guidance to project team leaders, providing training for project team leaders and their teams, assisting in obtaining needed resources, and so on.

Project plan—The several documents that comprise the details of why a project is to be initiated, what the project is to accomplish, when and where it is to be implemented, who will have the responsibility, how the implementation will be carried out, how much it will cost, what resources are required, and how the project's progress and results will be measured.

Project scope—A narrative covering project objectives, tasks, responsibilities, deliverables, and overall basis for measuring project results.

Project selection matrix—A tool (matrix) for displaying all pertinent factors affecting the potential selection of one or more projects over other projects.

Project sponsor—The person who supports a team's plans, activities, and outcomes; the team's "backer." The sponsor may be the same individual as the "champion."

Project status report—The project team leader's interim summary report to management and other stakeholders regarding the actual versus planned status of his or her project—time and cost being the principal factors.

Project team—A select group of individuals organized to carry out the activities associated with initiating a project, managing the project, and completing the project for the purpose of meeting a predetermined organizational strategy and objective.

Project team facilitator—A specially trained person who functions as a teacher or coach for a project team. The facilitator focuses on group process while the team leader focuses on content.

Project team leader—A designated individual who heads the project team; the chairperson; has the authority for and directs the efforts of the project team.

Project team members—The designated group of individuals selected to work on a project. Additional individuals may be on call to provide specific knowledge, insights from experience or skills. (See "SME.")

Project team scribe—A designated person assigned to record the critical information (e.g., decisions, actions taken, results of previous actions, etc.) from project team meetings. Formal meeting minutes may be required.

Project team timekeeper—The role of an individual project team member in keeping track of the team's use of allocated time.

Project variance report—The periodic report provided by the project team leader to designated management documenting the positive or negative variance in planned versus actual time and cost.

Project deliverables approval—Where needed, an approval form to document stakeholders' signing off for receipt of deliverables.

Project-oriented organization—An organization focused on serving stakeholders' needs and requirements through a project-oriented organizational structure; usually a matrixed organization.

Resource leveling—The analysis of the project network for the purpose of adjusting the schedule to better accommodate availability and use of resources.

Resources—All the personnel, facilities, equipment, material, contract services, funds, and so forth that are required to complete the project on time and within budget.

Risk assessment—The process of determining what potential risks may occur in the project as planned and what actions might be taken to eliminate or mitigate them.

ROI—Return on investment. An umbrella term for a variety of ratios measuring an organization's business performance and calculated by dividing some measure of return by a measure of investment and then multiplying by 100 to provide a percentage.

RONA—Return on net assets. A measurement of the earning power of the organization's investment in assets, calculated by dividing net profit after taxes by last year's tangible total assets and then multiplying by 100 to provide a percentage.

ROPI—Return on project investment. The net monetary results derived from project completion.

RRM—Resource Requirements Matrix. A matrix displaying the relationship of various types of project resources needed, by type of task and time period when needed, such as personnel, facilities, equipment, material, and contracted services.

S.M.A.R.T. W.A.Y.©—A guide for setting objectives:

S   Focus on *specific* needs and opportunities.

M   Establish a *measurement* for each objective.

A   Be sure objective is *achievable* as well as challenging.

R   Set stretch objectives that are also *realistic*.

T   Indicate a *time* frame for each objective.

W   Ensure that every objective is *worth* doing.

A   *Assign* responsibility for each objective.

Y   Ensure that all objectives stated will *yield* desired result.

Sarbanes-Oxley Act—The Sarbanes-Oxley Act of 2002 is aimed at improving the governance of public corporations through a requirement that a company's chief executive officer and chief financial officer certify the appropriateness of each financial statement released by the company. To conform, a company must ensure that its financial management processes, including internal controls, are effective and will improve over time. Additional documentation and traceability may be required. Inasmuch as the financial management of a project impacts the overall financial management of the company, project managers in public companies need to be aware of the requirements and consequences of this law.

Scope—A statement including project justification, project objectives, and major deliverables.

Scope creep—Deviations to the approved scope that are allowed/tolerated as "minor changes" and are not supported by renegotiated schedule and budget modifications. The accumulation of many such scope changes can seriously affect completion time and allocated resources.

Self-directed project team—A team structure whereby the team members control much of the decision making about how to handle the team's activities.

Slack time—The time a project activity can be delayed without delaying the entire project; it is determined by the difference between the latest allowable date and the earliest expected date. Also called "float."

SME—Subjectmatter expert. An individual who may be called into a project team to provide pertinent information, special knowledge and experience, or perform a specialized skill. Not an ongoing member of the project team.

SOW—Statement of Work. A description of the actual work to be accomplished. It is often derived from a preliminary Work Breakdown Structure and, when combined with the project specifications, becomes the basis for the contractual agreement on the project (also referred to as scope of work).

Stage-Gate™—Stage-Gate breaks a product development project into predetermined stages:

0—concept creation

1—defining, scoping, and building a business case for development

2—developing the product

3—testing and validating and launch of product

4—manufacturing and full-scale production

The "gate" before each stage is when a decision is made to move ahead or abort (go/no-go).

Stakeholder—Any individual or organization that will have a significant impact on or will be significantly affected by the outputs and outcomes produced by the project.

Strategic plan—The result of a process by which an organization envisions its future and develops strategies, goals, objectives, and action plans to achieve that future.

Task—A specific, definable activity to perform an assigned piece of work, within a certain time.

Task schedule—A simple sequential listing of the steps to be taken in completing a very small project.

Team dynamics—Interactions that occur among team members in different conditions.

Team meeting process—self-assessment—An assessment tool for project team members to use immediately after their team meetings. The goal is to identify ways to continually improve the team meetings.

Team stages—Four stages teams move through as they develop maturity: forming, storming, norming, and performing.

Tree diagram—A planning tool that depicts the hierarchy of tasks and subtasks needed to complete an objective. The finished diagram resembles a tree (when drawn vertically).

Virtual team—Remotely situated individuals who are affiliated with a common organization, purpose, or project and who conduct their joint effort via electronic communication. The individuals might not be employees.

Vision—An overarching statement of the way an organization wants to be; an ideal state of being at a future point.

WBS—Work breakdown structure. A project planning technique by which a project is divided into tasks, subtasks, and units of work (Work Packages) to be performed.

Work Package—The lowest level on the WBS for which estimates of time, cost, and resources are recorded for controlling purposes.

Resources

Books

Baker, Sunny, and Kim Baker, *The Complete Idiot's Guide to Project Management.* 2000. Indianapolis, IN: Alpha Books.

Baker, Sunny, and Kim Baker, *On Time/On Budget: A Step-by-Step Guide for Managing Any Project.* 1992. Englewood Cliffs, NJ: Prentice Hall.

Barkley, Bruce T., and James H. Saylor, *Customer-Driven Project Management: Building Quality into Project Processes,* 2nd ed. 2001. New York: McGraw-Hill.

Chapman, Chris, and Stephen Ward, *Project Risk Management.* 2003. New York: John Wiley & Sons.

Charvat, Jason, *Project Management Methodologies: Selecting, Implementing and Supporting Methodologies and Processes for Projects.* 2003. New York: John Wiley & Sons.

Cooper, Robert G., *Winning at New Products: Accelerating the Process from Idea to Launch,* 3rd ed. 2001. Cambridge, MA: Perseus Publishing.

Devaux, Stephen A., *Total Project Control: A Manager's Guide to Integrated Project Planning, Measuring, and Tracking.* 1999. New York: John Wiley & Sons.

Dinsmore, Paul C., *Human Factors in Project Management,* rev. ed. 1990. New York: AMACOM.

Dobson, Michael, *Project Management for the Technical Professional.* 2001. Upper Darby, PA: Project Management Institute.

Dobson, Michael, *Practical Project Management: The Secrets of Managing Any Project on Time and on Budget.* 1996. Mission, KS: SkillPath Publications.

Dorf, Richard C., ed., "Project Management," Chapter 15 in *The Technology Management Handbook.* 1999. Boca Raton, FL: CRC Press and IEEE Press.

Englund, Randall L., Robert J. Graham, and Paul C. Dinsmore, *Creating the Project Office: A Manager's Guide to Leading Organizational Change.* 2003. New York: John Wiley & Sons.

Ensworth, Patricia, *The Accidental Project Manager: Surviving the Transition from Techie to Manager.* 2001. New York: John Wiley & Sons. [Software project planning and development.]

Fleming, Quentin W., and Joel M. Koppelman, *Earned Value: Project Management.* 2000. Newtown Square, PA: Project Management Institute.

Frame, J. Davidson, *Managing Projects in Organizations: How to Make the Best Use of Time, Techniques, and People.* 1995. San Francisco: Jossey-Bass Publishers.

Frame, J. Davidson, *Managing Risk in Organizations: A Guide for Managers.* 2003. New York: John Wiley & Sons.

Frame, J. Davidson, *The New Project Management Second Edition: Tools for an Age of Rapid Change, Complexity, and Other Business Realities.* 2002. San Francisco: Jossey-Bass Publishers.

Fuller, Jim. *Managing Performance Improvement Projects: Preparing, Planning, Implementing.* 1997. San Francisco: Pfeiffer-Jossey-Bass Publishers.

GOAL/QPC and Joiner Associates, *The Team Memory Jogger: A Pocket Guide for Team Members.* 1995. Methuen, MA: GOAL/QPC.

Graham, Robert J., and Randall L. Englund, *Creating an Environment for Successful Projects,* 2nd ed. 2003. San Francisco: Jossey-Bass Publishers.

Greer, Michael, *The Manager's Pocket Guide to Project Management.* 1999. Amherst, MA: HRD Press.

Hicks, Robert F., and Diane Bone. 1990. *Self-Managing Teams.* Los Altos, CA: Crisp Publications.

Hitchcock, Darcy. *The Work Redesign Team Handbook: A Step-by-Step Guide to Creating Self-Directed Teams.* 1994. White Plains, NY: Quality Resources.

Jackson, Stephanie F., and Roger M. Addison, "Planning and Managing Projects," Chapter 5 in *Handbook of Human Performance Technology* by Harold D. Stolovitch et al. 1992. San Francisco: Jossey-Bass Publishers.

Juran, Joseph M., and A. Blanton Godfrey, eds. *Juran's Quality Handbook,* 5th ed. New York: McGraw-Hill, 1999. "Project Management and Product Development," Section 17.

Kendrick, Tom, *Identifying and Managing Project Risk.* 2003. New York: AMACOM.

Kerzner, Harold, Ph.D., *Applied Project Management: Best Practices on Implementation.* 2000. New York: John Wiley & Sons.

Kerzner, Harold, Ph.D., *Project Management: A Systems Approach to Planning, Scheduling and Controlling,* 8th ed. 2003. New York: Van Nostrand Reinhold.

Kerzner, Harold, Ph.D., *In Search of Excellence in Project Management,* 8th ed. 2003. New York: Van Nostrand Reinhold.

Kezsbom, Deborah S., Ph.D., and Katherine A. Edward, *The New Dynamic Project Management: Winning Through the Competitive Advantage,* 2nd ed. 2001. New York: John Wiley & Sons.

Kimbler, D. L., and William G. Ferrell, *TQM-based Project Planning.* 1997. New York: Chapman & Hall.

Knutson, Joan, ed., *Project Management for Business Professionals.* 2000. New York: John Wiley & Sons.

LaBrosse, Michelle A., *Accelerated Project Management.* 2002. New York: HNB Publishing.

Levine, Harvey A., *Practical Project Management: Tips, Tactics, and Tools.* 2002. New York: John Wiley & Sons.

Lewis, James P., *How to Build and Manage a Winning Project Team.* 1993. New York: AMACOM.

Lewis, James P., *Mastering Project Management: Applying Advanced Concepts of Systems Thinking, Control and Evaluation, Resource Allocation.* 1998. New York: McGraw-Hill.

Lewis, James P., *Project Planning, Scheduling, and Control: A Hands-On Guide to Bringing Projects in on Time and on Budget,* 3rd ed. 2001. New York: McGraw-Hill.

Lowenthal, Jeffrey N., *Six Sigma Project Management: A Pocket Guide.* 2002. Milwaukee: ASQ Quality Press.

Martin, Paula, and Karen Tate, *Getting Started in Project Management.* 2001. New York: John Wiley & Sons.

Martin, Paula, and Karen Tate, *Project Management Memory Jogger: A Pocket Guide for Project Teams.* 1997. Methuen, MA: GOAL/QPC.

Milosevic, Dragan Z., *Project Management Toolbox: Tools and Techniques for the Practicing Project Manager.* 2003, New York: John Wiley & Sons.

Mooz, Hal, Kevin Forsberg, and Howard Cotterman, *Communicating Project Management: The Integrated Vocabulary of Project Management and Systems Engineering.* 2003. New York: John Wiley & Sons.

Nelson, Stephen L., *Project 2000: Effective Project Management In Eight Steps.* 2002. Richmond, WA: Redmond Technology Press.

Okes, Duke, and Russell T. Westcott, eds., *The Certified Quality Manager Handbook,* 2nd ed. 2001, Milwaukee: ASQ Quality Press. Chapter 14, "Projects."

Paul, Gerard T., "Project Management and Product Development," in *Juran's Quality Handbook,* 5th ed. Joseph M. Juran and A. Blanton Godfrey, eds., 1999. New York: McGraw-Hill. Section 17.

Phillips, Jack J., Timothy W. Bothell, and G. Lynne Snead, *The Project Management Scorecard: Measuring the Success of Project Management Solutions.* 2002. New York: Butterworth Heinemann.

Pinkerton, William J., *Project Management: Achieving Bottom-Line Suce$$.* 2003. New York: McGraw-Hill.

Project Management Institute, *People in Projects.* 2001. Upper Darby, PA: Project Management Institute. Includes:

- Dewhirst, H. Dudley, "Project Teams: What Have We Learned?"
- Levene, R. J. and K. R. H. Goffin, "QFD in Project management—A Pragmatic Approach"
- Pitagorsky, George, "The Project Manager/Functional Manager Partnership"
- Schweriner, Jeffrey H., "Anticipating Team Roles and Interactions when Planning a Software Development Project"

Rad, Parviz F., and Ginger Levin, *Achieving Project Management Success Using Virtual Teams.* 2003. Boca Raton, FL: J. Ross Publishing.

Scholtes, Peter R., *The Team Handbook,* 2nd ed., rev. 1996. Madison, WI: Joiner Associates.

Stamatis, D. H., *Failure Mode and Effect Analysis: FMEA from Theory to Execution,* 2nd ed. 2003. Milwaukee: ASQ Quality Press.

Thamhain, Hans J., John L. Richards, Jeffrey K. Pinto, Howard Eisner, and E. Lile Murphree, Jr., "Project Management," in *The Technology Management Handbook,* Richard C. Dorf, ed. Boca Raton, FL: CRC Press. Chapter 15.

Thomas, Janice, et al., *Selling Project Management to Senior Executives: Framing the Moves That Matter.* 2002. Upper Darby, PA: Project Management Institute.

Thomsett, Michael C., *The Little Black Book of Project Management.* 2002. New York: AMACOM.

Verma, Vijay K., and Hans J. Thamhain, *Human Resource Skills for the Project Manager.* 1996. Upper Darby, PA: Project Management Institute.

Verzuh, Eric, *The Fast Forward MBA in Project Management: Quick Tips, Speedy Solutions, Cutting-edge Ideas.* 1999. New York: John Wiley & Sons.

Verzuh, Eric, *The Portable MBA in Project Management.* 2003. New York: JohnWiley & Sons.

Wysocki, Robert K., and James P. Lewis, *The World Class Project Manager: A Professional Development Guide.* 2001. Cambridge, MA: Perseus Publishing.

Articles

Arnett, Stephen, "Project Cost Justification," *Quality Digest,* April 1999, pp. 28–31.

Aust, Sarah, "Ensuring a Successful Simulation Modeling Project, *Quality Digest,* November 2000, pp. 28–31.

Conklin, Joseph D., "Smart Project Selection," *Quality Progress,* March 2003, pp. 81–83.

DeMeyer, Arnoud, Christoph H. Loch, and Michael T. Pich, "Managing Project Uncertainty: From Variation to Chaos," *MIT Sloan Review,* Winter 2002, pp. 60–67.

Elkins, Tony, "Virtual Teams: Connect and Collaborate," *IIE Solutions,* April 2000, pp. 26–32.

Greer, Michael, "ID Project Management: How to Organize the Project," *Performance & Instruction,* August 1988, pp. 39–47.

Harrington, H. James, "Project Management: It's a More Important Tool Than Six Sigma," *Quality Digest,* June 2000, p. 20.

Madden, Jerry, et al., "One Hundred Rules for NASA Project Managers," NASA Goddard Space Flight Center, July 9, 1996, pp. 1–9. Contact Sherman Jobe, Sherman.jobe@msfc.nasa.gov or (205) 544-3279.

McMahon, Patricia, "Project Management and Human Resources," *Proceedings of the 52nd Annual Northeast Quality Conference,* October 8, 1998. [Communication and status reporting]

Nanda, Vivek, "Keep Your QMS Implementation on Schedule," *Quality Progress,* October 2003, p. 104.

Peters, Tom. "The WOW Project," *Fast Company,* May 1999, pp. 116–121.

Prahalad, C. K., and Gary Hamel, "The Core Competence of the Corporation," *Harvard Business Review,* May 1, 1990.

Pyzdek, Thomas, "Selecting Winning Projects: Software Helps Select the Best Projects," *Quality Digest,* August 2000, p, 26.

Richard, Harry P., "Identify Big Payback TQM Projects," *Quality Progress,* March 2000, p. 120.

Snee, Ronald D., and William F. Rodebaugh, Jr., "The Project Selection Process," *Quality Progress,* September 2002, pp. 78–80.

Stamps, David, "Lights! Camera! Project Management! Work Imitates Hollywood, Every Job Can Now Be Turned into a Project, But Should It?" *Training,* January 1997, pp. 50–56.

Stanleigh, Michael, "Managing a Project . . . From A to Z," *Proceedings of ASQ's 53rd Annual Quality Congress,* May 1999, pp. 405–413.

Thompsen, Joyce A., Ph.D., "Leading Virtual Teams: Five Essential Skills Will Help You Lead Any Project—No Matter How Distant," *Quality Digest,* September 2000, pp. 42–46.

Ulfelder, Steve, "The Dirty Half-Dozen: Six Ways IT Projects Fail—And How You Can Avoid Them," *Darwin Magazine,* June 2001, pp. 58–64.

Westcott, Russ, "Quick & Easy Project Planning Techniques for small projects," *Connecticut Business & Industry Association* (Seminar), June 15, 1993.

Electronic Media

American Society for Quality, 1-800-248-1946 and www.asq.org:

- Webinars (live programs via the Web and a telephone)
  - Project Management from A to Z (archived)
  - Other periodic offerings—call for schedule
- E-Learning Center (Web-based courses)—call for schedule
  - Project Management Basics
  - Project Management Fundamentals
  - Project Management Certificate Program
  - Critical Chain Project Management
  - Quality for Project Managers

Software—Programs and Instructional Manuals

Chatfield, Carl S., and Timothy D. Johnson, *Microsoft Project 2000 Step by Step.* 2002. Redmond, WA: Microsoft Press.

Stevenson, Nancy. *Microsoft Project 2000 For Dummies.* 2000. Foster City, CA: IDG Books Worldwide.

Uyttewaal, Eric, *Dynamic Scheduling with Microsoft Project 2002.* 2003. Boca Raton, FL: J. Ross Publishing.

Standards, Criteria, Guidelines

American Society for Quality, 1997. *Quality Management—Guidelines to Quality in Project Management."* ANSI/ISO/ASQ Q10006-1997.

International Standards Organization, *ISO 10006:2003, Quality Management Systems: Guidelines for Quality Management in Projects.* Available in PDF format through ISO national member institutes.

PMI Standards Committee, *A Guide to the Project Management Body of Knowledge.* 2000. Upper Darby, PA: Project Management Institute.

References

Bauer, John E., Grace L. Duffy, and Russell T. Westcott, eds., *The Quality Improvement Handbook.* 2002. Milwaukee: ASQ Quality Press.

Bloom, Benjamin S., *Taxonomy of Educational Objectives Book I: Cognitive Domain.* 1956. Longman.

Campanella, Jack, ed., *Principles of Quality Costs,* 3rd ed. 1999. Milwaukee: ASQ Quality Press.

Cooper, Robert G., "The New Product Process: A Decision Guide for Managers," *Journal of Marketing Management* 3, 3 (1988), pp. 238–255.

Cooper, Robert G., *Winning at New Products: Accelerating the Process from Idea to Launch,* 3rd ed. 2001. Cambridge, MA: Perseus Publishing.

Fournies, Ferdinand F., *Coaching for Improved Work Performance.* 1978. New York: Van Nostrand Reinhold.

Kerzner, Harold, *In Search of Excellence in Project Management.* 1998. New York: Van Nostrand Reinhold.

Kezsbom, Deborah S., Ph.D., and Katherine A. Edward. *The New Dynamic Project Management,* 2001. New York: John Wiley & Sons, pp. 247–248.

Lewis, James P., *Mastering Project Management: Applying Advanced Concepts of Systems Thinking, Control and Evaluation, Resource Allocation.* 1998. New York: McGraw-Hill. Chapter 20, "Managing Vendors in Projects."

Okes, Duke, "APLOMETrics" in *APLOMET,* December 2003.

Okes, Duke, and Russell T. Westcott, eds., *The Certified Quality Manager Handbook,* 2nd ed., 2001. Milwaukee: ASQ Quality Press.

Peters, Tom, *Liberation Management.* 1992. New York: Alfred A. Knopf.

Prahalad, C. K., and Gary Hamel, "The Core Competence of the Corporation," *Harvard Business Review,* May 1, 1990, p. 12.

Pyzdek, Thomas, "Selecting Winning Projects," *Quality Digest,* August 2000, p. 26.

R. T. Westcott & Associates, "Behavior Management Training," *Human Resources Management & Development Handbook.* 1985. New York: AMACOM.

R. T. Westcott & Associates, "Return-on-Quality-Investment: The Overlooked Quality Tool," *The Quality Management Forum* (Quality Management Division, American Society for Quality Control). 1993. Milwaukee: ASQC.

R. T. Westcott & Associates, "Applied Behavior Management Training: Case Study: North County Electric & Gas," in *In Action: Measuring Return on Investment.* 1994. American Society for Training and Development.

R. T. Westcott & Associates, "Behavior Management Training (Revised)," *Human Resources Management & Development Handbook,* 2nd ed. 1994. New York: AMACOM.

R. T. Westcott & Associates, "ROQI: Overlooked Quality Tool" *The Total Quality Review,* November–December 1994.

R. T. Westcott & Associates, "Has Your Quality Initiative Overlooked ROQI?" (chapter), *Essence of Quality Management Anthology Series,* Volume 3. American Society for Quality Control, Quality Management Division, 1999.

Reichheld, Frederick F., *The Loyalty Effect.* 1996. Boston, MA: Harvard Business School Press.

Reichheld, Frederick, and Claus Fornell, "What's a Loyal Customer Worth?" *Fortune,* December 11, 1995.

Schmidt, Warren, and Robert Tannenbaum, "Management of Differences," *Harvard Business Review,* November–December 1960.

Snee, Ronald D., and William F. Rodebaugh, Jr., The Project Selection Process," *Quality Progress,* September 2002, pp. 78–80.

Stamatis, D. H., *Failure Mode and Effect Analysis: FMEA from Theory to Execution,* 2nd ed. 2003. Milwaukee: ASQ Quality Press.

Stewart, Thomas A., *Intellectual Capital: The New Wealth of Organizations.* 1997. New York: Doubleday/Currency, pp. 207–209.

Tieger, Paul D., and Barbara Barron-Tieger, *Do What You Are: Discover the Perfect Career for You Through the Secrets of Personality Type.* 1995. Boston: Little, Brown.

Tuckman, B. W., "Developmental Sequence in Small Groups," *Psychological Bulletin* 63, no. 6 (November–December 1965): 384–399.

Verzuh, Eric, *The Fast Forward MBA in Project Management.* 1999. New York: John Wiley & Sons.

Wysocki, Robert K., and James P. Lewis, *The World Class Project Manager: A Professional Development Guide.* 2001. Cambridge, MA: Perseus Publishing.

About the Author

Russ Westcott has visualized, sold, launched, and managed projects in a wide range of industries, organizational settings and disciplines, for more than 50 years. Some examples are design and implementation of information systems, a plant relocation, several office moves, training design and delivery, preparation of a Baldrige-type award application, many ISO 9000 quality management system implementations, a quality improvement initiative for a 2000-person division, reorganization of a storage facility, and even a personal 10,000-mile tour of the United States.

He has held management and internal consulting positions in manufacturing, aerospace, insurance, financial institutions, and a public utility. He is president of R. T. Westcott & Associates, a consultancy based in Old Saybrook, Connecticut, that assists clients with strategic planning, ISO 9001/9004-based Quality Management Systems implementation, Baldrige-based quality initiatives, the application of lean techniques, and benchmarking, as well as facilitating project management. He can be reached at russwest@snet.net.

Russ is an ASQ Fellow, an ASQ-certified quality manager, and quality auditor. He is a coeditor of the *Certified Quality Manager Handbook* (2nd edition) and the *Quality Improvement Handbook* and is a contributor to the *Certified Quality Engineer Handbook*. He writes for *Quality Progress, The Informed Outlook, Quality Digest,* and the *ASQ Quality Management Division Forum*. He is the author of *Stepping Up to ISO 9004:2000, Guidance for Your Organization's Journey to Become World Class*. Russ serves on the board of the Thames Valley ASQ Section (CT) and is editor of the section's newsletter, *The Sound View*.

Index